The Art of
Cooking
With
Love and
Wheat Germ
(And Other Natural Foods)

The Art of

Cooking With Love and Wheat Germ

(And Other Natural Foods)

by Jane Kinderlehrer
Author of Confessions of a Sneaky Organic Cook

 Rodale Press, Inc., Emmaus, Pennsylvania

Printed in the United States of America on recycled paper, containing a high percentage of de-inked fiber.

Library of Congress Cataloging in Publication Data

Kinderlehrer, Jane.
  The art of cooking with love and wheat germ (and other natural foods).

  Includes index.
  1. Cookery (Natural foods)   I. Title.
TX741.K56   641.5'63   76-49579
ISBN 0-87857-148-5 (Hardcover)
ISBN 0-87857-280-5 (Paperback)

4 6 8 10 9 7 5 3 (Hardcover)
4 6 8 10 9 7 5 3 (Paperback)

CONTENTS

CHAPTER 15

CHAPTER 16

CHAPTER 17

APPENDIX

INTRODUCTION

What I Mean By "Love And Wheat Germ"

When it comes to bringing up children and to living the good life yourself, love is not enough. It takes . . . "Love and Wheat Germ." This philosophy is so important to all of us that I believe it should influence every meal and snack from pediatrics to geriatrics.

That's what this book is all about.

By love I mean a gut-level urge to bring the glow of health to your children's faces, the desire to know your husband or wife (and yourself) will be unencumbered by the high blood pressure, the nerves, and the bad digestion that afflict so many as they swing into their later years.

This kind of love inevitably leads to "Wheat Germ," the term I use as a symbol for complete nutrition, the element vital to beaming health. And cooking with love and wheat germ means getting those nutrients we've been losing through refinement and processing back onto the dish. It means understanding special vitamin and mineral needs and finding a way, by hook or by crook, to provide them.

How do you put love and wheat germ into practice?

When our children were struggling with exams, I would put a bowl of my special mixture of sunflower seeds, almonds, and raisins on the table to take care of their "munchies." Now that was *real* brain food—and they never missed the pretzel sticks and Twinkies. When my husband worked extra hours at year's end to close the company books, I sent him off with a thermos of hot broth laced with brewer's yeast and the calcium-rich marrow from the soup bones, to help keep his nerves steady and his endurance high. These are gestures of "Love and Wheat Germ."

You can start right away to punch up muscle-making meals for your youngsters, to pack timesaving lunches that slim down while they build up, to plan heart-saving, bone-bracing, nerve-nourishing meals that have a freshness and flavor you thought were gone forever.

This book will show you how to bring "Love and Wheat Germ" into your life. Do it for your children; do it for yourself; do it for your husband or wife. For everybody! It's not difficult and you'll thank me when you see the payoff.

Part 1

Feeding Them Well, From Diapers To Dungarees

Chapter 1

A Little Advice to New Mothers from an Older One

Many times at my lectures mothers say to me, "If only I had known when my children were small what I know now, we could have been spared so much misery." Others say, "If I had started my children out on what you call 'love and wheat germ,' I wouldn't have to buck their poor eating habits now."

If you have a brand-new baby and a good working knowledge of how to apply "love and wheat germ," you are fortunate indeed and so is your baby. You can raise your child with built-in habits of good eating that will give him a great start in life, will help him sail through infancy with a minimum of sniffles and a maximum of smiles, he will be equipped to cope successfully with every new stage of his development. It has been demonstrated that what a child gets to eat during the first 15 months of his life can greatly influence his intelligence. With a boost from good nutrition, your child can equal and surpass his parents and his grandparents in all areas, even in the "brain" department.

The philosophy of 'love and wheat germ' starts at the breast.

I hope you are nursing your child. Nursing is not only an assurance of nutrition, it is an assurance of love. When you nurse your child, you give him—along with all the protein, vitamins, minerals, and enzymes he needs—a built-in sense of security. The child who is nursed is cuddled and loved. He and his mom develop a close and affectionate bond, a wonderful intangible quality that could never be put in a bottle.

For you, nursing can be a uniquely satisfying experience.

"A new mother needs to be shown that she is loved;" says Karen Pryor in her book, *Nursing Your Baby* (Harper and Row, New York, 1973), "and the behavior of a tiny baby at the breast is proof positive to that. His greed is flattering, his blissful enjoyment is contagious, his drunken satiety is a comical compliment. Then there are the rewards to her own physical health and beauty. Nursing helps the uterus to contract thus hastening the return to a youthful figure. A nursing mother can feel her organs returning to home base."

The baby's sucking stimulates the release of oxytocin from your pituitary gland. It is this hormone that causes the womb to contract and hastens recovery from childbirth. It also hastens the time when you can safely resume sexual relations.

When you are breast-feeding, you must eat well—for the sake of your own health as well as your baby's. There will be a heavy drain on your calcium supply because the baby has priority in this department, even if the calcium he needs must be extracted from your bones. Spare yourself weakened bones and decaying teeth. Take bone meal supplements, sesame seeds, wheat germ, lots of leafy greens, and four to six glasses of milk daily. Substitute yogurt or kefir for some of that milk and you will promote the growth of friendly bacteria in your intestinal tract, your mouth and throat—a protection against colds and intestinal upsets.

Here's a good way to get extra calcium and it doesn't cost a cent.

Save your eggshells. Wash and crush them, put them in a pan with water to cover, and add a teaspoon lemon juice or vinegar. Crush the shells with a potato masher or a smaller pot and bring to a boil. Simmer 20 minutes and strain. Keep it in the refrigerator and use it as part of the liquid in making broths or soups.

If you are producing plenty of milk but your little tyke still doesn't seem satisfied, you may need to eat more foods high in fat which increases the richness of breast milk and also slightly increases the flow.

If you haven't enough milk, go heavy on the foods rich in protein and the B vitamins.

A Bit of Beer?

When I was nursing our first child, one of my neighbors suggested that I drink beer. But, she said, it must be imported beer. It wasn't until many years later that I found out *why* domestic beer just doesn't have what it takes. Most imported beers contain about two tablespoons of yeast per pint. The yeast is removed from American brews. The B vitamins and the protein which stimulate lactation are in the yeast not in the foam.

You can make your own version of imported beer. Take three heaping tablespoons of brewer's yeast every day—in tomato juice, in soups, as a broth with a dash of vegetable seasoning, and you can look forward to a copious supply of nourishing milk for your baby. You'll feel wonderful, too. You'll find yourself capable of doing much more without experiencing the fatigue which is often the constant companion of the new mother.

Brewer's yeast, now also called nutritional yeast, is

almost 50 percent protein and contains all the known B vitamins. The B vitamins affect the quantity and the quality of your milk. The other vitamins A, C, D, E, and K in the milk you're providing for baby, depend on how much of each you get in your diet. They affect the quality of your milk—not the quantity.

In her book, *Let's Have Healthy Children* (Harcourt, Brace, Jovanovich, New York, 1972), Adelle Davis suggests that a nursing mother get 50,000 units of vitamin A, at least 300 mg. of vitamin C, and 2,000 units of vitamin D each day. Cow's milk contains little or no vitamin E or K. Here's where you have it all over the cow. Your milk contains both these vital elements—if you get them in your diet. Take at least 200 I.U. of vitamin E (mixed tocopherols) and eat cabbage in the form of coleslaw, raw spinach in your salads, and alfalfa sprouts. These are your richest sources of vitamin K, the vitamin necessary for blood clotting. Alfalfa also helps the mammary glands in the production of milk, says Dr. R. Swinborne Clymer in his book, *Diet, A Key to Health* (Franklin Publishers, San Francisco, Calif., 1966).

I'm going to give you several recipes for liver because you should enjoy it several times a week. (see "Great Foods for Nursing Mothers," at the end of this chapter.) It's a rich source of the B vitamins which stimulate milk production and enrich its quality. It's great for baby and it will help prevent fatigue in you. Make sure it's baby beef liver or calves' liver or the liver from cows who haven't got to the feedlots to be given hormones. Here's one you can try today. It's great because the enzymes and nutrients come to you intact because of the way it's prepared—it's almost raw, but delicious.

Heat up some chicken soup or beef broth or plain water enriched with two tablespoons of yeast and a dash of tamari soy sauce or some vegetable seasoning. Cut a small piece of liver in cubes about a half-inch square. Skewer a cube on a fork and dip it into the boiling liquid for a count of 10 and enjoy. See how easy it is? Then when you've finished the liver, add a handful of alfalfa sprouts to the liquid and you've got a bowl of delicious soup. You'll have enough milk to give your baby a banquet at every feeding. And what milk!

Babies Need Vitamin E

I cannot stress too strongly the importance of vitamin E to your baby. Vitamin E, unlike other nutrients does not readily cross the placental barrier to nourish the fetus. Therefore, infants, whether they are full term or premature, are born with low levels of vitamin E. The crucial determinant to the newborn infant in alleviating this deficiency is whether or not he receives an immediate dose of vitamin E at birth. This factor gives the breast-fed baby a firmer hold on the ladder of life right from the beginning. Human milk contains an average of 1.14 mg. of vitamin E per quart while the vitamin E content of cows' milk averages less than half that amount—.21 mg. per quart in early spring to a maximum of 1.06 mg. per quart in mid fall—according to David C. Herting, Ph.D., and Emma-Jane E. Drury, B.S., reporting in the *American Journal of Clinical Nutrition*, (March 1969).

The amount of vitamin E which your baby will get from your milk will depend on how much you get in your diet. Think of this when you're eating your wheat germ. Put some wheat germ oil in your salad dressing, and take your vitamin E supplement daily—at least 200 I.U. Why not play it safe and cover all bases? You'll sleep better and you and your baby will benefit in many other areas as well. Vitamin E promotes the life of the red blood cells whose job it is to carry oxygen to every cell in the body.

In cases involving premature babies born with vitamin E deficiency and accompanying anemia, doctors have used vitamin E therapy with success, even after iron supplementation has failed. Iron will help the blood produce more cells—but without vitamin E the cells break up and lose their hemoglobin. In the *New England Journal of Medicine* (November 28, 1968), California investigators, Drs. J. Ritchie, M. Fish, V. McMasters, and M. Grossman, told of giving 75 to 100 I.U. of vitamin E to five of seven premature infants with good results. Even though these babies were on a commercial formula supplemented with 15 to 30 mg. of iron daily, their anemia failed to respond until vitamin E was added to their diet. Then, after a few days, their plasma tocopherol levels rose, their red cell survival time lengthened and the anemia was corrected.

Anemia in infants is quite common and most pediatricians recommend added iron. But many times it is vitamin E deficiency that is causing the anemia. The California researchers cautioned, "The frequency with which this syndrome is observed will depend on the level of awareness of its existence and the care with which it is sought." In other words, your doctor may not be aware of this syndrome and therefore will not look for it. "Some of the manifestations, anemia, puffy eyes, and firm legs with shiny skins, not unusual in premature infants and often called 'physiologic' or 'characteristic of prematures', may prove in many cases to represent vitamin E deficiency."

Don't take any drugs while you're nursing (unless your doctor insists that they are absolutely necessary) not even aspirin, cold remedies, or cough medicines. The salicylates in aspirin can be upsetting to your child and are among the factors involved in hyperactivity. Any drug you take can have an adverse effect on the nursing baby.

Many pediatricians will insist that your breast-fed baby should have fluorides. This is a questionable chemical and I don't like the idea of using it. None of our children got fluoride supplements. They all have good teeth. Our grandchildren are not getting fluorides in spite of dire warnings about caries from their pediatricians. They all have good teeth. Of course they get very few sweets and they eat mineral-rich foods—sunflower seeds, blackstrap molasses, wheat germ, and yeast—no refined sugar or flour or soft drinks. This is the road to good health and good teeth—not fluorides. Our Jodi, who is four and a half, said to me last week, "You know, Grandma, it's all right to have candy—once in a while —like on Halloween."

If the pediatrician gives you a sample bottle of an all-purpose vitamin when you leave the hospital, don't use it. Commercial pediatric formulations routinely contain artificial color or flavor. You can buy one that is additive free at a natural food store.

You would be very wise indeed to avoid all additives all the time—but especially while you're nursing. Most of the chemicals have not been fully tested for safety and it is impossible, even with all the computers and the best brains in the world to predict the synergistic reaction of the innumerable combinations of these drugs in your system.

If you have a little extra fat on you during your nursing period, that is no problem. *Do not diet.* You will have plenty of time to slim down once you have weaned your baby. Remember that unless you are getting plenty of calories, your milk will not provide sufficient calories. And that's what baby needs right now.

This is really the time of your life for enjoying good food. You can eat 1,000 to 1,500 calories a day, in addition to your own normal needs, without gaining weight. That's a free ride on the calorie train you seldom have.

Don't waste those calories on foods that lack nutrients. Make every calorie count. Use no white sugar or white flour products. Keep a jar of raw wheat germ in the refrigerator and use it liberally. If you like hot cereal for breakfast, put a couple of tablespoons of wheat germ on top of it or add hot milk to a half-cup of wheat germ. Add some unhulled sesame seeds and you have a meal that's fit for a queen and which will help you feed your baby royally.

Eggs are an excellent source of protein and rich in iron. Enjoy them for breakfast. Chances are you won't have much time to prepare an elaborate breakfast for yourself before you nurse the baby. It's a good idea to have some pre-prepared eggnog in the refrigerator. Try this recipe:

Ever-Ready Eggnog

2 eggs, preferably fertile

2 tablespoons yeast

2 tablespoons blackstrap molasses
(good source of iron and B vitamin choline)

2 cups milk, preferably certified raw milk

1 teaspoon vanilla

Put everything in the blender and whiz. You may vary this eggnog by adding fruits like strawberries, raspberries, bananas, or crushed pineapple.

METRIC CONVERSION

1 teaspoon = 5 ml.	1 tablespoon = 15 ml.
1 ounce = 30 ml.	1 cup = 240 ml./.24 l.
1 quart = 950 ml./.95 l.	1 gallon = 3.80 l.
1 ounce = 28 gr.	1 pound = 454 gr./.454 kg.

F.°	200	225	250	275	300	325	350	375	400	425	450
C.°	93	107	121	135	149	163	177	191	204	218	232

If, for any reason, you are having trouble nursing, do contact your local La Leche League. This is a nonprofit organization founded by seven nursing mothers in 1956 for the express purpose of helping mothers breast-feed their babies. They now have over a thousand groups throughout the United States. They will give you lots of help and encouragement should the going get rough.

When one mother was told that nothing but mother's milk could save her bottle-fed baby, who was suffering severe diarrhea, allergic reactions, and convulsive seizures, members of the La Leche League not only provided mother's milk for this baby, they encouraged the mother to nurse even though the child was already three months old. "Put your baby to your breast at every possible opportunity," they told her. "The sucking will eventually stimulate milk flow."

Eight days after her first attempt, the milk began to flow—only a few drops, then more and more until the baby no longer needed supplementation from La Leche mothers. The diarrhea and all allergic reactions disappeared and the baby soon became a full-cheeked, happy little boy who radiated good health.

If you can't find a chapter of La Leche near you, write to La Leche League International, 9616 Minneapolis Avenue, Franklin Park, Illinois 60131. Ask for their excellent book, *The Womanly Art of Breast-feeding.*

If your baby is not breast-fed, his need for vitamin E is crucial. Not only do most infant formulas contain inadequate amounts of vitamin E, but the very content of the formulas tends to drain the baby's own supply of this vitamin.

One function of vitamin E is to combine with fatty acids to prevent the formation of toxic peroxides within the organism. Investigators at the University of Wyoming's Division of Biochemistry point out that the vitamin E stores of the newborn are being depleted by the high P.U.F.A. (polyunsaturated fatty acid) content of their diets. Synthetic formulas that use vegetable oil (rich in P.U.F.A.) as a fat source have become commonplace in recent years. These fats have been refined and stripped of their vitamin E, so they not only lack this vital element, but they steal from whatever stores the infant gets from other sources.

By all means give your bottle-fed baby a vitamin E supplement. It is available in dropper bottles at natural food stores. Build him up gradually to at least 100 I.U. a day. His health will benefit in many ways.

If you must give your baby a formula, ask your doctor about acid milk. About two tablespoons of orange juice to an eight-ounce bottle of milk—preferably certified raw milk. This is the formula my doctor recommended as a supplementary feeding for our babies. It is especially advisable for infants who have frequent bowel movements. The acid breaks up the curd of the milk making it more digestible. When you use this formula, you don't have to sterilize the bottles. Just wash them in hot soapy water and rinse well. The acid in the milk prevents the growth of bacteria to some extent. A very popular baby doctor in our town told me that when he first came to our community people were horrified because he put babies on a vinegar in milk formula. "But," they would say in astonishment, "look how the babies are thriving!" Incidentally, the small proportion of acid does not curdle the milk.

I don't know why this formula is so rarely used today or why pediatricians put such blind faith in commercial formulas. When our daughter-in-law Mimi asked her pediatrician about this formula, the doctor remembered a reference to it in med school but was fearful of allergic reaction to the orange. None of our children nor any of the many children our doctor put on this formula ever showed allergic reaction to the orange juice. It just might be that in the presence of milk, orange juice is less likely to be allergenic.

Freshly squeezed orange juice is a good source of vitamin C. When juicing oranges for baby, don't ream them down to the skin. The orange rind contains a substance which may cause allergies. Canned and frozen juices may contain this substance—probably one reason for the high rate of allergic reaction to orange juice that pediatricians are finding. Our babies got orange juice when they were three weeks old. They loved it and were never upset by it.

If your baby is bottle fed, at least hold him while you're feeding him. Let the dishes wait. Take the phone off the hook. Baby comes first. The cuddling he gets while you feed him will establish a good rapport between you two and it just might prevent lots of emotional problems in later life.

I cannot emphasize this point strongly enough, do not put the baby to sleep with a bottle. Sure, it seems like an easy way to quiet him, but you're making a lot more problems than you're solving. Even though you add no sweetening agent to that bottle, the lactose of the milk creates an oral climate conducive to decay. My dentist told me of a 16-month-old child brought to him with every tooth in his mouth decayed and as soft as chalk. The baby's mother said they came in that way. She said she put no sweetener in his bottle but the baby got his bottle at bedtime and kept it with him all night. He also walked around drinking from his bottle a good part of the day.

This condition is known as "bottle-mouth" caries and dentists are seeing quite a lot of it. It occurs in infants and children who have had prolonged bottle feeding, particularly when they receive a bottle of milk or fruit juice at night beyond 12 months of age.

Such decay may result in extensive and expensive surgery and may even produce damage to permanent teeth, according to Dr. Robert Cooley, chairman of the Pediodontics Department of Northwestern University Dental School and director of dental services at Childrens' Memorial Hospital. Dr. Cooley performs surgery on at least one child a week and sometimes two or three for this problem. Crowns are placed over the remnants of the children's teeth. If this is not done and the teeth fall out, the permanent teeth which emerge later are not properly spaced.

Instead of crowns, some dentists are filling the teeth by hand—and hardening the fillings with an ultraviolet ray. This is a long, drawn-out procedure, but it does have advantages over crowns, which necessitate sometimes three hours of surgery under general anesthesia at a cost of $700 to $900.

It isn't just fruit juices and sweet drinks that are causing the problem. Even milk can cause this decay when the bottle goes to bed with the child. The child dozes off, his mouth filled with the liquid which bathes the inside of the upper teeth. The child wakes a little later and reaches for his bottle, takes a few swigs, and continues the decaying process.

If liquids are consumed in shorter time periods, when the child is awake, this chemical reaction does not occur because the mouth is continually flushed out with saliva.

Dr. Francis A. Castano who observed this bottle-mouth caries so frequently when he was chairman of the Pediodontic Department at the University of Pennsylvania Dental School, told me that he has never found this syndrome in a nursing child. "You have to be awake to nurse. Milk can flow from a bottle without much sucking effort on the part of the child." Besides, not many babies take their mothers to bed with them.

By the time your baby is four months old, the protein content of your milk has diminished and the little tyke is ready for additional sources of nourishment.

Always go very easy with new food. Give very little at first—maybe a teaspoon—and look for rashes, sore bottoms, or stomach upsets. Give your baby four days on a new food before you pass that food as O.K. Remember, if you yourself have allergies, your child is more likely to have them, though they may be manifested in different ways.

At this stage your baby's stores of iron are about used up and he needs to get some in his diet. To get more iron into your infant, instead of relying on commercial formulations and iron-enriched, refined cereals, try this:

Pour a cup of boiling water over a quarter-cup of unsulfured raisins that have been prewashed. Let stand overnight. Next morning, give a teaspoon of this liquid to your baby, right off the spoon or in his bottle. Watch for reactions. If there are none, then do this: Pour a cup of boiling water over eight raw almonds and let stand overnight. Repeat the same procedure as with the raisins. No reaction? Good. Now pour a cup of boiling water over raisins and almonds combined. Now you are giving your little angel mineral-rich water that will charge every one of his batteries and it tastes delicious. Keep this water refrigerated and use it to prepare baby's first cereal.

Commercial baby cereals are expensive and over-refined but are recommended by pediatricians because they are fortified with extra iron. What kind of iron? The inorganic kind that fights with vitamin E. Use this raisin-almond water to prepare your baby's cereal and you are giving him a good source of organic iron and many other important minerals.

Our grandchildren's first cereal is brown rice. Here are some great ways to prepare it. When you prepare brown rice for your own dinner, set some aside and blenderize it, using the raisin-nut water to thin it to proper consistency and to get the blender going.

Or, do this. The night before, heat a cup of raisin-almond water with one quarter-cup of brown rice. Bring it just to the boil. Then, pour the whole thing into a thermos bottle pre-rinsed with hot water. Lay the thermos bottle on its side. In the morning, shake it a little and pour, or dig out, a most delicious cereal—ready on demand. No horsing around with pots and pans while the baby lets you know he's hungry—at the top of his voice. The rice will be mushy which is fine. You may not need to blenderize it or thin it. If it's too thick, simply add more raisin-nut water or some milk.

This thermos bottle of cereal can start your day with a smile and give your baby some fantastic nutrients.

Funny thing. It costs so much less to feed your baby well than poorly. Our daughter never bought a box of baby cereal nor a jar of baby food. Her daughter is the most beautiful baby you've ever seen. She's bright, impish, and she radiates good health. Go ahead, call me a prejudiced grandma. But, how many toddlers do you know who ask for wheat germ and yogurt for lunch?

Getting back to the thermos bottle. You can make all kinds of cereals in the same way as the rice and have them ready and waiting when you get down to the kitchen in the morning. You can give your baby the whole grains that provide a full spectrum of vitamins and minerals instead of the highly processed ones that have to be reinforced with synthetic substances. We use millet, which the children love and so do we, whole wheat grains, the ones you sprout, whole oats, whole rye, and pearl barley. After you've tried them out individually, you can mix and match to your baby's delight. Try the wheat last because wheat is allergenic to some people.

The best advice I, as an experienced mother, can give to you is—enjoy your baby. Let your housework go if necessary, don't worry about it and don't worry what others think about your housekeeping. You're not Mrs. Craig, thank heavens. The house will be there long after your baby has been weaned and joined the cub scouts or brownies. Invest in a comfortable rocking chair even if you have to go into hock for it. Better yet, since your relatives will all be asking what you need for the baby, it wouldn't hurt to include rocking chair along with high chair, baby bouncer, playpen and such.

I hope you remember some lullabies. If not, brush up on a few and croon to your baby. Our kids loved the

Russian Lullaby, Brahm's Lullaby and *Tell Me Pretty Baby* (are there any more at home like you?), which is not exactly a lullaby but lends itself very nicely to rocking with an infant cradled in your arms.

Great Foods for Nursing Mothers

Some people think they don't like liver. They may have been turned off by a piece that had a bitter aftertaste. If you sprinkle the liver with lemon juice before you cook it, it won't leave a bitter memory on your taste buds.

When liver is on the menu at Fitness House, the Rodale Press dining room, there's always a stampede to sign up. It is far and away the most popular dish served there.

Your success with liver depends on how you prepare it. Do not overcook and do not use a high heat. If it's tough, you've probably cooked it too long. Five minutes is usually enough.

Use a medium-hot frying pan and heat some oil or chicken fat in it. Cut up one medium-sized onion and sauté lightly. Put the lid on the pan and let the onions steam (you'll need less fat). Take the onions out, add a little more fat if necessary and put the liver in. I usually coat the liver (about one pound—one-fourth inch slices) with sesame seeds after sprinkling it with lemon juice, this adds crunch and calcium. You may sprinkle a little thyme, basil or parsley flakes on it. We don't use any salt on liver; it doesn't seem to need it. Experiment. It's delicious served with horseradish, a side dish of applesauce, string beans, broccoli or cauliflower and a crunchy baked potato. Now that's a real meal for a nursing mother—and the new father.

Chopped Liver

I always prepare more liver than we need and the next day we have chopped liver as a salad or as an *hors d'oeurve.*

Cut the liver up into a wooden bowl. Add whatever onions were left over. If none were, then sauté some with a few pieces of chicken skin, oil, or chicken fat. Take the onions out when nice and crisp and let the chicken skin crisp up. The resulting pieces are called *gribben* and they are sheer magic in chopped liver. When they are crisp add them to the chopping bowl. A good substitute for *gribben* is soy nuts, the roasted ones you get in natural food stores. The soy also contributes lecithin, more protein, and a nice little bundle of vitamins. Add a few lettuce leaves (they give moistness) and a hard-cooked egg and chop away. Serve as a salad with grated white radish or spread on whole wheat crackers. Keep some of this liver pâté in the refrigerator and scoop some onto a cracker or a piece of celery when you need a pickup.

This recipe for Crispy Liver Slices is a sure winner. I have adapted it from one that is included in the La Leche Cookbook, *Mother's in the Kitchen,* edited by Roberta Johnson, (published by La Leche League International, Franklin Park, Ill., 1971).

Crispy Liver

1 egg
1 tablespoon lemon juice
1 pound sliced liver in ¼-inch thick slices
½ cup mixed whole wheat bread crumbs
½ cup wheat germ with 2 tablespoons bran
2 tablespoons oil

Beat the egg with the lemon juice. Dip liver slices first in crumbs, then in egg mixture, then again in crumbs. Brown slowly in pre-heated oil for about eight minutes on one side. Turn and brown about five minutes on the other side. Cooking time varies according to the thickness of the liver, and the kind you choose.

METRIC CONVERSION										

1 teaspoon = 5 ml.
1 ounce = 30 ml.
1 quart = 950 ml./.95 l.
1 ounce = 28 gr.

1 tablespoon = 15 ml.
1 cup = 240 ml./.24 l.
1 gallon = 3.80 l.
1 pound = 454 gr./.454 kg.

F.°	200	225	250	275	300	325	350	375	400	425	450
C.°	93	107	121	135	149	163	177	191	204	218	232

This Carrot-Nut Loaf with brown rice is loaded with good nutrients for the nursing mother and the whole family. It's also very delicious the second time around though you probably won't have any left over.

Carrot-Nut Loaf

1 cup ground raw cashews, almonds,
    walnuts, or pecans
1 cup cooked brown rice
1 cup raw carrots, grated
½ cup wheat germ
2 tablespoons bran
2 tablespoons nutritional yeast
1 cup tomatoes or tomato sauce
2 tablespoons parsley, chopped
1 tablespoon chives, chopped (optional)
½ teaspoon kelp
½ teaspoon thyme (dry)

Preheat oven to 350° F.
Combine all ingredients, mixing thoroughly. Pack into a buttered or oiled loaf pan and
bake for 45 minutes.
Serve with a tossed salad, a bowl of soup,
and top it off with carob cream pie for a lovely
meal. Inexpensive, too.

I got this recipe from a Korean woman who told me
that in her country it is customary to serve it to new
mothers and to anyone who has undergone surgery.
The seaweed has a magical effect on the intestinal tract
and helps to alleviate the gas pains which so frequently
follow surgery and childbirth by Cesarean section. It is
also rich in lovely nutrients. A friend of mine made this

soup for his wife after she called in the middle of the night from the hospital where she had just had a hysterectomy. She was so uncomfortable and miserable with gas pains, she couldn't sleep. She said this soup was positively magic. She had two bowls of it and fell asleep like a baby.

New Mother Soup

3 sheets of seaweed or laver

1 cup water

3 tablespoons hamburger or
    a can (3½ ounces) of tuna fish

6 cups of beef bouillion or soup stock

3 tablespoons parsley, cut up

Wash the seaweed or laver and soak it in one cup lukewarm water for one hour. Cook it briskly in the same water for 15 minutes. Add the other ingredients and simmer gently 10 to 15 minutes. Serve with wheat germ sprinkled over it, or with whole wheat bread cubes or sprouts.

METRIC CONVERSION										
1 teaspoon = 5 ml.					1 tablespoon = 15 ml.					
1 ounce = 30 ml.					1 cup = 240 ml./.24 l.					
1 quart = 950 ml./.95 l.					1 gallon = 3.80 l.					
1 ounce = 28 gr.					1 pound = 454 gr./.454 kg.					

F.°	200	225	250	275	300	325	350	375	400	425	450
C.°	93	107	121	135	149	163	177	191	204	218	232

Carob Cream Pie

This is luscious and tastes as though it were loaded with calories. Actually it isn't. It's a great way to get your milk and eggs and relish every velvety smooth spoonful.

2 cups milk

2 two-inch pieces stick cinnamon

1 teaspoon vanilla

2 egg yolks

¼ cup honey or blackstrap molasses

¼ cup whole wheat flour

⅓ cup carob powder

METRIC CONVERSION										
1 teaspoon = 5 ml.					1 tablespoon = 15 ml.					
1 ounce = 30 ml.					1 cup = 240 ml./.24 l.					
1 quart = 950 ml./.95 l.					1 gallon = 3.80 l.					
1 ounce = 28 gr.					1 pound = 454 gr./.454 kg.					
F.°	200	225	250	275	300	325	350	375	400	425	450
C.°	93	107	121	135	149	163	177	191	204	218	232

Add the cinnamon sticks to the milk in a quart saucepan and bring to a boil. Remove from heat and add vanilla.

Beat the egg yolks and honey or molasses together with a wire whisk or with an electric mixer. Add the whole wheat flour a little at a time. Add the carob powder.

Discard the cinnamon sticks from the milk and slowly pour the milk into the egg yolk mixture, beating constantly. Return the mixture to the pan and cook over very low heat, stirring constantly with a whisk until the mixture gets thick as pudding.

You can use this mixture as a pudding topped with whipped cream or you can make a delicious pie, using any crumbs you have left over from cake and cookies that you have made yourself with wholesome ingredients. (I keep a can of such crumbs in the freezer.)

Take three-quarters of a cup of crumbs and one-quarter cup of wheat germ. Whiz in the blender. If it is not moist, add two tablespoons of oil. Press the crumb mixture in a pie plate bringing it up the sides.

Pour the cooled pudding into the crumb crust. To make it really fancy, beat up the egg whites with a little honey or blackstrap, spread the meringue over the pie and put it under the broiler for a few minutes. Sprinkle the pie with chopped walnuts and enjoy.

Salmon with the bones and skin is a marvelous source of calcium. Use the liquid, too, that comes in the can. At least once a week make a meal out of a can of salmon. It's so good, it doesn't even need mayonnaise—just a slice of onion and a little lemon. Heavenly.

If you want to stretch a can of salmon for the whole family, make salmon patties. Try this recipe.

Salmon Patties

1 lb. can pink salmon

2 eggs, slightly beaten

1 cup mashed potatoes, plus two tablespoons wheat germ

½ teaspoon kelp

dash cayenne

1 tablespoon lemon juice

¼ cup cold-pressed oil

1 teaspoon onion, grated or scraped

sesame seeds

Mash salmon fine including bones and skin. Stir in beaten eggs and potatoes, blending well. Add seasonings, onion and lemon juice and mix thoroughly. Divide in quarter-cup portions and shape in flat patties about half-inch thick. Coat with sesame seeds. Heat shortening in heavy skillet. Place patties in skillet and brown slowly on both sides to a rich golden color. (If you prefer, place on oiled baking dish in 350°F. oven till well heated.) Place on a hot platter and garnish attractively with parsley, lemon wedges, and black olives, if available.

This makes five servings. Serve with hot tomato sauce, a lovely, crisp, vegetable salad, pickled beets and either spaghetti or a rice creole.

METRIC CONVERSION

1 teaspoon = 5 ml. 1 tablespoon = 15 ml.
1 ounce = 30 ml. 1 cup = 240 ml./.24 l.
1 quart = 950 ml./.95 l. 1 gallon = 3.80 l.

1 ounce = 28 gr. 1 pound = 454 gr./.454 kg.

F.°	200	225	250	275	300	325	350	375	400	425	450
C.°	93	107	121	135	149	163	177	191	204	218	232

Café Au Lait for Two

If you still haven't kicked the caffeine habit, try *café au lait*. It's like the *capuccino* you get in Italy.

Warm up half-a-cup of milk and half-a-cup of cream or simply one cup of light cream. As it warms, beat it with a little wire whisk. It will froth up. Pour the whipped milk and the coffee into your cup at the same time using half-and-half. It's a delicious just like that. If you must have a sweetener, use a spot of blackstrap molasses or honey.

Try *café au lait* using Postum and you will soon kick the caffeine dependency. Postum is made from grains and molasses.

Chapter 2
Feeding the Busy Minds and Tricky Appetites of Tots and Toddlers

Isadora Duncan, the beautiful dancer, once suggested to George Bernard Shaw that he father her child because—"With my looks and your brains . . .!"

Mr. Shaw, legend has it, firmly declined the proposition saying, "What if the child got my looks and your brains!" Both Miss Duncan and Mr. Shaw, like many, many people were putting too much faith in the influence of genetics on intelligence.

A lot more goes into the development of intelligence or brain power than your genes or those of your ancestors can provide. Your child can have superior intelligence even though yours is average. And if your brain power is above average, that is no guarantee that your child will be a genius.

"Intelligence is not something fixed at conception, like an individual's sex," says Dr. Joseph McVicker Hunt, professor of psychology at the University of Illinois. "A child is endowed not with a ready-made intelligence, but only with an intellectual potential."

How can you help your child achieve his greatest potential?

That's where the love and wheat germ come in. At this stage of life, especially, love means the whole concept of tenderness, care, attention, and wise discipline.

Wheat germ, of course, means providing all the nutrition necessary for both physical and mental health and development.

There is no doubt about it. The child who is loved, cuddled, and introduced to a "lively environment" while he is still in the crib, cradle, or playpen, has a much better potential for more brain power, according to results of some fascinating experiments with laboratory animals as reported by Rosenzweig, Bennet, and Diamond in *Scientific American* (February 1972). When experimental animals placed in an enriched environment were compared with others kept in an impoverished environment, differences in brain anatomy and chemistry could actually be measured. Most animals who were kept in the enriched environment developed larger brains and more cholinesterase, a very important enzyme, and more glial cells and blood capillaries which form connections between cells.

These are all physical factors which enhance intelligence. While they can be observed and measured in experimental animals, they of course cannot be weighed and measured in humans. What can be seen in children are the behavioral effects of this kind of increased brain development. Children brought up in homes where they are played with and exposed to a wide variety of sights and sounds, do develop more fully than those brought up in circumstances where they are deprived of this loving attention.

Help Your Child to Learn

Based on these findings, what can you as a parent do that will help your child to learn how to learn? Give your baby a wide—not overwhelming—variety of things to hear, see, and handle, suggests Dr. Hunt. This does not mean expensive toys. A baby is intrigued just as much by boxes of various shapes and sizes, by pots and pans, pieces of paper of different colors and shapes, and simple household objects like clothespins and spoons.

I remember well our first son's reaction when Uncle Jack showed up with a new toy. Little Davie ignored the toy, but played for hours with the large and sturdy box it came in. He gleefully climbed in and out of it, tipped it, pushed it, and stuck his teddy bear into it. All these ventures called forth laughs, giggles, and squeals of delight. Weeks later he played with the dump truck which had come in the box.

Try to find household objects of different colors, sizes, shapes, and textures. Shoe boxes, small containers with lids, empty spools from thread, the cardboard rolls from waxed paper and from toilet tissue, all these are new to your baby and a source of endless experimentation and delight. They will give him sensory impressions from which he will build his own ideas of volume, form, dimension, and number.

Besides an opportunity to use all his senses, a child needs the freedom to try himself out on the world, to walk, climb, jump, manipulate, and throw things. He also needs loving adults who appreciate his efforts, who laugh and applaud, who answer his endless questions, who serve as models for imitation, and ask him questions that he must use language to answer. I know of a child who was four years old before he used words to ask for a glass of water. The youngest of four children, all his needs were anticipated and met by his siblings. So he didn't need language until his siblings went off to school.

How can you teach your child to use words? You

can't, says Dr. Hunt. Your child will learn for himself. But you can make it easier if you talk to him, read to him, think out loud for his benefit, and keep him bathed in the sound of words.

In colonial days, children were exposed from infancy to reading aloud from the Bible. Dr. Hunt thinks this practice may have contributed to the outstanding verbal mastery of our founding fathers.

Have you ever thought of reading Shakespeare to your three year old? The father of Welsh poet Dylan Thomas did just that. Young Dylan may not have caught the intricacies of "To be or not to be . . ." and "Parting is such sweet sorrow . . ." but the music of the language may well have permeated his young brain and contributed to the development of his poetic skills.

There is no greater pleasure for parent or grandparent than to cradle a small child in one's arms and read to him with great expression. At three, our Jodi insisted on reading each book back to us. Her mimicry was hilarious.

Demanding or Permissive?

What about discipline? Does it promote or impede intelligence? Stern discipline discourages your child from being curious and from using his head to find out the reasons for things. A child can actually gain I.Q. points between the ages of four and seven if he comes from a home where decisions and their consequences are discussed. Whereas, according to studies by Professor Alfred Baldwin of New York University, children whose parents are either nonchalantly permissive or who arbitrarily demand obedience show a loss of I.Q. points.

The parent who pushes, who punishes an infant for his voluntary efforts or says, "Do this because I say so," is really saying "Don't think for yourself." An infant should be free to try himself, free to throw things, to see the effects of his efforts on the things he throws. How far does a sock go, how far does a rattle go, how far does a ball go when he throws it? What kind of a noise do they make when they hit the linoleum, the rug, the sidewalk, or the wall? A child should be encouraged to figure cause and effect and should be free within the limits of safety to explore things, to climb stairs, to use simple tools. Later on he should be free to climb trees and slide down cellar doors.

Frequently parents push too hard. If you make your love for your child conditional on what you want him to do, you are setting the stage for a very real danger. As long as you provide only the opportunities for problem solving and let your child's motive for learning be that of pleasing himself and feeling a sense of accomplishment, you are on the right track.

It seems that love, attention, and cuddling, so pleasurable to give and receive, can bring about not only improved brain power but can increase the child's ability to cope. It was found in one study that just simply handling test animals, particularly the young ones, increased the weight of their adrenal glands. This is the "fight or flight" gland that helps one to handle stress.

As important as this enriched environment is in the development of the brain and intellect, there are other areas of concern which should get high priority. Foremost among these is nutrition. If a child is malnourished, he is apathetic and unresponsive to his environment no matter how loving it is.

And this is where love and wheat germ are partners. The enriched environment alone will not build intelligence, and neither will the best nutrition in the world if it is administered without love and attention.

You have a wonderful opportunity during the baby's first years to set up some good eating habits. I'm talking about the foods you don't give to baby as well as the foods you encourage him to eat. One food you should withhold now and forever is sugar.

Do not make the mistake of sweetening baby's food as an inducement to eat it—no matter how undernourished and washed out he may appear to you.

A few years ago, we had an Indian lad, an exile from Uganda, living with us while he waited for his wife and baby son to be admitted to the United States. When they did arrive, the mother was rail thin and the nine-month-old baby was monstrously fat. So fat, he hardly moved. When she fixed his first bottle at our house she asked for the sugar. "What for?" I asked. "To make his milk sweet so he will drink it," she answered. "Why not try giving it to him unsweetened?" I suggested. She did. The baby drank it avidly.

At breakfast, she fed him one of the baby cereals she had brought over from England—all superrefined pap. "Do you ever give him eggs for breakfast?" I asked. "He seems to be more in need of protein than starch."

"He doesn't like eggs," she said.

"Are you willing to try adding an egg yolk to his cereal tomorrow morning?" She did and the baby loved it.

Instead of pretzels for snack chewing, his mother began giving him raw apple slices and bone meal cookies. In two months that baby had lost quite a bit of fat; he smiled more and cooed more and started to bump the baby bouncer with great vigor.

At this very important stage of your child's life, he is not only building his brain which must have many nutrients in order to grow to its full potential, he is also establishing eating habits that will stay with him for the rest of his life.

My doctor once advised me, "Do not let your child have a taste of sugar until he is six, and the child will never develop a sweet tooth and will eat much more protein. He will not be subject to colds and will generally be a far healthier human being than most."

My doctor was a very wise man. Not only was I training my children away from sweets, I was also training myself to make wholesome appetizing dishes and desserts without sugar. For example, I found a wonderful source of natural sweetness in fruit juices. When I make applesauce, I use either unsweetened apple juice or pineapple juice as the liquid instead of water. It has a delectable flavor. If the apples are too sour, I add some blackstrap molasses or a tiny bit of honey. Sometimes I cook the apples with presoaked raisins and the water they've been soaked in. For tiny tots, I put some of this mixture through the blender. The raisins add extra iron.

To avoid sugar you must be wary of hidden sugar in supermarket desserts such as puddings, gelatin desserts, and canned fruits (except those that are water packed). Use nothing that has been artificially sweetened and pass up commercial fruit "drinks" and "ades" in favor of fresh juices.

Always check labels carefully on juice cans or bottles; if they don't say something like "no sugar added," they probably do contain sugar. The label should indicate 100 percent pure juice. Any other product probably has water and sugar added.

Don't get into the habit of giving baby a commercial teething biscuit, crackers, or pretzels to distract him when he cries. These products contain mostly empty calories that contribute nothing to health and displace the foods that do. Not all of his cries mean hunger. Sometimes baby cries when he is bored. What he needs is a smile, a hug, and a kind word from you, or maybe a change of scenery or something to play with.

For the periods of serious teething, give him a homemade bone meal cooky to gnaw on. It supplies important nutrients and provides comfort for his gums. A piece of crisp, whole wheat buttered toast (especially the heel of the loaf) is a good teether. So are manageable bones with no sharp parts, little fist-size chicken, lamb, or steak bones. Make sure there is nothing attached to the bone which baby can't handle.

When your tot is in the middle of his first year, introduce him or her to yogurt, wheat germ, and brewer's yeast. Now's the time to make these foods seem as natural to him as candy, cake, and coke are to most kids.

Why Yogurt?

Breast milk is known to support the growth of valuable intestinal bacteria better than cows' milk does. So if you are bottle feeding, I believe it is wise to introduce yogurt early, it will greatly improve powers of resistance. But until your baby is six months old, use only the yogurt culture, and gradually—a few grains to each bottle feeding. According to the medical journal, *Nederlands Tijdschrift voor Geneeskun De* (December 1975), there is evidence that infants can't tolerate the protein in incubated yogurt until they are six months old. You can use acidophilus culture powder instead— a capsule split up into bottles to total one capsule a day.

When baby is six months old, introduce him to the real thing—yogurt which you have made yourself from whole milk. Commercial yogurts are usually made from fat-free milk. Baby needs fat. If you must occasionally use the fat-free yogurt, give your baby bread and butter with it. But it is so cheap and easy to make your own, and the finished product is far superior to most commercial yogurts because, for one thing, you can add yogurt culture which contains the very important acidophilus strain not contained in most commercial yogurts, (Erivan does have acidophilus).

A yogurt maker is a nice convenience, but you don't need one. Use one of those styrofoam picnic hampers that cost about one dollar. Fill two mason jars with hot water and put them in the hamper while you prepare the yogurt. This will bring the box to a nice warmth for incubating the yogurt culture.

If you're using very fresh raw milk, simply warm it to 115°F. (If you're not sure of the freshness of the milk, bring it to a near boil to kill off competing bacteria. Cool to 115°F. and proceed.) Add the yogurt culture (available at natural food stores). Blend the ingredients thoroughly with a wire whisk or slotted spoon, then pour the mixture into very clean—preferably sterile—containers. Put the containers into the styrofoam hamper until set. It may take 12 hours or more.

Yogurt can also be incubated in an oven. Set the heat to 250°F. for about five minutes, then turn the oven off and put yogurt in. You can also make yogurt in a thermos bottle. First fill the bottle with hot water and let set for a few minutes. Pour the water out, add yogurt and let it set.

Do not be tempted to give your tot a sip of your coffee, tea, or soft drink. I see this happening so frequently always with the disclaimer "a little bit won't hurt him, and he likes it so much." All of these drinks contain undesirable ingredients. Why develop your baby's taste for them? There are so many good foods that will delight him just as much, if not more, and every empty calorie displaces a nutrient which could be vital to his brain and brawn.

If you must have soda in the house—and you too would be far better off if you didn't—then let it be known to your child that this is "for adults only, X-rated for kids" and no exceptions.

In one family the parents found it increasingly difficult to resist their child's demands for a taste of the cola drink they often had with their meals. They switched to club soda, unsweetened and certainly far better than the artificially colored, chemicalized, and caffeinic cola drink. Occasionally, the child gets some of mom and dad's club soda—just a little bit—in her orange juice. To her, this is a big treat.

When babies are overweight, some pediatricians remove the fat from the formula in order to decrease the calories, but they continue to add sugar. I think this is a mistake. Fat stays in the stomach longer than either protein or sugar and thus fat postpones hunger pangs. In fact, the best way to prevent an infant from becoming overweight is to allow him more fat than standard formulas supply, wrote Adele Davis in *Let's Have Healthy Children.* Such a baby gets hungry less frequently and sleeps soundly for longer periods. Of course, this is great for your morale. You get more rest and feel more like tackling the laundry, taking a nice brisk walk with baby, and being a loving wife to your husband, who sometimes feels like a stepchild.

You should acquaint your baby with the bottle even though you have an abundant supply of milk. There will come a time when you'll want to go out for the day or an evening and leave baby with a babysitter or your husband. It's a good idea too to have Daddy give baby that bottle, paving the way to a nice close rapport between the two most important people in your life. It doesn't have to be milk in the bottle every time. It could be unsalted vegetable cooking water, raisin and almond water, orange juice, or water with some brewer's yeast in it. You can also express milk from your breasts after several feedings and keep this in the freezer for emergencies.

Vitamins for Small Children

How about vitamins for small children? Yes. But, make sure they are not artificially colored or flavored.

Mrs. B., a lady from New Jersey told me that when her baby was four months old, the pediatrician prescribed a popular brand of children's vitamin. It was artificially flavored. Her child became fussy, could not rest comfortably and cried a lot. Mrs. B. called the pediatrician who said the baby must be teething and he prescribed a baby aspirin (containing salicylates, which many children cannot handle). Thus began an escalating case of hyperactivity. The child generally awoke several times every night, was so squirmy she would fall out of her high chair three times during a single meal and she whined and wept most of the time. This type of behavior continued for nearly four years. Then Mrs. B. heard about the additive-free diet advocated for hyperactive children by Ben Feingold, M.D. through a TV show, eliminated all additives from her daughter's diet, and three days later the baby slept 11 hours without a whimper. When she awoke she climbed out of her crib, grinned mischieviously as she stuck her head around the door and said, "Peek-a-boo."

Dr. Feingold estimates that there are 10 million children in the country suffering from hyperactivity due to additives.

The first and best supplement you can give your baby is cod liver oil. I don't know why cod liver oil has gone out of fashion. My doctor told me to use the whole cod liver oil—not the concentrated kind. Babies thrive best on the whole oil, he told me, and I found this to be true.

The need of the growing child for vitamins is relatively great in proportion to his size, wrote Mary Swartz Rose, Ph.D., in her book, *Feeding the Family*, (Macmillan, New York, 1940). She suggests starting with a quarter-teaspoon of cod liver oil daily with one breast feeding in the baby's second week and increasing to half-a-teaspoon by the third week. By his sixth week, a baby should be getting one teaspoon of cod liver oil and at the third month, it should be increased to two teaspoons daily.

Along with cod liver oil, introduce your infant to wheat germ oil. This oil is rich in polyunsaturates, something bottle-fed babies get very little of. It was reported many years ago by A. E. Hansen in the *American Journal of the Diseases of Children* that when infants suffering from a certain type of eczema are given unsaturated fatty acids, the eczema disappears. What blessed relief for mother and baby! If you start your child on wheat germ oil at the beginning you may be spared the problem completely.

Besides wheat germ oil, I recommend giving liquid vitamin E (mixed tocopherols) too. Start with a drop and build up to 20 drops over six months. Vitamin E is needed to prevent the oil from becoming rancid in the system by helping to preserve oxygen.

It's good to give liquid flavonoid C which has the bioflavonoids as well as ascorbic acid. Start with a few drops and build up to a teaspoonful. If anybody in our family has a cold, or if the baby has a sniffle, we triple the dosage of vitamin C. When my two-year-old granddaughter Becca has a runny nose, she asks for the vitamin C.

Just to make sure all the bases are covered, I recommend giving an all-purpose, liquid vitamin formula.

If you start your baby on these supplements when he or she is very young, they will become part of a routine and it just won't occur to the baby to reject them. Our granddaughter Jodi, age four, might leave her breakfast unfinished, but when she hears "Vitamin time," she perches on her chair and opens her mouth like a little bird. She especially likes to take her vitamins when she sees us taking ours. It makes her feel grown up.

Some people say, "Aren't you afraid to give a baby all those vitamins?" Frankly, I'm afraid not to. When certain nutrients are lacking, irreparable damage may result—especially in the first 15 months of life when the brain needs all kinds of nutrients in order to grow to its fullest potential. Giving supplements rarely causes harm. A nutritional shortage does cause damage.

Don't Be Satisfied with Minimal Amounts

When it comes to giving nutrients to your baby, don't be satisfied with the minimum amount that is deemed necessary to avoid an outright clinical deficiency. Better give more generous amounts which may help to build a higher degree of health resistence to disease. There is strong evidence that many nutrients are beneficial when given in more than the recommended amounts.

A child comes into the world iron rich and calcium

poor. That is why baby needs milk for calcium in liberal amounts from the day of birth and can get along on the meagre amount of iron milk contains to supplement his own body store.

By the end of the second month, according to Mary Swartz Rose, Ph.D., some special source of iron is needed to keep the baby growing at a good rate and building good red blood. It has been found that half-a-mg. of iron per pound of body weight is desirable. Thus if the baby weighs 10 pounds, he needs five mg. of iron. One tablespoon of blackstrap molasses contains 9.6 mg. of iron; two teaspoons would provide this baby with his iron requirements and a little more for good measure.

There is a distinct advantage in providing a considerable surplus over the recommended daily iron requirement. Infection interferes with the use of iron. Even a slight cold will cause a drop in the percentage of hemoglobin in the blood, requiring larger amounts of iron to restore the hemoglobin level to normal than were necessary to maintain it under ordinary conditions. Iron is used to best advantage when small amounts of copper are present in the diet. It just happens that blackstrap also provides a small amount of copper, so does nutritional yeast.

If you're going to use brewer's yeast or nutritional yeast as it is sometimes called (and I think it's a wonderful idea), start with very small quantities—about one-quarter teaspoon the first time you give it. Increase the amount to one teaspoon gradually, or by a quarter-teaspoon every four days. Don't worry about lumps of yeast, they will settle to the bottom of the bottle. The vitamins will leech into the liquid.

If your baby is not being nursed, use blackstrap molasses as the formula sweetener in an amount that will regulate the baby's bowels. If the baby has frequent movements, start the blackstrap at one-quarter teaspoon to an entire day's formula at first. If the stools do not become overly soft, increase gradually to as much as three teaspoons daily. Don't use any more than this unless the child is severely constipated.

If your baby wakes for feeding throughout the night, try giving him a special high-nutrient evening bottle that will stick to his ribs and encourage sound sleep. Once he is accustomed to the yeast and the blackstrap molasses, try putting a larger portion of his day's allotment in the evening bottle.

How to Start Your Baby on Solid Foods

Don't be in a hurry to add solid food to your baby's menu. These foods displace the milk which is a better source of protein and other nutrients than the solids you are pushing. And when you do add solid foods, for heaven sake, for baby's sake, and for your own sake, make your own. Do not be seduced by the loudly ballyhooed convenience of commercial baby foods. It is estimated that you will save as much as $25 a month if you make your own. I recently heard a pediatrician tell a television audience that the day of the commercial baby food is over. They have served their purpose. Since the advent of the blender, they no longer fill a crucial need. He suggested that parents keep a few jars just to use in emergency situations. Save the empty jars, wash them thoroughly. Whenever you have extra vegetables, meats, or soups, blenderize them and store them in these little jars in the freezer and you will always have an emergency supply of toddler food.

For daily feedings, use the same vegetables and meat that you serve the rest of the family for dinner and grind either in a Happy Baby Food Grinder (available at all department and drug stores, list $7.95) or blender. The Happy Baby Food Grinder is a convenient little device. It is easy to wash and so convenient to take with you when you travel or visit. You can keep the grinder at the table and use it on the spot to feed the baby the same food you are enjoying. You simply put his portion in the grinder, give the handle a few turns and spoon the food right out of the little container. This saves transfering food from one dish to another—a process which encourages bacterial growth and diminishes nutrients. It also means fewer dishes for you to wash.

You can grind a nice piece of liver, pot roast, chicken, fish, some lamb or veal—whatever is on your menu. And be sure to include the cooking liquid—that's where some of the minerals and water soluble vitamins are.

Be sure to introduce baby to organ meats—brains, sweetbreads, kidneys, as well as liver. Then he won't develop a hang-up about these meats which hold excellent nutrition, and are of a good consistency for the beginning eater, if not overcooked. Baby beef or calves' liver, cut into cubes and dipped into boiling broth for a half-minute tastes great, and will retain almost all of the good nutrients of the raw liver. The organ meats can also be cooked by slicing thin and quickly sautéing on both sides in hot fat or oil.

Handling Problem Eaters

Some children are good eaters. And some children are problem eaters. Practically all the books on child care, and all the pediatricians, too, will tell you that your child will eat when he is hungry. Just leave him alone.

I know one mother who went along with this advice. Her child ate very little and when the child was hungry she drank milk. Eventually the girl became listless and anemic and then the pediatrician changed his tune. "Sit her down and make her eat," he advised.

Our first child was never interested in food when he was a baby. I devised all kinds of ways to get him into the high chair and then to get him to eat. I would place an interesting object on the high chair tray and then he would eagerly climb in. I would save small jars with lids, and he would busy himself trying to match jars and lids while I spooned his food into him. I know this is not what the psychiatrists and child guidance experts endorse, but it gets important nutrients into them when they need them most, and it saves a mother from going out of her mind with worry.

It is important to realize however that there is quite a difference between a small appetite and a poor appetite. Our granddaughter Jodi has a small appetite. She fills up quickly. But she is a vegetable freak. She'll eat string beans and broccoli till she's ready to burst. She'll leave no room for meat and potatoes. Her mother soon learned to offer the meat and potato first and then let her indulge her passion for vegetables.

Jodi went off the bottle at a year, which was probably too soon, and she never drank much milk after that. Our big challenge is to get enough calcium into her. According to the Food and Nutrition Board of the National Research Council, a child's daily requirement for calcium from birth to six years of age is one gram (1,000 mg.). Jodi loves yogurt and cottage cheese. One cup of yogurt (eight ounces) provides 300 mg. of calcium; a half-cup of cottage cheese has 240 mg.; blackstrap molasses, which she loves, has 259 mg. in a tablespoon; an egg has 32 mg.; broccoli flowers have 64 mg. to three-fourths of a cup, (she eats both). Raisins, on which she *noshes,* have 20 mg. to one-quarter cup and brown rice, which she loves, has 22 mg. to three-fourths of a cup. She also loves Muenster cheese which provides a whopping 33 mg. per slice.

Add it all up and you get 1,465 mg. of calcium which should satisfy her daily need if she ate all these foods every day. But, who knows if she eats her daily quota? So, we fill in by making creamed soups, rice pudding (using brown rice, raisins, milk, and eggs) and bone meal cookies.

Calcium for Children Who Won't Drink Milk

For a child who isn't a milk drinker, it's a good idea to use blackstrap molasses as the sweetener in all baked goods and puddings. Always use carob instead of chocolate. For one thing there are 352 mg. of calcium to 100 grams, or about one-fourth pound of carob, versus semisweet chocolate with only 30 mg. per 100 grams, plus lots of sugar, theobromine, and oxalic acid which tends to bind with calcium so it is lost to the system.

Calcium is necessary for the strength of the bones, the hardness of the teeth, firmness of muscle tone, for the nerves, for coagulation of the blood, for every beat of the heart, for digestion, for kidney functioning and the workings of other vital organs, and for the general health of the body.

Meat does not provide enough calcium for the formation of the bones. Meat is rich in phosphorus which ushers excess calcium out of the body. Dr. Carl J. Reich,

M.D., of Canada, would have us serve bone meal powder on every cut of meat, since the body needs twice as much calcium as phosphorus.

It is not a bad idea at all to sprinkle some bone meal powder onto meats the same as others do salt. But do it sparingly, because the bone meal powder might be gritty. Start your baby on meat with bone meal while he is still in the high chair and the combination will be a natural to him. The child will be less subject to broken bones, will sleep better, be more relaxed, and sweeter tempered. Lack of calcium can lead to crankiness and insomnia.

Calcium is excreted from the body in wounds, open sores, and ulcers. If your tot has a diaper rash, he's losing calcium.

An excellent source of calcium, frequently overlooked, is sesame seeds—the brown ones with their hulls on. Sesame seeds are definitely included in the "love and wheat germ" approach to child raising. Besides being rich storehouses of B vitamins and minerals, they are one of the very few sources of vitamin T.

Chances are you have never heard of vitamin T. You will not find it at the drug store or even at the natural food store. Sometimes called Goetsch's vitamin, vitamin T, according to the *Merck Index of Chemicals and Drugs* (seventh edition, Merckling Co. Publishers, Rahway, N.J., 1960) is a complex of growth-promoting substances. This combination is encased in the tiny sesame seed, which is practically the only source of vitamin T for human use. Very small amounts are present in animal tissues, like liver and spleen.

Apparently, there is some mysterious quality in vitamin T which promotes and encourages appetite. When used back in 1953 to strengthen the lifeline of premature infants, it produced marvelous results. Dr. H.

Schmidt presented his observations on the use of vitamin T in 28 premature infants and in 52 full-term infants whose development was retarded in *Die Medizinische Stuttgart.* Dr. Schmidt administered five drops of the vitamin T preparation twice daily, even to weak, premature infants. To the older infants he gave 10 drops twice daily and later three times daily. The drops were usually given in milk. One premature infant who weighed only 1,300 grams (2.09 pounds) received the treatment for eight weeks, but most of the other children received vitamin T for only nine to 21 days.

Apparently the vitamin T was able to fan the breath of life for these tiny infants because Dr. Schmidt reports that they showed a tendency to increase in weight where previously their weight gain was almost nil. Although premature babies frequently show intolerance to many foods, this vitamin preparation was well tolerated. The babies' stools remained normal, and no intestinal disturbances resulted, even in the weakest premature infants. In my opinion, any substance which can so strengthen the tenuous hold on life of such tiny little babies certainly rates intensive study.

Adding Sesame to Baby's Diet

The following recipes will help you to incorporate the mighty sesame seed into your baby's daily eating plan. These are great dishes for all youngsters but come in especially handy when a child is allergic to milk.

One hundred grams, or slightly less than one-fourth pound of *whole* sesame seeds contains a whopping 1,160 mg. of calcium. When they are hulled, they contain only 110 mg. of calcium.

Look for tahini (sesame butter) that is made from

unhulled seeds. Make your own tahini by grinding sesame seeds in a little seed mill or pulverizing them with a mortar and pestle. Add a tiny bit of sesame oil to get peanut butter consistency.

Use tahini the same as you would peanut butter, only more so. Add a little lemon juice to tahini—diluted with water—and it's a great salad dressing for you and your child. Combine with ground coconut, wheat germ, and a little honey or blackstrap molasses and you have a delectable confection—*halvah*.

I make a special hummus of tahini, lemon juice, garbanzos, garlic, and chopped parsley. I put it out with a platter of carrot sticks, turnip slices, and any other raw vegetables we have in the refrigerator, and we have a dip party.

Sometimes we put small portions of hummus in dolly dishes and give each child her own dip dish. This is a good idea for even a one year old, and will preclude the use of candy and cookies that are the usual fare at children's parties.

Hummus for Tiny Tots

In your blender combine one-half cup cooked chick-peas with six heaping tablespoons tahini, one half-teaspoon salt, the juice of one clove of garlic, and about three tablespoons of lemon juice. Whiz until smooth. This makes a thinner consistency than the usual hummus.

If baby has not been introduced to all of these ingredients, add tahini to mashed potatoes for his version of the dip.

Sesame Seed Milk

2 cups water

¼ cup sesame seeds

Whiz in blender for about two minutes, strain to remove hulls.

Vary the flavor by adding any of these nutritional flavor enhancers; one tablespoon of carob powder, a few pitted dates, a little honey, molasses, a banana, a few raisins, any fresh fruit concentrate, or date sugar. After adding, reblend the mixture thoroughly.

You can also make sesame seed milk simply by beating tahini and water very thoroughly with a rotary beater, or by combining tahini and water in your blender. Use about four tablespoons of tahini to two cups of water. If sweetening is desired, add a little honey before blending.

METRIC CONVERSION

1 teaspoon = 5 ml.		1 tablespoon = 15 ml.
1 ounce = 30 ml.		1 cup = 240 ml./.24 l.
1 quart = 950 ml./.95 l.		1 gallon = 3.80 l.
1 ounce = 28 gr.		1 pound = 454 gr./.454 kg.

F.°	200	225	250	275	300	325	350	375	400	425	450
C.°	93	107	121	135	149	163	177	191	204	218	232

Sesame Cream

1 cup warm water

1 cup sesame seeds

Whiz in your blender until smooth. Add one tablespoon of honey or a little pure vanilla if you like, and whiz again.

Sesame Seed Yogurt

This yogurt is made much the same as cow's milk yogurt. Add yogurt culture to sesame seed milk and let it stand overnight in a warm place for about 12 hours.

Sesame Seed Cheese

First make a sesame seed clabber by letting the sesame seed milk stand overnight in a warm place. You might add some lemon juice to hasten the souring process. Clabber should be ready in 24 to 36 hours. Put the clabber in a cloth bag and hang overnight the same as when making cottage cheese from sour milk. Collect the whey in another utensil. Whey may be drunk as a good laxative or used as a skin lotion. It is very good for chapped hands. The whey can also be used in baked goods or you can cook rice or potatoes in it.

METRIC CONVERSION

1 teaspoon = 5 ml.	1 tablespoon = 15 ml.
1 ounce = 30 ml.	1 cup = 240 ml./.24 l.
1 quart = 950 ml./.95 l.	1 gallon = 3.80 l.
1 ounce = 28 gr.	1 pound = 454 gr./.454 kg.

F.°	200	225	250	275	300	325	350	375	400	425	450
C.°	93	107	121	135	149	163	177	191	204	218	232

Finger Foods

While they're learning to handle a spoon effectively, tots love finger foods. Try these:

Banana slices are a favorite with our grandchildren.

Apple slices and orange segments from which the seeds have been removed are popular.

Avocado is a great finger food for babies. It's rich in the whole alphabet of vitamins. It has a soft as velvet mouth feel, especially comforting to teething gums, and even toothless infants can gum it to a swallowing consistency. Let your baby feed himself little cubes of this most delectable fruit.

Whole grain bread, cut in finger strips and allowed to air dry can be spread with dairy butter or sesame butter. To make bread lots of fun, cut out forms with animal cooky cutters and toast or air dry.

Be sure to stay close by baby when he is finger feeding to make sure he doesn't get any pieces that he can't handle into his throat.

Cottage cheese pancakes mixed in the blender are good tasting, highly nutritious, and can be easily handled by the toothless tot who likes to feed himself. Here are two recipes. Try them both. Make them for breakfast, and count baby in if he has been introduced to all the ingredients in the recipe.

Cottage Cheese Pancakes

6 eggs

1½ cups cottage cheese

¼ cup whole wheat flour

¼ cup wheat germ

1 tablespoon nutritional yeast

½ teaspoon kelp or salt

Combine all ingredients in blender and whiz till smooth. Drop by tablespoon on lightly greased griddle. Bake until nicely browned. This makes two dozen three-inch pancakes. Serve with sour cream or yogurt. Serve baby his own portion of yogurt in an unbreakable dish and let him dip his pancakes in it.

METRIC CONVERSION										
1 teaspoon = 5 ml.					1 tablespoon = 15 ml.					
1 ounce = 30 ml.					1 cup = 240 ml./.24 l.					
1 quart = 950 ml./.95 l.					1 gallon = 3.80 l.					
1 ounce = 28 gr.					1 pound = 454 gr./.454 kg.					

F.°	200	225	250	275	300	325	350	375	400	425	450
C.°	93	107	121	135	149	163	177	191	204	218	232

Make sure your baby has been introduced to every ingredient in this recipe before you give him these:

Bone Meal Cookies

To help cut strong teeth, strong bones, and pleasant dispositions. (The combination of wheat and soy makes these cookies a complete protein.)

3 tablespoons blackstrap molasses

2 tablespoons oil

1 beaten egg yolk

½ cup whole wheat flour

¼ cup soy flour or rice polish

¼ cup wheat germ

¼ cup bone meal powder

Combine molasses, oil, and egg yolk. Add the dry ingredients. If batter is too thick, add one tablespoon orange juice, apple juice, milk, or vegetable water. Roll dough about one-quarter inch thick. Cut into easy to handle shapes. For tiny babies, the rectangular shape—about three-quarters of an inch wide and twice as long. Bake at 350°F. for 12 to 15 minutes or until lightly browned. When baby is a year old, he will be delighted with animal shapes. These cookies have so many good nutrients, you will be delighted to see your baby gnaw away at them. Jodi loved these cookies when she was tiny.

These cookies freeze well and can be eaten straight from the freezer. Baby welcomes something cold when his gums hurt.

For those days when baby is fretful and doesn't want to eat—and everybody has days like that—a few of these cookies will satisfy his need to gnaw on something, at the same time supplying him with almost every nutrient in the book.

Chicken Soup

(for baby and family)

Everybody loves chicken soup—even the little high chair thumper. I always have some in the freezer, stored in individual servings. There are times when Jodi doesn't want what's on the menu. She'll always settle for chicken soup with brown rice and *einlauf* (egg dumplings) which is absolutely delicious and nutritious.

You probably have your own favorite recipe for chicken soup. I start mine with marrow bones and always include the well-washed gizzard, heart, neck, and feet along with a well-cleaned, cut-up, approx. five-pound chicken. I cook the bones first with a little lemon juice (about two tablespoons). This is to release the calcium. Then I skim, but I save the skimmings for a meat or lentil dish where they won't show. Add the chicken and parts, bring to a quick boil, then simmer for about a half hour. Then add:

2 onions, with a little of the onion
    skin (to be removed later)

1 large carrot, well scrubbed but
    not pared, cut into lengthwise strips

2 stalks celery, including leaves

1 bay leaf

2 sprigs fresh dill, if I'm lucky enough to
    have it, otherwise, one teaspoon dill weed

1 scrubbed parsnip (optional but very good)

1 piece parsley root with tops
    (I should be so lucky)

½ teaspoon ginger

1 teaspoon kelp

papaya seeds (dried and grated in a
    pepper mill), optional

Cook another half hour or until chicken is tender.

Put some of the chicken in the blender with a little chicken soup to engage the blades and you have baby's meat course. Fix the rest for the family—any way you like—see chicken recipes in index.

METRIC CONVERSION										

1 teaspoon = 5 ml.
1 ounce = 30 ml.
1 quart = 950 ml./.95 l.

1 tablespoon = 15 ml.
1 cup = 240 ml./.24 l.
1 gallon — 3.80 l.

1 ounce = 28 gr.

1 pound = 454 gr./.454 kg.

F.°	200	225	250	275	300	325	350	375	400	425	450
C.°	93	107	121	135	149	163	177	191	204	218	232

Blenderize some cooked brown rice and some carrots from the soup either together or separately for a second course for baby. If baby is ready for finger foods, just cut up the carrots. Give the chicken soup last. If you give it first, baby may not have room for the rest of his dinner. Somehow there's always room for chicken soup.

If baby didn't eat much of the meat and you think he needs more protein, then make an *einlauf,* which is an egg dumpling.

Einlauf

(Eggdrop for Soup)

1 egg

2 tablespoons whole wheat flour
   (or 1 tablespoon soy and
    1 tablespoon whole wheat)

pinch of salt

Blend ingredients until smooth. Pour into boiling soup from a spoon, either in small drops or in a steady, thin stream. Cover and boil for about five minutes. This is delicious. It beats penicillin for helping sick kids battle the blues.

Take some of the marrow out of a bone and serve a little to baby. Serve the rest to your hearty, happy eaters. Bone marrow is so delicious and so strengthening you can almost feel it charge your batteries as you eat it.

METRIC CONVERSION

1 teaspoon = 5 ml.　　　　　　　　　1 tablespoon = 15 ml.
1 ounce = 30 ml.　　　　　　　　　　1 cup = 240 ml./.24 l.
1 quart = 950 ml./.95 l.　　　　　　1 gallon = 3.80 l.

1 ounce = 28 gr.　　　　　　　　　　1 pound = 454 gr./.454 kg.

F.°	200	225	250	275	300	325	350	375	400	425	450
C.°	93	107	121	135	149	163	177	191	204	218	232

Cereals

Instead of commercial dry cereals, most of which have B.H.A., B.H.T., and a rainbow of artificial colors, the kind that can trigger hyperactivity in susceptible youngsters, make your own delicious cereals. You'll feel a nice warm glow when you feed baby a cereal you know is health building and free of harmful substances.

This recipe for Muesli is adapted from one by Gena Larsen in her excellent book, *Better Food for Better Babies* (Keats Publishing, Inc., New Canaan, Connecticut, 1972, © by Gena Larson).

Beginner's Muesli Cereal

(for one year old or older)

Soak overnight:

1 tablespoon oat flakes

1 teaspoon wheat germ

2 tablespoons apple juice or
raisin nut water or plain water

Next morning add:

1 teaspoon lemon juice

½ large apple, grated (Use skin for older
child, if apple has not been sprayed.)

1 tablespoon cream, top milk, or
sesame milk, mixed with

1 teaspoon almond butter or tahini

A word about oatmeal: rolled oats and oatmeal, like brown rice, are essentially whole grain products from the nutritive standpoint. When oat groats are milled, very little is removed. Most of the bran, the aleurone layer and the germ, which are rich in protein, lipids, vitamins, and minerals, remain with the part used as human food. Therefore, rolled oats and oatmeal are higher in protein, fat, and energy value as well as in calcium, phosphorus, iron, and thiamine content than other processed cereal foods.

Millet Cereals

For babies over six months old, familia cereals (a muesli-type cereal) are available at practically all natural food stores and at many supermarkets. We find them much too sweet. However, I do keep a package in the freezer for emergency use, and add wheat germ to it to dilute the sweetness. Jodi loves this cereal sprinkled on her hot oatmeal, hot millet, or hot wheat cereal which we make in a thermos bottle and have ready and waiting when we come down in the morning and the kids are ravenous.

Millet is high in protein and mineral values and is hypoallergenic—that is, there are no recorded cases of allergy to this grain. Very popular in Europe, it is not well known in the United States. However, you'll find it in most natural food stores.

Thermos Millet

To make millet in a thermos, add a half-cup of millet to two cups of water and bring to a boil, add one-fourth teaspoon salt and pour the mixture into a hot, glass-lined thermos. After corking the bottle, lay it on its side. This will facilitate removal of the contents. For older babies, you may add raisins to the mixture before putting it into the thermos, in which we use a bit less millet.

METRIC CONVERSION										
1 teaspoon = 5 ml.					1 tablespoon = 15 ml.					
1 ounce = 30 ml.					1 cup = 240 ml./.24 l.					
1 quart = 950 ml./.95 l.					1 gallon = 3.80 l.					
1 ounce = 28 gr.					1 pound = 454 gr./.454 kg.					
F.° 200	225	250	275	300	325	350	375	400	425	450
C.° 93	107	121	135	149	163	177	191	204	218	232

When your baby gets to be about three years old and becomes a social gadabout, he's going to see a lot of candy and store-bought cookies. And if he indulges once in a while, don't make an issue of it. So long as your child realizes that this kind of eating is an occasional thing, you've got it made.

Last week I told Jodi, "Next time you come to visit me we're going to make some candy that you can eat every day." She counted the days to her next visit when we had a most happy session making:

Molasses Dreams

½ cup blackstrap molasses

½ cup peanut butter

½ cup dry milk

½ cup wheat germ

Mix all ingredients into a ball. Break off small pieces, the size of a marble, and roll in any of these ingredients: sesame seeds, unsweetened coconut crumbs, sunflower seeds, crushed walnuts, pecans, almonds, or cashews. I let Jodi choose. She sampled them all and liked the sesame best.

Incidentally, this is a great treat for children's parties. Make a big platter using different coatings.

Everything in this recipe contributes to health. Even though it is sweet and delicious, it contains no no-no's. Nevertheless, since they are of a sticky consistency, it's a good idea to encourage mouth rinsing after eating them.

The Terrible Twos Don't Last Forever

If your child is now into the terrible twos, relax. This too will pass. On their way from diapers to dungarees, kids go through many stages. In exasperation I once asked my sister, whose children are older than mine, what the most difficult stage is. "The one they're in," she answered.

If there's anything more frustrating than the terrible twos, it's the terrible two and a halfs, a pediatrician once observed.

The two year old has learned how to say "No," and he uses his veto power more frequently than the veto was ever used at the U.N. At this stage it is wise to avoid giving your child the opportunity to say no to something that's good for him. Don't ask, "Do you want an egg for breakfast?" Ask instead, "Do you want your egg boiled or scrambled this morning?" All youngsters like to be given a choice. Make sure both alternatives you offer are acceptable to you. Do not ask, "What do you want for breakfast?" I know of one youngster who answered "Fried worms and I want you to eat some too!" Ask instead, "Would you like to start with cereal or an egg this morning?" or "Do you want your bread plain or toasted, and do you want butter or cream cheese on your bread?" Get the idea? Either answer would be fine so you're both happy.

The two and a halfer goes on food jags. He likes the same things over and over. He likes things that are familiar. Play along with him. He'll soon be ready to branch out. In the meantime, thank heaven you're giving him the whole spectrum of vitamins and minerals in his supplements so you don't have to worry about a deficiency that can hurt.

Eventually, baby turns three, and then it's "thank heaven for little boys and girls." Threes are absolutely delightful.

Now that my own children are grown, what I miss most around the house is a three year old spinning around the corner on a bicycle and making strange noises as he shifts the gears into high speed. Every household needs one.

At three, he usually has a full complement of teeth and he loves to use them. He gives up his two-year-old food jags and develops a passion for raw vegetables. He likes the taste and the texture of raw carrots, raw beans, raw peas, raw sweet potatoes, raw broccoli, raw potatoes, and even raw cooky dough.

Taking a cue from your three year old, you have a wonderful opportunity to provide some powerful nutrition for your whole family. In this respect, the three year old is wiser than his mother who insists on cooking everything to death. Let him crunch it up in the raw— and get the whole family to join him!

Chapter 3
Coping With —
and Cooking for —
Teenagers, the Nonstop Crowd

My mother had a favorite expression she used to bolster my spirits when our four kids were little and rambunctious. "Little children—little problems," she would sigh. "Big children—big problems."

This little saying was supposed to be a great source of comfort. I must confess it didn't comfort me. Here I was surrounded by those "little problems" she talked about and what did I have to look forward to?—bigger problems! I mean, what problem could seem more life-and-death than getting your close-mouthed baby to eat his egg? Or getting your toddler to tell you—before he goes? (Sure, he finally gets the idea and tells you before, but it always happens when there's a cab at the curb tooting its horn, and you have your darling all bundled up in six layers of snowsuit.)

I once said to my mother—in desperation. "Mom, you raised five. How did you ever train us?"

"Look," she said, "I never trained you—and you all know how."

Funny thing, they did learn how. They grew out of toidy seats, out of diapers, and before I realized it I had tweeners and teeners to cope with—a whole new ball game.

The tween years are particularly frustrating for girls. These are the in-between years when they are too old for toys and too young for boys. I remember the classic comment of a daughter grumbling about her lack of status as a tweener because, "I'm past the stage of childhood but haven't reached the stage of adultery."

When they get to be teenagers, the challenges really begin. They are trying to untie the apron strings—not without considerable trepidation which they try to conceal with a show of bravado.

"As teenagers their greatest need is not to need us," says Dr. Haim G. Ginott, in his excellent book, *Between Parent and Teenager* (Macmillan, New York, 1969). But, "As parents, our need is to be needed. Conflict is real; we experience it daily. This can be our finest hour. To let go when we want to hold on, requires utmost generosity and love."

I found a very helpful poem in the old *Saturday Evening Post* (February 21, 1959), which expresses so well what you feel but cannot say:

"The Invisible Line"
by Louise McNeill

Mothers must draw a subtle line
Finer than any thread is fine;
Must firmly hold but never clutch,
Must freely give but not too much,
Must stand apart but never far,
Must heal the wound but bless the scar;
And falsely speaking, truly tell,
And, guarding, never guard too well;
And hearing, fail to overhear;
And, fearing all things, have no fear;
And loving, love each child the best
Yet no child dearer than the rest.

At this age, perhaps more than ever, love and wheat germ can make all the difference. Love and wheat germ can help both parent and teenager to weather the inevitable storms of this turbulent period, and to come up smiling. Also, it can have a profound effect on the future.

Consider this: it is now known that the kind of food a girl eats in her teens, affects not only her present well-being, but can actually affect the baby she bears when she's 20 or 30. Good nutrition is vital during puberty because this is the time when ovaries develop their lifetime supply of egg cells that will later be used in the reproductive process, says nutritionist Dr. Helen Swenerton of the University of California at Davis. In the later stages of pregnancy, the fetus takes its nourishment from the placenta. At the beginning it feeds on the nutrients already in the egg. Therefore, even a crash nutrition program during pregnancy can't entirely make up for the earlier poor nutrition of the potato chip-cola diet typical of the teenager.

No matter how earnestly you caution your teeners about the importance of good diet, they will challenge you—challenge your right to "practice medicine without a license." But don't despair. It does get through to them. At this age they have to challenge you. It's part of the ritual of cutting the apron strings.

Ground Rules for Harmony

There are a few ground rules to be observed with teenagers which will make life more pleasant all around and make it easier for you to keep adding the love to the wheat germ. Most important, try not to take your role as a nutrition missionary too seriously. I know good food is important, but like those hell-fire and brimstone sermons, an overdose can turn people away from a good thing.

I began sneaking nutrition into my family long before most people could spell 'granola.' I must admit that in the beginning I got carried away and many times I overdid it. I was willing to sacrifice taste for quality. That's a mistake. If it doesn't taste good, no matter how nutritious it is, it won't do them a darn bit of good, because they're not going to eat it.

I once spent a whole morning baking all kinds of goodies and enriched them thoroughly with wheat germ, yeast, rice polish, soy powder—the whole works. I had all kinds of 'good goodies' waiting for the kids when they got home from school. I can still recall the frustration I felt when Bob swept in, opened every cupboard and drawer in the house and then, with hands on hips said, "Don't we have a decent store-bought cooky in the house?" So I learned to put the damper on the zeal that was infiltrating my baked goods.

I know of one mother who was even more zealous than I was. She would put wheat germ in the spaghetti sauce! Her family did not like it and, of course, ate very little of it. She was defeating her own purposes. She could have used the whole wheat spaghetti which is delicious and available at natural food stores, and she would have gotten all the wheat germ portion right there in the spaghetti without affecting the taste of the sauce.

There are some foods which can take wheat germ without shouting about it. Meat loaf and hamburger dishes, for instance. Some people coat their liver with wheat germ. I don't. I think wheat germ has a sort of sweet flavor that does not marry well with liver. However, taste is a very individual thing. Some people do like it. I prefer to coat my liver with sesame seeds, which for me enhances the flavor and crunch of the liver. You'll have to do a little experimenting there. You've got to remember this: If your family does not like it, then for heaven's sake, don't persist in doing it. You must, at all cost, avoid any kind of confrontation over food appeal.

If you have overdone some ingredient, and someone remarks about it, don't argue the point. Admit that you may have been carried away, and will try the recipe again a different way. Otherwise, they won't even try the dish when you present it again.

My children, who are a product of their generation and subject to the prevailing notions of the day, resisted many of my efforts, of course.

Shortly after I had learned of the dangers of chemicals, and had cleaned out my shelves of all the no-no's, but had not yet learned to substitute the goodies, my son David said in total desperation, "I'll never die of cancer, or of a heart attack. But I sure as heck am going to starve to death."

Now the Kids Think *They* Discovered Natural Food!

Many young people who never heard of wheat germ at home, get turned on to the whole natural food thing by their peers, and then, like with sex, they think they discovered it. When I sent a copy of my first book, *Confessions of a Sneaky Organic Cook,* to the daughter of a friend who just got married, she told her mother that she was amazed that anyone "my age" should be so "into" natural foods.

In fact, many young people suffer the same kind of

frustrations you are experiencing when they try to convert their parents to better eating habits. I thought I was good at changing labels until I heard of one family where a high school senior changed the label on the wheat germ jar. When menopausal Mom came down to breakfast, could she resist a healthy helping of "anti-hot flash granules?"

By far the best way to turn your children on to good nutritious foods is to let them observe its effect on you. I remember one occasion at a country square dance when we were sashaying and promenading with the kids long after their parents had quit, all gasping for breath and nursing sore muscles. I heard one youngster remark, "Look at those Kinderlehrers; there must be something to this wheat germ thing."

Some mothers tell me, "I tried to give them the right foods, but they gave me too much sass. I gave up."

Then there is the other side of the coin. A mother of five children who has been cooking with love and wheat germ for many years told me that one Sunday her husband dialed a football game on TV and her ten-year-old son asked, "Which one is that, Dad?"

"I believe it's the Sugar Bowl," he said.

"You might as well change the channel," the boy said, "Mom will never let us watch it."

Whatever you do, avoid hassles at the table. It is tiresome to be forever carping about how important this or that food is to your child's welfare now and forever. Tiresome for him; tiresome for you.

Most teenagers are notoriously snack-happy. They rarely want to sit down to a meal with their parents. At our house dinner was at six and all hands aboard. We tried to make the dinner hour a most pleasant time so nobody would want to miss it. I always prepared extra food—for the big teenage appetites of our own kids—

and the kids who came for homework and stayed for dinner. We always maintained a sincere interest in everything that was going on in their world and the world at large, so dinner conversation was lively.

I remember well how the kids enjoyed the games we played around the table. If one of them was having trouble with arithmetic or some branch of mathematics, we'd play a game or have a quiz designed to strengthen his skills in that area. If one of the children was boning up for a spelling match, we'd have our own spelling bee. We always played the quiz games with the kids and we flubbed just as frequently as they did.

Our children knew their friends were always welcome at the dinner table, so long as everyone pitched in to help clean up.

Sometimes the visitors would ask questions—out of honest curiosity—about some food we were eating that was new to them. By their questions they created a new interest in food among our own teenagers. At this age, what kids care about most is peer approval. While your youngsters might put you down now and then about your penchant for wheat germ, they like it when their peers show admiration for your superior knowledge about nutrition. You will be pleased too by the intelligent contributions your own children can make when the conversation gets around to nutrition. They absorb a lot more of your patter than you think they do.

I was amazed and delighted on one occasion to hear one of mine advise a friend to eat his salad first because, "When you eat something raw first, the cells that protect your body from attack by germs can travel faster to the weak places that need reinforcement, like that brushburn you have on your arm from when you were fouled. If you eat something cooked first, these cells are needed in your stomach, so they leave the other positions like cuts and sores unguarded longer. Get the idea?"

To Relieve Acne, They'll Eat Almost Anything!

Acne and other complexion problems are the bane of most teenagers' existence. They'll do anything—even eat liver—if they believe it will help to prevent or cure the condition.

When it comes to acne, liver can be a teenager's best friend. There is as much as 53,400 I.U. of vitamin A in as little as a quarter-pound of beef liver; even more in lamb liver—74,500 I.U. That's a lot of vitamin A, and scientific studies have shown vitamin A to be useful against acne and other skin diseases.

The strange thing is that even though vitamin A is easily obtained in a well-rounded diet, a survey done in the schools of New York City and published in the *American Journal of Clinical Nutrition* (August 1967), revealed that a deficiency in vitamin A is a common dietary shortage in children.

Isn't it possible that this vitamin A deficiency in children paves the way for the acne, which makes so many teenagers miserable?

When one of our sons first started to date the girl who later became his wife, she was undergoing a series of X-ray treatments for her skin problem. Knowing about the dangerous consequences X-ray treatment can have, I suggested to her that she try vitamin A instead. She began to take 50,000 I.U. of vitamin A in halibut liver oil daily. Within a few weeks her skin improved tremendously and soon it became fresh looking, smooth, and absolutely innocent of eruptions. She then went on

25,000 I.U. daily as a maintenance dose and stayed on that.

When Danny was 13, he once wrote from camp, "Send all my vitamins and doubles on vitamin A. Randy, my bunkmate has terrible pimples." At the end of the summer Randy's mother thanked us for the tremendous help Dan had been to her son whose face had cleared up to a point where he finally had the courage to ask a girl to a school dance.

This treatment sure beats the use of antibiotics such as tetracycline, which are sometimes given for a period of several years though there is no significant evidence that they are effective. And it sure beats the contraceptives which are currently given to teenage girls to help them overcome acne. Think of some of the possible side effects of this kind of estrogen treatment!

Besides giving our kids 25,000 units of vitamin A daily as a routine procedure, I made sure that there were lots of vitamin A-rich foods on the menu. Besides liver, which I always managed to serve twice a week— once broiled and once chopped—I put the emphasis on sweet potatoes, broccoli, carrots, and apricots. Incidentally, sweet potatoes are delicious raw in salads. Peanut butter spread on raw sweet potato slices makes a great snack for hungry teeners.

Fresh fruits and vegetables rich in minerals play an important part in the overall treatment of acne. So does vitamin D. However, a major role of vitamin D is to facilitate the body's absorption and use of calcium. For best results from Mr. Sun you should be eating plenty of fresh calcium-rich vegetables.

Emotional stress is recognized as a factor in teenage vulnerability to attacks of acne. Improved calcium absorption can also alleviate emotional turmoil, so we have another indication that increased calcium consumption can help to improve an acne condition.

For many teenage girls the menstrual period is announced by a distressing pimple on the chin or at the corner of the nose, or even worse, a boil. The amount of calcium in a woman's blood falls so low during the week prior to menstruation that irritability, nervous tension, and mental depression frequently set in. Added calcium at this time might ease the acne and the anguish.

Sunflower seeds are an excellent source of calcium and also offer a vegetable source of vitamin D. I used to put out a bowl of sunflower seeds, sesame seeds, and raisins for nibbling whenever I noticed one of those little premenstrual eruptions on my daughter's face or my own. I also added a few extra bone meal tablets to our daily vitamin ration. Bone meal contains calcium, phosphorus, and magnesium in the proper proportions.

What About Drinking and Drugs?

Every parent of a teenager trembles at the thought of the alcohol and drugs that dominate the teen scene. No matter what you do or say, sooner or later your teenager is probably going to try alcohol, if not drugs. For a teenager, alcohol is a symbol of maturity. "He drinks to stimulate sophistication and to defy authority," Dr. Ginott points out *(Parent and Teenager)*, "The drinking represents a daring gesture, a declaration of virility, a proclamation of adulthood."

You may not be able to prevent this alcohol experimentation, but you can try to make sure that your children's bodies are well nourished enough to withstand its harmful effects. It has been shown that deficient diets increase the tendency to abuse alcohol.

In a research project reported in *The Journal of the American Dietetic Association* (Vol. 61, 1972), groups of rats were fed a marginal "teenage-type" diet, and a control was fed a "human-type" diet. Some of the diets were supplemented with vitamins, spices, and coffee. Alcohol solutions were added on the basis of free choice by the animals. Those animals fed the diets with either coffee or caffeine added consumed significantly more alcohol than those on the diet without additions. When the marginal teenage diet was supplemented with vitamins, the animals consumed less alcohol.

When "heavy drinkers" on the teenage diet were shifted to the control or human diet, representing better nutrition, alcohol intake dropped significantly.

When we send our children off to high school, or even junior high, we tremble because of the drug pushers that have become so prevalent. And yet, the greatest pusher of them all may well be holding a prominent place right in your own living room. Dr. Stephen Homel, a Pennsylvania pediatrician whose practice is limited to adolescents, told a meeting of professional personnel of the character building agencies of eastern Pennsylvania (February 10, 1970) that "The notion, perveyed through the nation's advertising media that there is an instant 'up' and an instant 'down,' an instant relaxation, instant excitement, instant tune in and instant tune out is perhaps the greatest drug pusher of them all . . . And," he pointed out, "there is a whole respectable industry pushing these drugs without medical advice."

How can you help your own youngster to resist this trend. Nobody seems to have the perfect answer and I'm no exception. Most parents do their best to instill a good sense of right and wrong and an appreciation of personal responsibility. Who knows how successful you will be in this? You can only try. I know this much: if you have taught your child from his earliest years that he doesn't need any kind of drugs to help him through life, you have taken a giant step in the right direction.

In the end a parent cannot grow his child's muscles, make his friends, or secure his values. But a parent can provide the food and the environment that will help a child to have the best of these.

Teenagers are like young saplings in the spring. Their juices are flowing. Their bodies are budding and maturing. All these processes require a full complement of nutrients. Unfortunately, most teenagers, because of their poor snacking habits, fall far short.

Let Them Snack on Wholesome Foods

Let your motto be, "If you can't beat 'em—join 'em." If they're going to snack, let them snack on wholesome foods. Get rid of the empty calorie, highly sugared junk foods and stock up on raw nuts, seeds, lots of fresh and dried fruit. A bowl of homemade granola is great for snacks and your teenagers will enjoy making it themselves. Popcorn is a fine snack, too, especially when it is freshly made. Incidentally, popcorn (if not too heavy on butter and salt) is low in calories.

Your sons may be trying to gain weight. But chances are your daughters are either trying to lose weight or at least keep their curves under control.

Youngsters' tastes for foods may vary. One child will take doubles on the salad; another will take doubles on the potatoes. But one thing you can be certain of, they all love pizza. For snacking, mini pizzas on squares of whole wheat bread with lots of cheese, oregano, and garlic salt, broiled to a nice bubbly consistency, are always welcome. Try making some of the mini pizzas on thick slices of tomato or on eggplant, omitting the bread and its calories. Then just offer a tray of mixed pizzas to the crowd.

Do not say to a weight watching teenager, "Take this one, it's low calorie." It may be a sensitive area. I once made the mistake of offering a smaller portion of potatoes to my daughter who was at the time struggling to look more svelte in her ballet costumes. I thought she would be grateful for my concern with her problem. Not a bit.

"What's the matter with me?" she protested, tears glistening in her big brown eyes, "Am I a stepchild?"

However, when you are handing out the pizzas, if your daughter should protest that she would love some but it's too fattening, then you can tell her about the low calorie ones. She'll be delighted and grateful.

When you have teeners in the house, the refrigerator door gets a constant workout. They no sooner finish a meal when they've got the munchies. Keep your refrigerator well supplied with cheeses, cold chicken, clean raw vegetables, lots of fruit, carob confections, peanut butter-molasses balls, sunflower seed candies, oatmeal-wheat germ cookies, or banana nut bread, and eliminate the empty calorie chemical concoctions.

Back in the flapper days, which you probably don't remember, teenagers would get together for an evening of fudge making. This was great fun and everyone vied for the privilege of cleaning out the pan. Nowadays we know the danger sugar holds, so we don't make that kind of fudge anymore. But teenagers can still have a lot of fun in the kitchen making raw carob fudge which is just as tasty as the other kind and is rich in the nutrients we want to get into growing bodies.

Raw Carob Fudge

½ stick butter (¼ cup)

¼ cup honey

1 tablespoon vanilla

Cream above ingredients together and add:

⅓ cup carob powder

⅓ cup soy milk powder

⅓ cup arrowroot or protein
     powder or rice polish

Mix all ingredients well and form into balls, pressing a half nut meat into each ball. This must be kept refrigerated because of the butter.

METRIC CONVERSION										
1 teaspoon = 5 ml.					1 tablespoon = 15 ml.					
1 ounce = 30 ml.					1 cup = 240 ml./.24 l.					
1 quart = 950 ml./.95 l.					1 gallon = 3.80 l.					
1 ounce = 28 gr.					1 pound = 454 gr./.454 kg.					
F.°	200	225	250	275	300	325	350	375	400	425	450
C.°	93	107	121	135	149	163	177	191	204	218	232

Another good fun-in-the kitchen activity is popping corn.

Popcorn

Heat a heavy saucepan or skillet and add enough oil to coat the bottom. When a drop of water sputters in the oil, it is hot enough to add just enough popcorn kernels to cover the bottom of the pan. Cover the pan and slowly shake it. In about a minute you will hear the corn start to pop and you will smell the appetizing aroma we've learned to associate with the lobby of a movie theater. When the corn is all popped, turn it into a large bowl and add salt and butter. For a change, you can add some blackstrap molasses instead of the salt and butter and make little popcorn balls by hand. (Just be sure to smear some butter or vegetable oil on your palms first, or they'll get awfully sticky.) Molasses is rich in iron and calcium, so very necessary for teenagers.

You might not consider cream puffs or eclairs as good examples of health-building foods. But when you make them with good health-building ingredients, they are. Make them for a surprise and expect enthusiastic response. These recipes are from the *Mini-Guide to Living Foods* by Pat Connolly (Price-Pottenger Foundation, 5662 Dartford Way, San Diego, Calif., 1975).

Cream Puffs and Carob-Covered Eclairs

1 cup boiling water
¼ pound butter
1 cup brown rice flour or
　　other whole grain flour
4 eggs

Preheat oven to 425° F.

Melt butter in boiling water and stir in flour. Add eggs one at a time beating constantly until dough forms a ball in center of pan. Remove from stove and shape into rounds for cream puffs or oblongs for eclairs. You may chill in refrigerator or bake at once on a baking sheet. Place into preheated oven for five minutes, then lower heat to 325° F. and bake 20 minutes for teaspoon-sized puffs or 30 minutes for larger puffs or eclairs. After cooling they may be frozen or used at once.

To fill, make a slit in side of puff or eclair and insert flavored whipped cream or custard. Eclairs may be topped with shavings of raw carob fudge as an icing.

METRIC CONVERSION										
1 teaspoon = 5 ml.					1 tablespoon = 15 ml.					
1 ounce = 30 ml.					1 cup = 240 ml./.24 l.					
1 quart = 950 ml./.95 l.					1 gallon = 3.80 l.					
1 ounce = 28 gr.					1 pound = 454 gr./.454 kg.					
F.°	200	225	250	275	300	325	350	375	400	425	450
C.°	93	107	121	135	149	163	177	191	204	218	232

Oatmeal and sesame cookies are irresistibly crunchy. Double this recipe and have plenty around to take care of the "munchies." These are also a good survival snack when the kids are cramming for exams.

Oatmeal and Sesame Cookies

1 cup whole wheat pastry flour

½ cup soy flour

1 cup oatmeal

½ cup unhulled sesame seeds

½ cup honey

½ cup oil

¼ cup peanut butter or
  tahini (sesame seed butter)

⅓ cup fruit juice or water

½ cup raisins

Preheat oven to 350° F.

Combine ingredients and mix well. Drop from a tablespoon onto an oiled cooky sheet and bake in oven for about 15 minutes or until they are golden brown. The soy flour complements the wheat making a complete protein.

Keep these cookies crisp by storing them in a loosely covered container.

Always have some good homemade granola around, and your teenagers will take the time to enjoy breakfast. Not only is granola good for breakfast, it's great for snacks, it can be used as a basis for a pie crust, it can be used as a dessert topper, or it can be eaten in the usual way with milk, with yogurt, with sour cream, or fruit juice.

Granola

3 cups rolled oats

1 cup wheat or rye flakes

½ cup wheat germ

½ cup bran

½ cup sesame seeds

½ cup cashews or walnuts

½ cup sunflower seeds

½ cup coconut, shredded

¼ cup oil

¼ cup honey

1 teaspoon salt

Preheat oven to 225° F.

Spread this mixture very thin on a cooky sheet and put it in the oven for about one hour. It should turn a golden brown.

When the granola is browned, add some raisins, chopped dates, chopped apricots, dried apples, chopped prunes, or whatever.

METRIC CONVERSION										
1 teaspoon = 5 ml.					1 tablespoon = 15 ml.					
1 ounce = 30 ml.					1 cup = 240 ml./.24 l.					
1 quart = 950 ml./.95 l.					1 gallon = 3.80 l.					
1 ounce = 28 gr.					1 pound = 454 gr./.454 kg.					
F.° 200	225	250	275	300	325	350	375	400	425	450
C.° 93	107	121	135	149	163	177	191	204	218	232

We know that teenagers are patsies for pizza, and what's good can be better if you make it yourself using whole wheat flour for the dough. If the dark-colored dough turns them off, use unbleached white flour and add a few tablespoons of wheat germ.

Homemade Pizza

For the dough, you'll need:

1 package yeast or 1 tablespoon
  yeast granules

1 cup warm water

3 cups whole wheat flour or
  2½ cups whole wheat flour
  and ½ cup soy flour (this will
  improve the protein value) or
  2½ cups unbleached white flour
  and ½ cup wheat germ

½ teaspoon salt

2 tablespoons oil

Soften yeast in a little of the warm water.
Combine the flour, salt, the rest of the water,
oil, and yeast mixture to form a stiff dough.
Cover and set aside to rise.

For sauce:

1 medium-sized onion, minced

1 medium-sized clove garlic, minced

2 tablespoons oil

1 can tomato sauce

1 teaspoon dried basil

METRIC CONVERSION										
1 teaspoon = 5 ml.					1 tablespoon = 15 ml.					
1 ounce = 30 ml.					1 cup = 240 ml./.24 l.					
1 quart = 950 ml./.95 l.					1 gallon = 3.80 l.					
1 ounce = 28 gr.					1 pound = 454 gr./.454 kg.					
F.° 200	225	250	275	300	325	350	375	400	425	450
C.° 93	107	121	135	149	163	177	191	204	218	232

Brown onion and garlic in the oil until golden; add tomato and basil and simmer for about five minutes.

For topping:

1 tablespoon oregano

¼ pound sliced mozarella or jack
   cheese or any good melting cheese

anchovy fillets (optional)

¼ cup grated Parmesan cheese

Preheat oven to 400° F.

Pour two tablespoons of oil into each of two large, shallow baking pans. Divide the dough, placing half in each pan and turning so that dough is well oiled over the entire surface. Use your fingers to spread the dough over the pan to about one-quarter inch thickness. Pour sauce over all and arrange the anchovy fillets and sliced cheese on top. Sprinkle with the Parmesan cheese. Bake 15 to 20 minutes.

You can, of course, make quite a pizza using English muffins, whole wheat bread, or pita as a base.

Eggplant Pizza

1 medium-sized eggplant, sliced ½-inch thick

tomato sauce

sliced mozzarella, jack, or cheddar cheese

¼ teaspoon each of thyme, basil, oregano, and garlic powder

Cook eggplant with a little water in a tightly covered skillet—just enough to take the rawness out. Then carefully place the slices on a cooky sheet or pizza pan. Combine the spices and tomato sauce and spread the mixture on the eggplant slices. Top with cheese and place under broiler till the cheese bubbles.

METRIC CONVERSION										
1 teaspoon = 5 ml.					1 tablespoon = 15 ml.					
1 ounce = 30 ml.					1 cup = 240 ml./.24 l.					
1 quart = 950 ml./.95 l.					1 gallon = 3.80 l.					
1 ounce = 28 gr.					1 pound = 454 gr./.454 kg.					
F.*	200	225	250	275	300	325	350	375	400	425	450
C.*	93	107	121	135	149	163	177	191	204	218	232

Discover frozen bananas and you can treat your teen-agers to the sweet life without sugar. Bananas, when frozen, are incredibly sweet and when they are whipped up, they make a variety of creamy desserts. Always peel your very ripe bananas before freezing. You can freeze them in chunks on a cooky sheet, and when frozen, put them in plastic bags. You can make a kind of banana ice cream by mashing or blending two cups of frozen bananas and then mixing it with one-half cup of whipped cream. Return it to the freezer, for about one-half hour, then top it with nuts or fresh fruit. This is a gorgeous dessert.

Part 2

How To Eat Healthfully When You're Out On Your Own

Chapter 4
Surviving College, or How to Dodge the Dismal Fare of the Dormitory Dining Room

I know quite a few sickly adults who date the start of their poor health to breakdowns suffered while they were at college. At college the emphasis is on building your mind. Some very basic things—like building your body or even just maintaining your health—are placed in the hands of a commercial catering service, that is often chosen primarily for its ability to work within a tight budget. These catering services generally provide what they think you expect, lest they be accused of cheating you.

The catering service at one local college agreed to try to improve the food value of the meals being served, but refused to eliminate such additive-laden foods as maraschino cherries, white bread, and sugar-laden cereals. The owner feared that the students would stage a protest. I think this is a lot of bunk. It's also very sad, especially in view of research which proves that good nutrition and good health march side by side in the same parade with a good mind, the ability to cope with school, and with the complex problems of growing up.

So, if the food served in your college dining room is not inspiring you, if in fact, it's plain lousy, heavy on the starches and low on the nutrients, don't just grin and eat it, or fill up on pizza and beer at the local hangout. Do something about it.

I get mail from college students all over the country. "The food here is awful," they say. "I find myself filling up on starches; my skin is breaking out. I'm always tired and feel sluggish. I have trouble keeping up with my work. What do you suggest?"

First of all, I recommend a vitamin C supplement to help get a student through all the pressure days of that first year at college. Every stress situation drains your body of vitamin C. Today it is easy to get lots of vitamin C without drinking a gallon of orange juice. High-potency vitamin C supplements are sold everywhere, and you should never be without them.

Another way to get added vitamin C is to eat sprouts daily. You can grow them right in your own room. (See index for method.)

If for some reason you must eat at the dorm, at least do this: double up on the salad, and skip the white bread. If whole wheat bread isn't being served bring a loaf from home or buy a good loaf and keep it in the refrigerator. Tell the kitchen staff you're allergic to white bread. Maybe they'll get whole grain just for you.

If dessert is pie or cake, skip it and ask for a piece of fresh fruit. They may not have it, but keep asking until they get it. Meantime, go to the market and buy some.

I used to send care packages to our kids—fresh fruit, homemade bread, survival snacks—a mixture of nuts, seeds, raisins, and coconut—honey cake, oatmeal cookies, and granola, and all kinds of dried fruits. Our kids lost very few college days to illness; they all made dean's list, and two won Phi Beta Kappa keys.

Is it possible to get the college to serve good food? It is, if you insist on it. Why should you have to eat over-cooked, overprocessed meals, lacking in the very elements of nutrition most needed to keep body and soul together and to study and retain information?

Where Fine Food Service Is in Force

Students at several colleges have mounted campaigns to improve the quality of the food service. At Florida Presbyterian in St. Petersburg, as a result of student action, there are now two food lines. Line one serves the usual commercial plastic food products; line two offers an interesting choice of truly health-building foods:

The breakfast menu lists fresh fruit—apples, oranges, dates, and other dried fruits—cereals such as granola, familia, cracked wheat, and always a jar of wheat germ. Organic apple juice and milk are available as beverages. Nut butters like sesame, cashew, peanut, and almond are on a help yourself basis. Eggs any style are made up to order. The bread is a special whole grain loaf baked at the school from stone-ground flour, cornmeal, and cold-pressed oil. Lunch includes a smorgasboard of raw nuts and seeds, yogurt, cottage cheese, and whole grain bread.

One of the finest food plans I know of is provided for students at Northland College in Ashland, Wisconsin. In a letter sent to all students, the food service committee wrote:

"Yes, we are discarding the canned fruits, vegetables, soup and dessert mixes with additives and preservatives, the bleached and processed grains and flours. The meals will not taste as though they are from the same pot. Besides being fresh, the meals will be nutritious. We are offering a high-protein, low-carbohydrate diet.

"You might ask why the program? The answer is simply, we want to present a healthy balanced diet that gets us out of our unconscious attitudes. We want you to participate, experiment, and give your mind and body a new feeling toward dining hall food."

Here is the menu plan for the new food service:

BREAKFASTS

To accompany breakfasts they serve fresh fruit, home-made granola, and eggs with herbs, cheeses, or sprouts.

LUNCHES

With crisp salads offering color, seasonings, and textures they serve one of a variety of hot soups each day: hearty vegetable, miso, lentil, split pea, greek egg-lemon soup, chicken, and chili. Sandwiches are self-service; fillings include vegetarian spreads, cheese, sprouts, vegetables, peanut and sesame butter with honey and seeds, besides egg and tuna salad.

DINNERS

Poultry, fish, and vegetable entrees are prepared according to international recipes: chicken cacciatore, shrimp fried rice, baked chicken with herbs, trout almondine, and ratatouille.

DESSERTS

Desserts are served at lunch and dinner. Ingredients are all-natural fruits and unprocessed flours. Sweets range from traditional brownies, cakes, cookies to yummy seed, nut, coconut, and honey combinations. Fruit and yogurt are served as well.

BEVERAGES

Hot and iced herbal teas are served along with fruit juices and coffee. Natural herbal teas contain no dyes or chemical treatments. According to Chinese thought they provide a way to soothing harmony in the body

Northland College Menu

	Sunday	Monday	Tuesday
Breakfast	Granola Breakfast juice Oranges Whole wheat toast Western omelet	Cinnamon oatmeal Breakfast juice Bananas Blueberry muffins Hard-soft boiled eggs	Granola Breakfast juice Grapefruit Coffee cake Scrambled eggs with alfalfa sprouts
Lunch	Miso soup Curried eggs on whole wheat toast Marinated cucumbers and tomato slices Dried fruits and nuts	Lentil soup with rye krisp crackers Fresh green salad with sunflower seeds and alfalfa sprouts Oriental fried rice Chocolate chip cookies	Chicken salad spread Whole wheat bread Fresh cucumber and carrot sticks Cottage cheese with fruit Creamed potato soup
Dinner	Soybean burgers with cheese sauce Brown rice Green beans with sautéed mushrooms Sesame crisp cookies Molasses bread	Shrimp fried rice Fresh spinach boiled with diced eggs Ambrosia fruit salad Pumpkin cake	Baked cottage cheese squares Fresh garden salad with blue cheese dressing Strawberry yogurt Curried rice salad Nut cake

Condiments available for all meals: Natural peanut butter spread • Sesam butter spread • Natural honey • *Hot* and *chilled* teas (Sassafras Rose hip Peppermint Chamomile)

Wednesday	Thursday	Friday	Saturday
Familia cereal Breakfast juice Grapes Whole wheat toast Cheddar cheese omelet	Granola Breakfast juice Pears Sesame orange muffins Buckwheat pancakes	Rice cereal with raisins Breakfast juice Oranges Coffee cake Scrambled eggs	**Brunch** Poached eggs Grilled sausage links Granola Breakfast juice Banana Cheese soufflé Soybean stew Potato salad with yogurt dressing Asst. dried fruits and nuts
Vegetable soup Egg salad spread Assorted natural cheeses-rye krisp crackers Peanut sunflower waldorf salad Lemon custard pudding	Cream of tomato and rice soup Garden sandwich— cukes, tomatoes, cheese Cucumber salad Banana break	Whole wheat macaroni casserole Cabbage coleslaw Fresh fruit bowl Pineapple- corn muffins	**Dinner** Oven baked chicken with dry herbs Scalloped corn Fresh green salad Cornmeal bread Cottage cheese cake
Roast sirloin of beef Sautéed vegetables Parsley buttered potato Red kidney bean salad Pineapple cake	Baked lasagna French bread with Parmesan cheese Garden salad Broiled tomatoes with herbs Cherry cobbler	Baked lake trout Brown rice Fresh broccoli spears Vegetable gelatin salad Molasses bread Baked apples	

and help to maintain the yin-yang balance. Oriental healers prescribed herbal teas: peppermint for headaches, indigestion, chamomile flowers for the stomach and digestive system, and rosehips for aiding blood circulation and providing vitamin C.

I have gone into the Northland plan in considerable detail to provide a blueprint for change at any college. Don't be deterred by such administration objections as, "It's too expensive. Our budget can't stand it." Mr. Kenneth R. Nielson, Vice President for Student Affairs at Northland told me that the cost of the foods provided under his alternative eating program is about the same as the cost of the regular program. Northland found too, that when natural foods are served, quantities needed are lower.

After a two week trial of this food program, the response from the students was overwhelmingly in favor of continuing it.

Stocking Your Own Pad

If you have your own private pad while at college, you're in luck. At least you are in full control of the food you eat. If you're sharing a place with someone who has different views on nutrition, don't wrangle. But don't compromise your eating habits either. Eat your way.

If it works out that you are the only one in the crowd who cares about sensible eating, let the rest of the crowd follow you. Stick to your wheat germ philosophy. Soon they will be coming to you for advice. "How come you always have so much energy, and I am always pooped?" That's the time to invite them over for some "love and wheat germ."

On your shelf of staples, keep a good supply of sardines. They are inexpensive, high protein, and very tasty. Sardines require no cooking. Just the flick of a can opener and you've got yourself a meal.

They make a stick-to-your-ribs breakfast, lunch, or supper. Sardines, because they are so small are at the bottom of the sea food chain and therefore much less subject to contamination. Get the sardines that come with their skin and bones. They are a wonderful source of calcium as well as protein. You get as much as 20.6 mg. of complete protein in 100 grams of these tasty little fish. One hundred grams of liverwurst has only 16.2 mg. and meat loaf has 15.9 to 100 grams. For variety try:

METRIC CONVERSION

1 teaspoon = 5 ml.	1 tablespoon = 15 ml.
1 ounce = 30 ml.	1 cup = 240 ml./.24 l.
1 quart = 950 ml./.95 l.	1 gallon = 3.80 l.
1 ounce = 28 gr.	1 pound = 454 gr./.454 kg.

F.°	200	225	250	275	300	325	350	375	400	425	450
C.°	93	107	121	135	149	163	177	191	204	218	232

A Sardine Dip

1 can sardines—use the oil

2 eggs, hard-cooked

1 teaspoon lemon juice

1 teaspoon dry mustard

1 teaspoon parsley flakes or
    several sprigs fresh parsley

½ teaspoon tarragon or oregano

2 scallions or ½ small onion

Put everything in your blender or mash with a fork.

Try this great nut loaf, which you can make ahead of time. Heat it up and serve to your pals when they drop in for a buzz session and chow. Then stand back and watch the gusto with which they enjoy it. Sure, they'll ask for the recipe:

Carrot Nut Loaf

1 cup chopped onions

2 tablespoons parsley, minced

2 tablespoons celery, minced

½ cup raw carrot, grated

1 cup chopped nuts or seeds or combination of both

½ cup tomato sauce

1 egg, beaten

½ cup wheat germ

½ teaspoon thyme, crushed

½ teaspoon kelp

1 teaspoon vegetable salt (Spike is good)

METRIC CONVERSION										
1 teaspoon = 5 ml.					1 tablespoon = 15 ml.					
1 ounce = 30 ml.					1 cup = 240 ml./.24 l.					
1 quart = 950 ml./.95 l.					1 gallon = 3.80 l.					
1 ounce = 28 gr.					1 pound = 454 gr./.454 kg.					
F.°	200	225	250	275	300	325	350	375	400	425	450
C.°	93	107	121	135	149	163	177	191	204	218	232

Preheat oven to 350°F.

Combine all ingredients, pack into a buttered loaf pan and bake for about 40 minutes.

To put something good together quickly, for yourself, or a group, here's an inexpensive, no-cook snack or meal that works out well:

No-Cook Vegetable Nut Pie

2 cups carrots, grated

2 cups celery, chopped

½ cup peanut butter or tahini

2 cups ground nuts (pecans, walnuts, cashews, or peanuts)

2 tablespoons parsley, chopped

1 teaspoon onion, minced

1 teaspoon salt

½ teaspoon dried basil

¼ teaspoon paprika

sesame seeds (optional)

Combine all ingredients thoroughly and press into an oiled pie plate. Cover with sesame seeds. Chill. Serve in wedges to six people or enjoy it six times yourself.

When you have a delicious vegetable nut pie in the refrigerator, you'll be less tempted to snack on junk food. (This same mixture makes an excellent spread for crackers or sandwiches.)

If you're using meat, you're very likely specializing in hamburger for economy's sake. Look for a butcher who will grind some heart or tripe into your ground chuck. This will cut the price per pound and increase the nutrition considerably. It will also give you a good tasting, juicy, lean mixture. For a change of pace, try:

METRIC CONVERSION

1 teaspoon = 5 ml.	1 tablespoon = 15 ml.
1 ounce = 30 ml.	1 cup = 240 ml./.24 l.
1 quart = 950 ml./.95 l.	1 gallon = 3.80 l.
1 ounce = 28 gr.	1 pound = 454 gr./.454 kg.

F.°	200	225	250	275	300	325	350	375	400	425	450
C.°	93	107	121	135	149	163	177	191	204	218	232

Spinach Burgers

1 pound ground meat

1 teaspoon salt

½ teaspoon kelp

a few grindings of fresh pepper

½ cup sour cream or yogurt

½ teaspoon salt

2 teaspoons prepared horseradish

¼ teaspoon paprika

1 small onion, finely chopped

1 tablespoon parsley, chopped

½ cup chopped fresh or
frozen spinach, uncooked

sesame seeds

Mix the meat with one teaspoon salt, the kelp, and the pepper, and shape into 12 hamburger patties. At this point you can freeze what you don't intend to use right away.

Combine the rest of the ingredients. Put a spoonful of this mixture on top of six patties, cover with the other six and sprinkle with sesame seeds. Pan fry or broil in the regular way. All you need is a piece of whole grain bread and a salad, and you've got a meal. Dessert: fruit and cheese.

Here's another way to make hamburger go further nutritionally and economically—extend the meat with grated potato or zucchini like this:

Mom's Hamburgers

1½ pounds ground meat

3 tablespoons onion, minced

2 cloves garlic, minced

1 teaspoon salt

1 teaspoon kelp

¼ teaspoon pepper

¼ teaspoon paprika

½ cup grated raw potatoes
    or zucchini (drained)

1 egg

¼ cup wheat germ

¼ cup water or tomato juice or stock

3 tablespoons oil or chicken fat

2 onions, sliced

Mix all ingredients except the fat and the sliced onions. Form into 10 or 12 patties.
Brown the hamburgers with the onions in the hot fat.
Serves four to eight

METRIC CONVERSION										
1 teaspoon = 5 ml.					1 tablespoon = 15 ml.					
1 ounce = 30 ml.					1 cup = 240 ml./.24 l.					
1 quart = 950 ml./.95 l.					1 gallon = 3.80 l.					
1 ounce = 28 gr.					1 pound = 454 gr./.454 kg.					
F.°	200	225	250	275	300	325	350	375	400	425	450
C.°	93	107	121	135	149	163	177	191	204	218	232

These garbanzo and rice burgers are delicious served with hot tomato sauce or used as the base for quick pizzas. For this purpose it is good to have them always on hand. They can be frozen.

Garbanzo and Rice Burgers

1 onion, chopped

2 stalks of celery, including tops

2 tablespoons oil or butter

1 cup cooked brown rice

1 cup cooked garbanzos or
  raw sprouts, finely chopped

¼ cup wheat germ

½ cup pecans or walnuts, chopped

½ teaspoon vegetable salt

½ teaspoon kelp

¼ teaspoon thyme

¼ teaspoon oregano

¼ teaspoon basil

sesame seeds

2 tablespoons oil or butter

Sauté onions and celery in oil or butter till golden. Add to other ingredients and mix well. Shape into patties and either sauté in a little butter or oil or bake until brown—about one hour.

For a quickly made breakfast that will stick to your ribs till lunch, spread a piece of whole grain bread with peanut butter to which you have added wheat germ and brewer's yeast. Top with apple or banana slices, yogurt and sunflower seeds, and a dusting of cinnamon. Absolutely fantastic. You can enjoy this for lunch or supper, too.

This soup really hits the spot and makes you feel kind of special. Make it when you need a boost.

Creamy Carrot Soup

2 tablespoons butter

½ cup onion, chopped

2 cups carrots, diced

3 tablespoons whole wheat flour

3½ cups chicken broth,
     vegetable cooking water, or water
     from soaking seeds for sprouting

¼ teaspoon salt

¼ teaspoon kelp

⅛ teaspoon nutmeg, ground

1 cup evaporated milk or light cream

3 tablespoons parsley, chopped

Melt butter over moderate heat; sauté onion and the diced carrots until onion is soft. Stir in the flour and cook another minute. Add the broth and cook until liquid bubbles and thickens. Reduce heat to low, cover pan, and simmer 15 minutes more, or until carrots are fork tender. Add seasonings. Pour half the soup in your blender, blend until smooth and pour it back into the pan. Repeat with the other half.

At this point, if you're making the soup for tomorrow, you can refrigerate it. Next day you simply stir in the evaporated milk or cream and heat to serving temperature. Do not boil. Pour into bowls for yourself and three friends. Garnish with parsley and dig in. The lift you get from that nicely flavored velvet on your palate will set you up for days.

METRIC CONVERSION

1 teaspoon = 5 ml.	1 tablespoon = 15 ml.
1 ounce = 30 ml.	1 cup = 240 ml./.24 l.
1 quart = 950 ml./.95 l.	1 gallon = 3.80 l.
1 ounce = 28 gr.	1 pound = 454 gr./.454 kg.

F.°	200	225	250	275	300	325	350	375	400	425	450
C.°	93	107	121	135	149	163	177	191	204	218	232

Chapter 5

If You Plan to Be a
Vegetarian — Be a Healthy One

Sixteen-year-old Ricky, a very talented, bright, and sensitive young man told me that he had decided to go vegetarian because he was against killing animals for food. He hadn't eaten meat for two weeks. He felt fine, but he could not take his mother's constant carping and warnings ... "Eat your meat or you'll fall apart." ... "A growing boy must have meat." ... "How do you expect to do well in school, play on the basketball team, keep up with your music if you don't have meat?" I sympathized with Ricky, but I certainly could understand his mother's concern, too.

Several months passed before I met Ricky again. He had developed a terrible case of acne and he told me he was taking antibiotics for it. "How are you doing on your vegetarian diet?" I asked him.

"Oh," he said sheepishly, "I'm eating meat now. I couldn't take the hassle with my mother. She took me to the doctor and he said 'A growing boy needs meat'."

I do not wish to imply that Ricky's acne condition was caused by eating meat. But I'm convinced that eating the meat against the dictates of his conscience did cause an emotional upheaval in this sensitive lad, and that could have triggered the acne. If your children decide to become vegetarians, don't fight it. Don't ridicule them. Instead, help them to plan a meatless diet that will give them the complete nourishment they need.

For years we have had it drummed into us that eating meat is essential to good health and it's hard to give up a long held belief. A friend of mine told me that her daughters became vegetarians a year ago at the ages of 13 and 11. Both girls are very active, they are good students, and haven't slowed down at all. "They are both in good health, love vegetables, fruits, cheeses of all kinds, and eggs, and I keep plenty of these foods in the house," she said. "I must confess that although I was worried about their becoming 'veggies', I can't find a single argument against it."

Many young people—some of the best—are changing their ancestral eating habits. Because of their deep reverence for all living creatures, they eat no meat or fish; some also avoid all foods of animal origin, such as eggs or milk products. A few even go so far as to refuse honey and gelatin.

At some colleges so many of the students follow a vegetarian diet, that the food service contractor is instructed to provide good vegetarian meals. For example, at Purchase College in New York, vegetarian entrees that combine beans and grain, nuts and seeds, and greens for proper amino acid patterns, are on the menu every day.

Can You Stay Healthy If You Don't Eat Meat?

The number of vegetarians in the United States has more than doubled since 1970, swelling their ranks to an estimated 10 million. These millions all have their own valid reasons for sticking to a diet of vegetables, fruits, and grains, be it health, ethics, ecology, or economics.

There are about 50 vegetarian cookbooks currently in print. In 1975, a 13-day meeting of vegetarians at the University of Maine drew 4,000 people from all over the country.

Vegetarians delight in the anecdote about the lady in the restaurant who ordered only vegetables. When a man at the next table did likewise, she asked, "Are you a vegetarian, too?" He replied, "No, lady, I'm a meat inspector."

What about the idea that you must eat meat to be a he-man?

Historian Will Durant wrote this about the Roman soldiers in the Punic Wars: "Food in camp was simple; bread or porridge, some vegetables, sour wine, rarely fish; the Roman army conquered the world on a vegetarian diet."

An experiment conducted many years ago at Yale University wiped out another myth: It takes "steak every day" to make a football hero. Dr. Irving Fisher, a professor at Yale University and himself a vegetarian, got the football coach to cooperate in putting all the Yale rookies on a strict vegetarian diet for several weeks. He then pitted them against the varsity men who had been eating their regular red meat diet. As it turned out, the inexperienced rookies showed twice the endurance of the meat eaters.

As a group, vegetarians live longer than meat eaters. Meat eaters are likely to have heart attacks and strokes an average of 10 years earlier than vegetarians might, said Dr. Lawrence Lamb, according to the *Pittsburgh Press* (February 21, 1974). A study by Drs. F.M. Sacks, B. Rosner, and E.H. Kass of Harvard Medical School revealed that those who eat mostly a vegetarian diet tend to have significantly lower blood pressure (*American Journal of Epidemiology*, November 1974).

So, you see, it is possible to maintain health and vigor on a purely vegetarian diet. The list of famous people who lived long and productive lives without eating meat—Henry David Thoreau, Benjamin Franklin, Voltaire, Leonardo da Vinci, Milton, Pope, Gandhi, and Bernard Shaw, to name a few—shows that vegetarianism doesn't interfere with wisdom, genius, or moral strength either. But I firmly believe that a modern no-meat diet demands nutritional awareness and careful planning. Even if a person is eating vegetables of superior quality, he still must plan his diet with care because at best the protein in individual vegetables is incomplete. No single one has enough of all the amino acids in the proper balance for the body's needs.

When planning an adequate vegetarian diet, the quality of the protein is a vital consideration. Some foods contain all the known protein building blocks (amino acids) needed for the construction of tissue and the maintenance of body function while other foods are deficient or entirely lacking in certain of these constituent protein parts.

How to Balance Amino Acid Intake

One of the basic problems with a vegetarian diet is the possibility of an amino acid imbalance. Not only must you have all the essential aminos in adequate amounts, you must get them all at the same time. Meat, fish, eggs, and milk products are all complete protein foods, that is, they contain all the essential amino acids in the correct proportions. The eight known amino acids which you must include in your diet (essential amino acids) because the body cannot make them are: leucine, methionine, phenylalanine, valine, lysine, isoleucine, threonine, and tryptophan. (A ninth, arginine, is considered essential for growing children.) Because all of these protein elements depend on each other to make body tissue, each one must be present, or none of them is used. The tryptophan you consume in the morning does not hang around waiting for the matching methionine you consume in the evening to make it a complete protein. Unless they are eaten together, both the tryptophan and the methionine are lost to the body.

How do you balance your amino acids properly on a vegetarian diet?

If you are a whiz at mathematics you could learn the quantities of all the amino acids in the various foods, match them against your body's requirements for each (they differ) and plan your meals accordingly.

A simpler method is to measure the content in a food of three building blocks of protein—lysine, methionine, and cystine. Dr. J.A. Campbell told an American Chemical Society meeting (September 1959) that "Since most common foods are deficient in these amino acids, such a technique is quite reliable . . ." In other words, in virtually all incomplete proteins, it will be one or more of these three that is missing or in short supply.

Lysine is heat sensitive. As the heat goes up and the length of cooking time is increased, the amount of lysine available from the food goes down. To make sure all the amino acids aren't killed in cooking, vegetarians should serve a raw vegetable, salad, raw fruit, raw sprouts, or unroasted seeds at every cooked meal. The one food which improves its protein picture with cooking is the soybean.

As a guide in your planning, here are some amino

acid values from *Metabolism* published by the Federation of American Societies for Experimental Biology (1968).

Grams of Amino Acid per 100 Grams of Nitrogen

	Histidine	Isoleucine	Leucine	Lysine	Methionine	Phenylalanine	Threonine	Tryptophan	Valine
Eggs	15	41.5	55	40	19.6	36.1	31.1	10.3	46.4
Sesame Seeds	12.1	26.1	46.1	16	17.5	40	19.4	9.1	24.4
Soybeans	14.9	33.6	48.2	39.5	8.4	30.9	24.6	8.6	32.8
Turnip Greens	11.0	23.0	44.7	27.8	11.3	31.5	27.0	9.8	32.1
Chick-Peas (dried)	16.8	35.9	46.2	43.1	8.3	30.4	22.2	5.1	30.8
Broccoli	11.9	23.9	30.8	27.8	9.4	22.6	23.1	7.1	32.2
Sweet Potato	12.4	30.1	35.8	29.5	11.6	34.8	29.4	10.9	46.8
Sunflower	13.5	29.4	40.0	20.0	10.2	28.1	21.0	7.9	31.2
Yeast (brewer's)	16.9	32.4	43.6	44.6	11.3	25.7	31.8	9.6	36.8
Peanuts	15.2	25.7	38.0	22.3	5.5	31.6	16.8	6.9	31.1
Rice	10	27.9	51.3	23.5	10.7	29.9	23.3	6.4	41.6
Wheat	13	26.2	42.7	10.9	9.9	31.0	15.1	6.1	27.0
Corn	12.9	28.9	81	18	11.6	28.4	24.9	3.8	31.9

Eggs provide protein that is biologically complete. Dr. Roger Williams of the University of Texas was able to keep experimental laboratory animals alive and well for several generations on a diet of nothing but eggs.

Try to Match the Egg

Notice the distribution of the amino acids in eggs. A vegetarian should try to plan his meals for the same kind of balance. Notice the methionine content is 19.6 grams per 100 grams of nitrogen, as compared to its lysine content of 40. This is the proportion in which the body needs these amino acids. Sesame seeds come very close to the methionine content of eggs—17.5 but they fall down in lysine—16. Soybeans, on the other hand, fall way down in methionine—8.4—but are high in lysine—39.5. But if a person eats sesame seeds with soybeans, they will combine internally into high-grade protein.

Notice that corn is very low in tryptophan: 3.8 compared to the egg, 10.3. Corn is also low in lysine: 18 compared to the egg, 40. Sweet potatoes complement corn very nicely. They are high in tryptophan, 10.9, and a good source of lysine, 29.5.

Most people don't serve corn and sweet potatoes at the same meal because they are both starchy. Together, however, they do provide a good amino acid balance, and vegetarians must keep trying for such balances at every meal.

Okay. But how can a vegetarian be assured of a proper balance of the amino acids without using a slide rule at the dinner table? Dr. Roger J. Williams of the University of Texas gave this simple guide: "Don't restrict yourself to one part of a living organism, try to get the whole works. In the plant world, do not restrict yourself to green leaves (spinach), or to roots (parsnips), or to seeds (corn or wheat), or to fruit (apples, tomatoes). Each of these is in itself incomplete. A combination diet containing leaves, roots, tubers, seeds, and fruits is a vast improvement. Early in the history of animal nutrition it was found that seeds and leaves have a profound supplementary action."

Nuts, seeds, avocados, whole grains, considered "incomplete proteins" should, according to Dr. Williams' formula, be eaten with raw, green leafy vegetables to provide a complete amino acid pattern that is well utilized by the body.

In her booklet, *Fundamentals in Foods,* Gena Larson, who has researched the subject with great care, suggests these combinations as examples of complete amino acid patterns:

1. Raw greens in salad plus raw cashews or other nuts.
2. Raw green vegetables with mashed avocado dressing.
3. Sprouted grains or seeds plus raw green salad.
4. Large green salad plus sesame seed dressing.
5. Raw green vegetable plus raw egg mayonnaise.

Yeast is rich in the very amino acids that are low in soy or peanut flour. In using soy or peanut flour in baking, a little nutritional yeast can be added. Those avoiding dairy products and using soy milk should add yeast to it.

Whenever vegetarians use whole wheat flour, one-fifth should be soy flour, to complement the amino acids of the wheat.

Combining nuts is important in vegetarian eating. Brazil nuts are a good source of methionine; cashews rate high in lysine. Sunflower seeds and sesame seeds are good sources of methionine. Mixed nuts with raisins make an even more complete amino pattern.

Millet is a good high-protein cereal that fits well into a vegetarian diet. The same goes for buckwheat groats, whole unpearled barley, natural whole grain rice and, of course, soybeans which come closest of all plant food to being a complete protein.

Of course, a single dish that takes care of all protein needs at once is the ideal. The key to preparing protein-complementary casseroles appears in the chart at the end of this chapter. When in doubt, get this out!

B_{12} Is a Problem

The one essential vitamin frequently in short supply in a vegetarian diet is B_{12}. Vitamin B_{12} is associated especially with animal proteins. Liver is the richest source. Kidney, muscle meats, milk, eggs, cheese, and fish are other sources. Vegetarians who eat eggs and milk in generous amounts are not quite so vulnerable to B_{12} deficiency as are vegans who avoid all animal products and animal by-products. Pernicious anemia in vegetarians can escape diagnosis. A vegetarian diet is rich in the green vegetables which provide lots of folic acid that keeps the blood picture normal and can mask the evidence of vitamin B_{12} deficiency.

Yeast, wheat germ, soybeans, comfrey leaves, and sprouted garbanzos are about the only foods from which a vegan can get some B_{12}. To be nutritionally safe, it would certainly be wise for everyone on a vegetarian diet and especially vegans to take a daily vitamin supplement that is rich in B_{12}, which, in supplements, is made from molds. It is not of animal origin.

In a study of the effects of veganism, conducted in collaboration with the Department of Nutrition, Queen Elizabeth College, London, three scientists, Ellis, Path, and Montegriffo found nine of the 26 vegans had serum B_{12} levels that were low; three of the nine had a frank B_{12} deficiency, whereas only one control had a serum B_{12} deficiency.

Other than the B_{12} deficiency, there was no significant difference in the clinical states of the vegans and the meat eaters except that the vegans were lighter in weight.

Vegans may be interested in these substitutes for eggs as suggested by the publication, *The Vegan Kitchen*, by Freya Dinshah, published by the American Vegan Society, Box H, Malaga, New Jersey 08328.

Create Protein Complementary Casseroles!

1. Choose one ingredient from each of the five columns.
2. Mix together ingredients from first four columns.
3. Pour into greased casserole dish (1 quart) and bake 30 minutes at 375°F.
4. Top with one choice from column 5 and bake 15 minutes longer at 325°F.
5. Salt to taste at the table. Serve with bread and a salad. (Each casserole serves four to six)

Complementary proteins

1	2	3	4	5
Two Cups Cooked	One Cup, Cooked	Sauce: One Can soup + 3/4 cup water	Vegetables to make 1 1/2 Cups	Three to five Tablespoons Topping
Brown Rice	Soybeans	Cream of Tomato	Browned Celery and Green Onions	Wheat Germ
Macaroni, enriched	Lima Beans	Cream of Potato	Mushrooms and Bamboo Shoots	Slivered Almonds
Corn	Peas	Cream of Mushroom	Browned Green Pepper and Garlic	Fresh Whole Wheat Bread Crumbs
Spaghetti, enriched	Kidney Beans	Cream of Celery	Cooked Green Beans	Sesame Seeds
White Rice, converted	Black Beans	Cheddar Cheese Soup	Cooked Carrots	Brewers Yeast, debittered

1	2	3	4	5
Noodles, enriched	Garbanzos (Chick-peas)	Cream of Pea	Browned Onion and Pimento	Sunflower Seeds

Prepared by: Anna Gordon, Nutrition Educator,
Community Food and Nutrition Program,
West Chester, Pennsylvania

Vegan Mayonnaise

2 baked sieved potatoes

½ pint vegetable oil

chopped parsley, sage,
    green and red sweet pepper,

celery, and cucumber. Mix in blender.

Binder to be used as substitute for one egg
in conventional recipes:

1 teaspoon arrowroot flour

1 teaspoon soya flour

Mix in ½ cup warm water.

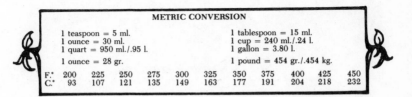

METRIC CONVERSION										
1 teaspoon = 5 ml.					1 tablespoon = 15 ml.					
1 ounce = 30 ml.					1 cup = 240 ml./.24 l.					
1 quart = 950 ml./.95 l.					1 gallon = 3.80 l.					
1 ounce = 28 gr.					1 pound = 454 gr./.454 kg.					
F.° 200	225	250	275	300	325	350	375	400	425	450
C.° 93	107	121	135	149	163	177	191	204	218	232

Since soy is a staple on a vegetarian or vegan diet, try
this:

Soya Cheese

Mix a quart of soy milk made from soy powder and bring to a boil. As the soy milk begins to rise, pour in three-quarters tablespoon of fresh lemon juice. Let stand. Then strain.

Making nut butters is easy. Grind some nuts or seeds; add water or oil a little at a time until the mixture has a good spreading consistency.

Avocados are a natural butter and delicious.

To make nut cream, add more water to nut butter. Add even more water to make a delicious nut milk.

Soy milk is made by blenderizing four heaping teaspoons of pure soy powder with a pint of water. To sweeten use the juice of soaked dates, raisins, apricots, figs, or prunes.

To most vegetarians, the perfect stand-in for the T-bone is the long neglected and now honored soybean. The "life pill for an overcrowded world," said a large ad in the *Wall Street Journal* which pictures one little soybean regally encased in a jeweled pill box.

Try these pancakes for breakfast. They not only look good and taste great, they also provide good well-balanced protein.

Soy-Sesame Pancakes

¾ cup whole wheat flour (you may use buckwheat flour, or finely ground wheat germ, corn flour, or cornmeal)

½ cup soy flour

¼ teaspoon salt

¼ teaspoon kelp

¼ teaspoon nutmeg or cinnamon (or both)

2 tablespoons unhulled sesame seeds

2 eggs, separated

1¾ cups buttermilk or
    1 cup milk and ¾ cup yogurt

Combine all the dry ingredients in one bowl. Beat the egg yolks and combine with buttermilk or milk and yogurt in another bowl. Combine both mixtures. Beat egg whites until stiff, and fold in last. This will make about two dozen three-inch pancakes. They are especially good served with applesauce, sliced fresh fruit, or yogurt.

Soy balls can be an excellent substitute for meatballs that you serve with spaghetti, macaroni, or rice.

METRIC CONVERSION										
1 teaspoon = 5 ml.					1 tablespoon = 15 ml.					
1 ounce = 30 ml.					1 cup = 240 ml./.24 l.					
1 quart = 950 ml./.95 l.					1 gallon = 3.80 l.					
1 ounce = 28 gr.					1 pound = 454 gr./.454 kg.					
F.°	200	225	250	275	300	325	350	375	400	425	450
C.°	93	107	121	135	149	163	177	191	204	218	232

Soy Balls

½ cup soy powder

¼ cup wheat germ

3 tablespoons nutritional yeast

1 teaspoon salt

½ teaspoon kelp

3 eggs

3 tablespoons milk or water

1 tablespoon sesame oil

Combine all ingredients and stir vigorously until the mixture is smooth. Chill for about one hour.

Drop small amounts (about a teaspoon) of batter into a large pot of boiling water—same as you would for dumplings. Cover the pot, turn the heat down to simmer for about 10 minutes. Do *not* overcook. You can also drop the soy balls into a soup or stew. If you serve these soy balls on brown rice with a tomato sauce, you will further enhance the protein power of this dish.

Serves four

METRIC CONVERSION										
1 teaspoon = 5 ml.					1 tablespoon = 15 ml.					
1 ounce = 30 ml.					1 cup = 240 ml./.24 l.					
1 quart = 950 ml./.95 l.					1 gallon = 3.80 l.					
1 ounce = 28 gr.					1 pound = 454 gr./.454 kg.					
F.°	200	225	250	275	300	325	350	375	400	425	450
C.°	93	107	121	135	149	163	177	191	204	218	232

Soy Cheeseburgers

¾ to 1 cup soybeans (preferably
   small variety)

Crack or split beans in food mill. Soak overnight and cook in the soaking water for two
hours with these ingredients:

3 cloves garlic, pressed

⅛ teaspoon cayenne pepper

1½ teaspoons oregano

1 teaspoon paprika

1 teaspoon salt

½ teaspoon kelp

½ cup sherry

Cool beans completely and mix:

2 eggs, beaten

2 tablespoons milk

½ onion, chopped fine

¼ cup sesame seeds

Make five generous-sized patties by spoon-
ing out the mixture into either a large greased
frying pan or a greased baking dish. Flatten
patties slightly with spoon. Do not turn them.
They should cook on one side only. Now top
with one-quarter pound of grated cheddar
cheese. Place them in a medium oven until
cheese is nicely melted. If you are doing them

in a frying pan, on low heat, covered, cook for five to seven minutes until the cheese is melted and the patties are set.

You can also enjoy all the nutrients of soybeans in the form of soy grits and soy meal. Grits have a slightly different taste from the chopped beans because they have been toasted. This gives them a pleasant nut-like flavor and crunchy texture. It also precooks them making them ready for use. When you pour two parts boiling water over one part grits, the grits will absorb the water within five to 10 minutes. They are now ready to be used in a variety of ways—like in meat loaves, tuna casseroles, hamburgers, soups, and with brown rice as a complementary source of protein.

Many young people of the Jewish faith are passing up the traditional chicken soup and chopped liver and going vegetarian. Jonathan Wolf, a young staff member of the Synagogue Council of America entertains his vegetarian friends frequently and suggests this version of the traditional *cholent* for the *Shabbat* afternoon meal.

Meatless Cholent

½ pound great Northern beans
½ pound pinto beans
2 large onions, sliced
4 large, or 6 to 10 small potatoes
⅓ cup pure vegetable oil
2 cups dry red wine
2 cloves garlic, minced
salt

pepper
4 bay leaves

Soak beans in enough water to cover for several hours. Remove beans from water but retain the water. Place the beans in a heavy Dutch oven or in a crockpot. Cut potatoes into chunks and add together with the sliced onions. Add oil, wine, garlic, and seasonings. In a saucepan bring the soak water to a boil, then pour over the potato and onion mixture adding enough to cover. Place the bay leaves on top and cook on low heat from early Friday afternoon until *Shabbat* lunch to achieve a thick consistency. Remove bay leaves before serving. Jonathan serves this *cholent* with brown rice for complementary protein.
Makes about three quarts or eight servings

METRIC CONVERSION									

1 teaspoon = 5 ml.   1 tablespoon = 15 ml.
1 ounce = 30 ml.   1 cup = 240 ml./.24 l.
1 quart = 950 ml./.95 l.   1 gallon = 3.80 l.

1 ounce = 28 gr.   1 pound = 454 gr./.454 kg.

F.°	200	225	250	275	300	325	350	375	400	425	450
C.°	93	107	121	135	149	163	177	191	204	218	232

Triticale Is a Triumph

Anyone who is into vegetarianism will certainly be glad to know about triticale, the new super grain. The first time I told my kids we were having triticale for dinner they really gave me the business:
"Is it Ms. or Mr.?"
"Do you eat it, or dance to it?"
"Sounds to me like something you do on Halloween."
Triticale (trit-i-kay-lee) is the result of research which had its beginnings some 100 years ago. This new grain

is the child of a wheat mother and a rye father. Its name is a combination of the scientific names for wheat (triticum) and rye (secale).

Dr. S. P. Yang, chairman of the Department of Food and Nutrition at Texas Tech University has found the new grain to contain 16.4 percent protein—some 40 percent more protein than most other cereal grains. Commonly available wheat and/or rye flour contains only 12 percent protein.

But the true value of triticale is its high content of lysine and methionine, amino acids which are low in most grains.

Triticale contains 3.95 percent lysine which is the limiting amino acid in wheat (2.7 percent lysine) and it contains as much as 2.83 percent methionine which is a limiting amino acid in rye (1.6 percent). This improved amino acid balance gives to triticale a far better protein efficiency ratio or a biological value closer to that of eggs and meat than either rye or wheat alone.

How do you use triticale? One way is to sprout it. It sprouts quickly and easily and has a wonderful chewy texture. Add the sprouts to salads, casseroles, to brown rice dishes, to soups, or just snack on them. (Don't let sprouts get any longer than the grain itself. They will continue to grow in the refrigerator and must be used quickly.)

A most delicious instant soup can be made from triticale sprouts.

Quick Triticale Soup

2 cups water in which the grains were
soaked or plain water or stock

2 tablespoons brewer's yeast
    for each cup liquid

1 teaspoon salt

dash kelp

1 cup triticale sprouts

Heat the liquid but do not boil it. Add the
yeast and seasonings and add the sprouts last.
A garnish of parsley and watercress is particularly nice on this soup.

METRIC CONVERSION										
1 teaspoon = 5 ml.					1 tablespoon = 15 ml.					
1 ounce = 30 ml.					1 cup = 240 ml./.24 l.					
1 quart = 950 ml./.95 l.					1 gallon = 3.80 l.					
1 ounce = 28 gr.					1 pound = 454 gr./.454 kg.					

F.°	200	225	250	275	300	325	350	375	400	425	450
C.°	93	107	121	135	149	163	177	191	204	218	232

Triticale Sprout Milk

To make triticale sprout milk, blend one
cup of slightly sprouted triticale with one cup
of soak water or plain water. After whizzing
in the blender for a few seconds, strain it.

Triticale Sprout Bread

You can add triticale sprouts to any bread
dough for a superior, moist, and delicious loaf.
You can chop them, blend them, or use them
whole. Work the sprouts into the dough during the last kneading. You can use up to one
cup of sprouts for every cup of liquid in the

recipe without making any adjustment in the other ingredients.

Triticale Dessert

1 cup triticale sprouts

2 tablespoons honey, or maple syrup

1 tablespoon coconut, shredded

2 tablespoons raisins, chopped dates, avocados, or any fresh fruit

Combine all ingredients and serve with yogurt, cream, or some kind of nut milk.

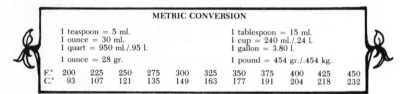

METRIC CONVERSION										
1 teaspoon = 5 ml.					1 tablespoon = 15 ml.					
1 ounce = 30 ml.					1 cup = 240 ml./.24 l.					
1 quart = 950 ml./.95 l.					1 gallon = 3.80 l.					
1 ounce = 28 gr.					1 pound = 454 gr./.454 kg.					

F.°	200	225	250	275	300	325	350	375	400	425	450
C.°	93	107	121	135	149	163	177	191	204	218	232

The kitchens of some of our southern universities are sending up some appetizing aromas as the Home Economics laboratories try out triticale flour and develop new recipes. Margarette Harden, assistant professor of Food and Nutrition at Texas Tech says that triticale flour adds a very pleasing, nutty flavor and has proven to be quite versatile. The triticale flour can be substituted for regular flour in most recipes but to produce attractive loaves of bread, it is best to blend the triticale with wheat flour. A blend of 30 percent wheat flour to 70 percent triticale may be used if you like a heavy bread. But, for those who are accustomed to a light loaf of bread, the 50–50 ration is better, Mrs. Harden says. Triticale does not contain so much gluten as does wheat and, when used alone, makes a rather heavy bread.

Triticale biscuits for breakfast send up a teasing fragrance that will bring the sleepyheads into the kitchen before they're fully dressed. This recipe was developed by Mrs. Harden.

Triticale Biscuits

½ cup triticale flour

½ cup wheat flour

½ teaspoon salt

2¼ teaspoons baking powder

2 tablespoons dry milk powder

2 tablespoons butter

⅓ cup water

Preheat oven to 450°F.
Sift dry ingredients together. Cut in butter. Add water, stir quickly. Knead for one minute. Roll one-inch thick. Cut with biscuit cutter or inverted glass dipped in flour. Bake for 10 to 15 minutes.

These peanut butter cookies are lovely high-protein snacks for the lunch box and the after-school hunger pangs.

Peanutty Peanut Butter Cookies

½ cup oil
½ cup honey or molasses
½ cup peanut butter
1 egg
½ teaspoon vanilla
1½ cups triticale flour
¼ teaspoon salt
peanuts

Preheat oven to 375°F.
Combine oil, honey, peanut butter, and egg. Beat well. Add rest of ingredients. Shape into balls and use a fork to flatten on a greased or parchment-lined cooky sheet. Top each with a peanut half. Bake for 8 to 10 minutes.
Makes about four dozen cookies

In just about any recipe that calls for flour, triticale can be substituted for half the amount of flour, Dr. Harden has found. It makes lovely pizzas, superb breakfast pancakes, gingerbread, carrot-nut cakes, banana bread, pumpkin bread, and even doughnuts.

METRIC CONVERSION										
· 1 teaspoon = 5 ml.					1 tablespoon = 15 ml.					
1 ounce = 30 ml.					1 cup = 240 ml./.24 l.					
1 quart = 950 ml./.95 l.					1 gallon = 3.80 l.					
1 ounce = 28 gr.					1 pound = 454 gr./.454 kg.					
F.·	200	225	250	275	300	325	350	375	400	425	450
C.·	93	107	121	135	149	163	177	191	204	218	232

Kitchen Chart

SOME SIMPLE RULES OF THUMB for combining meatless foods to produce more nutritionally usable protein:

1 PART LEGUMES and 2 PARTS MILK

2 PARTS LEGUMES and 3 PARTS SEEDS

1 PART LEGUMES and 3 PARTS WHOLE GRAINS

4 PARTS MILK and 3 PARTS WHOLE GRAINS

1 PART MILK (scant) and 1 PART SEEDS

1 PART MILK (scant) and 1 PART PEANUTS

1 PART MILK and 1 PART POTATO

Please note that the legumes, grains, and seeds in this chart are in dry measure. In cooking, grains expand approximately by three, as do most legumes. Lentils and split peas approximately double in cooking. Also note that in recipes calling for one part milk you may substitute one-third as much cheese or instant powdered milk.

This chart is reprinted with permission from
Cooking with Conscience by Alice Benjamin and Harriett Corrigan.
Order from Vineyard Books, Noroton, Connecticut 06820 ($2.00).

Chapter 6

Don't Tell Me
You Can't Afford to Eat Well
— You Can't Afford Not To!

A young mother approached me after I spoke at a luncheon meeting not long ago and said, "I would love to feed my husband and four children only natural, healthful foods, but how can I afford to on a schoolteacher's salary?"

My answer to her was, "With four children in the house, how can you afford *not* to?"

Just forget for a minute the price of the food and consider some other expenses. With four kids in the house how frequently do you visit the doctor? How much are you giving to the dentist? How much did you spend last year on prescription drugs and over-the-counter medications? How is your health and your husband's? What did your medical bills amount to last year?

I can tell you from personal experience that after we switched to natural foods our doctor bills dropped off, our dental bills took a nose dive, and we were soon able to stop listing prescription drugs as a fixed budget expense.

I have found too that cutting out the junk foods leaves a surprising amount of budget money for good food, and the natural foods stick to the ribs, so that your kids are not forever looking for something to *"nosh."*

Mrs. R. of Canada, mother of a hyperactive child, decided to adopt the additive-free diet Dr. Ben Feingold devised for such children. (That means virtually no processed foods.) She served the same diet to the whole family. Not only did her child improve as though a fairy had waved a wand over him, but everybody in the family felt better *and* she saved $15 a week on the food budget for a family of four.

Sarah Bell, who runs the food program for the tiny tots at a day care center in Allentown, Pennsylvania, told me that she saved $3,000 the year she changed the food program to natural foods and stopped buying the prepared entrees—fish sticks, prepared cabbage rolls, pre-prepared chicken, turkey rolls, and lasagna—that the food service purveyors were constantly pushing. She makes everything herself and Sarah says it doesn't take any more of her time than it took to put the pre-cooked stuff together.

You too will save money if you learn how to make your own. Make your own yogurt, salad dressings, granolas, soups, mayonnaise, confections, and bread.

You think you have no time? You have as much time as I do. We all have 24 hours in every day. What you might need is the motivation and the determination to organize your time. You'll find, for example, that you can do two things at once quite effectively. You can watch your favorite television programs while you're making carob fudge. You can bake bread while entertaining friends in the kitchen.

Where do you start with your new, natural foods money-saving program? Let me show you.

Are Cereals Breaking You?

Almost every household where there are children has a cupboard lined up with boxes of dry cereals. Just read the fine print on some of these packages.

Frosted Flakes: 10 ounces for 88 cents—that's almost nine cents an ounce. (Prices do vary from store to store and month to month. The prices that follow are in force at this writing, June 1976.) And what do you get? The first ingredient is sugar, which means sugar is the most plentiful substance in that package. Cereal comes in second. The third ingredient is another sweetner. So you're really buying sugar plus some overprocessed cereal, some synthetic vitamins, and a bunch of chemical additives.

Maybe your kids reach for the Coco-Puffs, the Lucky Charms, the Super Sugar Crisp, the Fruit Pebbles, or any one of the 67 varieties of sugar-coated doodles on the shelf. Every single one of them lists sugar as the first or second most plentiful ingredient and all but one on the shelves I examined contained BHT (the butylated antioxidant which has caused liver and kidney damage and other adverse metabolic effects in laboratory animals).

Have you any idea how much you are paying—not for food—but for the additives? Let's examine one of the better known cereals on the shelf—one which has been there for years, Cheerios—10 ounces cost 65 cents. Here's what Cheerios contain: oat flour, wheat starch, sugar, salt, calcium carbonate, sodium phosphate, sodium ascorbate, artificial color, niacin, iron, gum acacia, vitamin A, palmitate, vitamin B_6, riboflavin, thiamine, vitamin D, vitamin B_{12}, and BHT.

Is there nothing good on the cold cereal shelf? Yes, in one little unobtrusive corner, I found wheat germ.

Seventy nine cents for 16 ounces. That's only five cents an ounce as compared to almost nine cents an ounce for the empty calorie fluff in the big psychedelic packages. From end to end on that cereal shelf, there was no other cereal which could claim to contain anywhere near all the nutrients listed on the label of the wheat germ. Every penny of that 69 cents you invest in the pound of wheat germ goes toward good solid muscle-building protein, vitamins, and minerals. Not one cent are you paying for sugar, salt, BHA, BHT, or synthetic vitamins. It's the *real thing.*

All right, let's face it. Some kids don't exactly drool over the prospect of a bowl of wheat germ and milk even when it's served with love and bananas.

But they do get excited over Almond Crunch Granola—available at your natural food store for roughly 99 cents for 16 ounces—which comes to less than seven cents an ounce—below what you pay for Vanilla Crunchies and not much more than the Cheerios. But the difference in eating pleasure as well as nutrients cannot be calculated in dollars and cents.

But since it's economy we're talking about, why not make your own granola?

At the Rodale Fitness House Experimental Kitchen we did a time-and-cost study. We used this recipe:

Almond Crunch Cereal

6 cups uncooked rolled oats (not the quick cooking kind)

3 cups dry coconut shreds, unsweetened

1 cup wheat germ

1 cup sunflower seeds

1 cup sesame seeds

1 cup honey

½ cup corn, soy, or safflower oil

1 cup cold water

1 cup slivered blanched almonds

1 cup unsulfured raisins (optional)

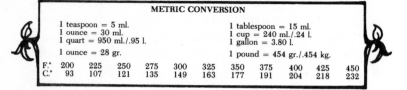

METRIC CONVERSION

1 teaspoon = 5 ml.					1 tablespoon = 15 ml.					
1 ounce = 30 ml.					1 cup = 240 ml./.24 l.					
1 quart = 950 ml./.95 l.					1 gallon = 3.80 l.					
1 ounce = 28 gr.					1 pound = 454 gr./.454 kg.					

F.°	200	225	250	275	300	325	350	375	400	425	450
C.°	93	107	121	135	149	163	177	191	204	218	232

Preheat oven to 225°F.

In a large mixing bowl, combine rolled oats, coconut, raw wheat germ, sunflower seeds, and sesame seeds. Toss ingredients together thoroughly.

Combine honey and oil. Add to dry ingredients, stirring until well mixed. Add the cold water, a little at a time, mixing until crumbly.

Pour mixture into a large, heavy, shallow baking pan which has been lightly brushed with oil. Spread mixture evenly to edges of pan. Place pan on middle rack of a preheated oven and bake for two hours, stirring every 15 minutes. Add one cup slivered almonds and continue to bake for one-half hour longer or until mixture is thoroughly dry and light brown in color. Cereal should feel crisp to touch.

When cereal has baked sufficiently, turn oven off and allow cereal to cool in oven. If raisins are to be added to cereal, do so at this point.

Remove cereal from oven—cool and store in a tightly covered container. Store in a cool, dry place.

Serve with fresh fruit or plain as a snack. This recipe will give you about 12 cups.

Cost per delicious ounce: six cents. And an ounce of this cereal has real satiety value. It goes a long, long way.

Bread-baking Adventure

Let's take a look at bread. Sunbeam Stone-Ground Whole Wheat Bread. Sounds good, doesn't it? But besides the stone-ground whole wheat flour, it contains sugar, diglycerides, monoglycerides, sodium stearoxyl, and artificial color—one of the worst offenders—and calcium propionate—another no-no. The price? A one-pound loaf costs 57 cents.

If you bake bread yourself without any of those nasty additives and add a good dollop of wheat germ, you have a far more nutritious, far more tasty loaf, and *at half the price.* Here's a recipe I use.

No-Knead Whole Wheat Bread

From County Cork, Ireland

4 teaspoons dry yeast
⅔ cup lukewarm water

2 teaspoons honey

5 cups whole wheat flour

3 tablespoons molasses

⅔ cup lukewarm water

1 tablespoon salt

⅓ cup wheat germ

1⅓ cups lukewarm water

1 teaspoon butter (for greasing pan)

1 teaspoon sesame seeds

Preheat oven to 375°F.

Sprinkle yeast over lukewarm water and add the honey. Leave to "work" while preparing the dough.

Warm whole wheat flour by placing it in a 250°F. oven for about 20 minutes.

Combine molasses with two-thirds cup of lukewarm water and add yeast mixture. Stir this into the warmed flour, then add the salt and wheat germ, and finally the one-and-one-third cups lukewarm water. The dough will be sticky.

Butter a large loaf pan (9" × 5" × 3"), taking care to grease the corners of the pan well. Turn the dough into the buttered pan. No kneading is necessary. Sprinkle sesame seeds over the top. Leave to rise to one-third more of its size in bulk (45–60 minutes).

Bake for 50 minutes until crust is brown. Remove pan from oven and cool on rack for 10 minutes. Loosen loaf, turn out onto rack and cool completely before slicing.

METRIC CONVERSION										
1 teaspoon = 5 ml.						1 tablespoon = 15 ml.				
1 ounce = 30 ml.						1 cup = 240 ml./.24 l.				
1 quart = 950 ml./.95 l.						1 gallon = 3.80 l.				
1 ounce = .28 gr.						1 pound = 454 gr./.454 kg.				
F.°	200	225	250	275	300	325	350	375	400	425	450
C.°	93	107	121	135	149	163	177	191	204	218	232

The cost? Fifty-five cents and we got a big two-pound loaf. It took exactly 20 minutes of preparation time and 45 minutes rising time. And there's no charge for the lovely appetizing aroma that fills your whole house and brings the kids out of the woodwork hankering for a hunk of whatever it is that smells so good. Get the kids involved with the bread making. There's nothing like it for bridging the generation gap.

If you have never baked a loaf of bread, then you have never experienced the deep satisfaction and elemental joy of providing your family's basic nutritional needs. Back in the good old crinoline days, any mother who bought bread was an object of pity. "One of the memories from my childhood in New England," says Dora Morrell Hughes, who wrote *Thrift in the Household* back in 1918, "is hearing the discussion of a woman new to the neighborhood and what I remember is this, spoken in pitying accents: 'Yes, poor thing, she does the best she can, but she hasn't any faculty. Why, she *buys* her bread!' "

The practice of bread making, I am happy to report, is returning. "Today bread is being made by men as well as women, from teenagers to octogenarians," says Beatrice Trum Hunter in her *Whole Grain Baking Sampler* (Keats Publishing, Inc., New Canaan, Connecticut, 1972). "All who make bread admit enthusiastically that bread baking is a creative, satisfying experience. It gets down to the essentials in life."

For a large family, I might add, it also saves a lot of cash.

Simple Salad Dressings

Do you buy prepared salad dressings? That's squandering your food dollar. An eight-ounce bottle of Kraft salad dressing costs about 43 cents and contains several undesirable chemicals and sugar. I make a delightful salad dressing using cold-pressed oil, good apple cider vinegar, fresh lemon juice and onion juice and it costs only 38 cents for eight ounces.

METRIC CONVERSION										
1 teaspoon = 5 ml.					1 tablespoon = 15 ml.					
1 ounce = 30 ml.					1 cup = 240 ml./.24 l.					
1 quart = 950 ml./.95 l.					1 gallon = 3.80 l.					
1 ounce = 28 gr.					1 pound = 454 gr./.454 kg.					
F.° 200	225	250	275	300	325	350	375	400	425	450
C.° 93	107	121	135	149	163	177	191	204	218	232

Oil and Vinegar Dressing

1 tablespoon lemon juice (½ lemon)	4 cents
4 tablespoons vinegar	3 cents
⅔ cup pressed oil	30 cents
few drops onion juice	1 cent
¼ teaspoon salt	———
One cup or eight ounces costs	38 cents

Six minutes to prepare.

Another way in which you can save on your food dollar is to make your own yogurt. Half a pint of plain unfruited yogurt costs from 29 to 35 cents. Make it yourself and it will cost you only nine cents for a half pint, whether you make it from powdered milk or liquid milk.

Yogurt

Blend:

¾ cup skim milk powder   16 cents

1 cup water

1 tablespoon yogurt   <u>2 cents</u>

    18 cents

Place in yogurt maker or in oven at temperature of 110°F. for about eight hours. You get more than one cup for 18 cents, and it takes four minutes to prepare. Save some yogurt as a starter for your next batch.

I like to use yogurt that contains the acidophilus strain so I start with the dry yogurt culture which can be purchased at most natural food stores or by mail from the International Yogurt Company, 628 N. Doheny Drive, Los Angeles, California 90069. This yogurt culture, which is the original Bulgarian strain, contains the lactobacillis and acidophilus along with the Bulgaricus and thermophilis. Most commercial yogurts include the latter two but no acidophilus which is indigenous to the human intestine where it implants itself and thrives—thus providing continuous digestive benefits. Bulgaricus, on the other hand, is a one-time thing. It does its job and goes away. There is a small company in Pennsylvania producing acidophilus yogurt (Erivan) which is available in natural food stores in New York, New Jersey, and in some parts of Pennsylvania. On the West Coast and in Canada there is a yogurt called Yami which does contain acidophilus. You could use a container of one of these acidophilus yogurts as a starter for your own supply.

Because I use whole raw milk, I do not heat it to the boil which tends to destroy enzymes and protein values. I heat it only to 112°F. You could do the same with whole pasteurized milk. After the milk is heated, I add the yogurt culture, mix well, then pour the mixture into clean pre-warmed glasses, cups or jars. And then I cap the jars and incubate them in a yogurt maker or in any warm place where the temperature is above 110°F. An oven with a pilot light can be used if you first give the oven a brief blast of heat. You can also simply pour the yogurt mixture into a pre-warmed thermos bottle and leave it for six to eight hours.

When your yogurt is thick as custard, take some off the first batch and put it in the freezer to be the mother batch for later culturing. It's a good idea to put it away in an ice cube tray in three tablespoon portions so that the yogurt freezes very quickly. You can make succeeding batches of yogurt by culturing each quart of luke-warm milk with three tablespoons from your most recent batch. After about a month, the yogurt culture may be weakened by competing strains. Then you pull out a reserve mother culture from the freezer and start a fresh batch. When you follow this procedure, you can make your original "mother" culture go a long, long way.

Your yogurt costs you the price of the milk plus the small investment you made in the starting culture.

Now that you're making your own yogurt, try this salad dressing.

Yogurt Dressing

1 cup yogurt	8 cents
4 tablespoons lemon juice	5 cents
¼ to ½ teaspoon dry mustard	1 cent
1 minced clove garlic	1 cent
½ teaspoon salt	1 cent
½ to 1 teaspoon paprika	<u>1 cent</u>
	17 cents

Combine ingredients and let stand in refrigerator for 15 minutes before serving. Positively delicious, and the cost? Seventeen cents for a whole pint—one-third the price of the commercial varieties.

METRIC CONVERSION										
1 teaspoon = 5 ml.					1 tablespoon = 15 ml.					
1 ounce = 30 ml.					1 cup = 240 ml./.24 l.					
1 quart = 950 ml./.95 l.					1 gallon = 3.80 l.					
1 ounce = 28 gr.					1 pound = 454 gr./.454 kg.					
F.° 200	225	250	275	300	325	350	375	400	425	450
C.° 93	107	121	135	149	163	177	191	204	218	232

If you like the fruited yogurts, add your own fruit to your own homemade yogurt and avoid the sugar that you get in the commercial varieties. Try grated apple and a touch of cinnamon—tastes better than apple pie.

Try orange sections and a sprinkling of unsweetened coconut and who needs ice cream? Wheat germ and bananas with a sprinkling of sunflower seeds make a good breakfast or brown-bag lunch.

Piima, Another Kind of Fermented Milk You Should Know About

Piima, a freeze-dried Finnish milk culture, long popular on the West Coast is now making the scene in other areas of the country. Its great advantage is that it cultures at room temperature. It's as easy as pie to prepare and I've never had a failure with it. If you can't find it in your natural food store, it is available by mail from Piima, P.O. Box 2614, La Mesa, California 92041. It costs $2.50 plus 25¢ postage.

You will receive a small envelope of the dry culture. All you do is sprinkle the contents into a cup of milk—right from the refrigerator. No heating. Stir it up and let it stand at room temperature 24 to 36 hours. I put the jar in a cupboard over the stove at night and it is ready in the morning. It's not quite so tart as yogurt but you can blend it with fruits or make it into custards, Bavarian creams, cheese pies, popsicles, and all kinds of goodies.

To make subsequent batches, you take one teaspoon from your last batch and mix it with a quart of milk. It just keeps on going and going. From my one starter, I have started at least 20 people on Piima. One of my friends who is allergic to all milk products—even yogurt, finds that she can handle Piima without any reactions. You can use Piima in any recipe that calls for yogurt.

Try these recipes:

Natural Custard

(very nice)

1 tablespoon gelatin
¼ cup cold water or juice
2 cups Piima
2 fertile eggs
1 teaspoon vanilla
¼ cup honey
nutmeg
cooky crumbs

Soak gelatin in water, then melt over low heat, stirring constantly. Place the next four ingredients in the blender. Blend briefly, then turn to low and add melted gelatin while blender is whirling. Pour into custard cups and sprinkle with nutmeg and cooky crumbs.
Variations:

Add any of the following:
½ medium banana
1 or 2 tablespoons carob powder
Omit honey and use 5 or 6 pitted dates
For a butterscotch flavor, add ¼ cup fig juice

METRIC CONVERSION									
1 teaspoon = 5 ml.					1 tablespoon = 15 ml.				
1 ounce = 30 ml.					1 cup = 240 ml./.24 l.				
1 quart = 950 ml./.95 l.					1 gallon = 3.80 l.				
1 ounce = 28 gr.					1 pound = 454 gr./.454 kg.				
F.° 200	225	250	275	300	325	350	375	400	425	450
C.° 93	107	121	135	149	163	177	191	204	218	232

Party Bavarian

2 tablespoons gelatin

½ cup cold water or fruit juice (any kind)

4 egg yolks

2 cups strawberries or other fresh fruit

2 to 4 tablespoons honey
(depending upon sweetness of fruit)

2 tablespoons lemon peel, grated

4 egg whites

2 cups Piima

Dissolve the gelatin in water. Melt over hot water or low heat, stirring constantly. Place egg yolks in blender and add the strawberries, honey, lemon peel, and fruit juice or water. Add melted gelatin with blender on low. Place the mixture in the refrigerator. Beat egg whites until stiff. Stir the gelatin mixture into the Piima and fold in beaten egg whites. Turn into a large mold or individual serving dishes and chill. Garnish with fresh berries.

METRIC CONVERSION

1 teaspoon = 5 ml.	1 tablespoon = 15 ml.
1 ounce = 30 ml.	1 cup = 240 ml./.24 l.
1 quart = 950 ml./.95 l.	1 gallon = 3.80 l.
1 ounce = 28 gr.	1 pound = 454 gr./.454 kg.

F.°	200	225	250	275	300	325	350	375	400	425	450
C.°	93	107	121	135	149	163	177	191	204	218	232

Convenience Foods are Budget Crushers

Your food dollar will go much further if you avoid all pre-cooked convenience foods like instant mashed potatoes, TV dinners, and cake mixes. These foods are

The High Cost of Food Processing

	Package size	Price	Price/ pound
Fresh potatoes	20 lb.	1.99	.10
Fresh potatoes	5 lb.	.79	.16
Sliced, canned potatoes	1 lb.	.25	.25
Frozen french fries	1 lb.	.35	.35
Frozen potato puffs	1 lb.	.35	.35
Frozen french fries (extra crisp)	10 oz.	.35	.56
Instant mashed potatoes	1 lb.	.71	.71
Potato sticks	7 oz.	.47	1.07
Potato chips	10 oz.	.69	1.10
Tuna Helper (potatoes with artificial mushroom flavor sauce)	7.5 oz.	.59	1.26
Crisp-i-Taters (potato snack)	6 oz.	.55	1.47
Hamburger Helper (sliced potatoes with a sour cream and beef-flavored sauce)	7 oz.	.63	1.53
Instant potato soup mix	5 oz.	.49	1.57
Munchies (potato crisp snack)	5 oz.	.56	1.70
Chipsters (potato snack)	4.75 oz.	.51	1.72

*From *Organic Gardening and Farming*® April 1974.

loaded with chemicals. A good part of your dollar is going toward the price of the additives you don't want.

What about produce? The price of lettuce and other salad greens when out of season is enough to discourage salad eating. But you never have to slight the salad no matter how expensive the greens are. You can have inexpensive organic greens every single day, by growing your own sprouts. In fact, sprouts can be your first line of defense against spiraling costs. It is the only food I know of that gives you more than you pay for. One pound of mung bean seeds gives you eight pounds of sprouts. It is also the only food I know of that actually increases its nutrients from garden to table instead of diminishing in food value.

Anyone can be a kitchen gardener and grow his own sprouts. You don't need a green thumb. You don't even have to talk to your plants. Here's how you do it:

Wash one-quarter cup of seeds or grains and place them in a glass jar with four times their volume of lukewarm water. Let them stand from four to 10 hours or overnight. Next day cover the top of the jar with two layers of cheesecloth or nylon net and secure it with a rubber band. Or make yourself a screen top lid (or buy a set at the natural food store).

Next morning pour off the rinse water and save it for use as soup stock or cook your vegetables in it, or simply add it to juices. It contains many important nutrients. Now rinse the seed with fresh water—not cold and not hot, just lukewarm. After rinsing the seeds, place the jar under your sink on its side. The hot water pipe provides a nice warm temperature which will encourage sprouting. Rinse the seeds two or three times each day and by the second day you will see little white roots starting to push out. If you are doing alfalfa seeds, shake them apart each time you rinse them so that they will not grow into a tight mat. Use a fork to stir them if necessary, but be gentle so that you do not break any.

When the tiny leaves begin to appear, bring your alfalfa seeds out into the light in order to develop the chlorophyll. When those tiny leaves turn a bright green, they are ready to enjoy. Be sure to eat the whole sprout—the old seed, the shell, the tiny root, the stem, leaves, everything in the jar.

Alfalfa sprouts are a wonderful substitute for lettuce if you are packing sandwiches. The sprouts, because they are alive, tend to retain their crispness.

Start a new seed or grain or bean sprouting every single night and you will always have a plentiful supply of fresh organic vegetables at practically no cost.

Carol Ann, a lovely young lady who lives largely on raw foods and has sapphires for eyes, makes sprouts a large part of her diet. She shared her sprouting procedure with me. Her method is simple and very satisfactory.

"We do our sprouting in old, glass, refrigerator storage dishes—the ones with flat bottoms and sides, and glass lids," she told me. "We find them at flea markets for 25¢–$1.00 depending on size and condition. Our other item is a plastic plant mister that emits a very fine, uniform spray with little effort.

"We soak the seeds overnight. The next morning we drain off the soak water (saving it to drink, to use in food preparation or to water plants), and spread the seeds out over the bottom of the container—thinly for alfalfa. We then water the sprouts, usually three times a day, depending on their stage of growth. If they dry out too quickly between waterings, the glass covers help retain moisture. The jars are kept in a dark place, or a towel is put over them, during germination. The watering process consists of spraying the sprouts so they are moist, but stopping before puddles form on the bottom. With the glass you can see through the bottom to check. Pour out any water that does collect.

"We especially like this method of sprouting as it conserves our limited supply of pure, unchlorinated, unfluoridated water—all water aside from the initial soak is used by the growing sprouts. Also alfalfa is sensitive to adulterated water and may not grow as well using some cities' water. We find that because our sprouts do not get tumbled about, they send their roots down and grow up, as nature intended. Alfalfa sprouts will crowd together, growing upward in unison, providing each other support. The result is a kind of luxurious green "lawn" of one-to-two-inch sprouts when left in the light a couple days. Soy, mung and lentil should be eaten when less than an inch (one–three days) when they are very tender and sweet. With soy and mung, any seeds that do not germinate, or look like they will not, should be taken out to keep them from molding or fermenting. Ungerminated alfalfa seeds remain on the bottom and can be shaken out as the sprouts are removed. As we consume them, we usually let alfalfa continue to grow. Other sprouts we often want to keep at one level of development, so we put the jar in the refrigerator, with the top on to retain moisture.

"For anyone who wants to sprout seeds, it is important to try different methods to find what works best for you, to get a feel for sprouting the different seeds, and to discover at what stages of growth you like them best. Do not be afraid to experiment and, above all, enjoy this wonderful live food fresh from your own indoor garden."

I find that soy beans and garbanzos do best in a collander. After soaking, put them in a collander and cover with a dampened tea towel. Rinse several times daily right through the towel. In warm weather cover the whole works with a piece of plastic to prevent drying out. Punch some holes in the plastic for ventilation.

I bought a pound of soybeans for sprouting for 45 cents last week. One pound will give me six to eight pounds of big, chewy soybean sprouts that I can use just slightly cooked. Soybeans themselves take hours to cook. The sprouts lose their raw bean flavor after only 10 minutes of cooking.

Soybean sprouts can be very lightly sautéed and served as a hot vegetable. Use very little oil because the soybean has its own built-in supply.

Try this recipe: lightly brown some sliced onion, add the bean sprouts and a very small amount of water, cover and cook for about 10 minutes. Season to taste. Great with brown rice.

Here is a really great recipe for a sprout curry.

Sprouted Soybean Curry

1 medium onion

1 medium apple

2 to 4 stalks celery

2 tablespoons oil

1½ cups meat stock or tomato juice

2 tablespoons soy flour

1 teaspoon curry powder

1 teaspoon salt

⅛ teaspoon paprika

½ cup raisins, seedless

3 cups sprouted soybeans

Cut onion, apple, and celery up fine. Lightly brown at a low temperature in the oil. Keep the pan covered. Add stock or tomato juice. Mix flour, curry powder, salt, and paprika together and make a paste with a small amount of water. Stir paste into vegetable mixture thoroughly. Add raisins and sprouted soybeans. Let simmer 15 minutes.

METRIC CONVERSION										
1 teaspoon = 5 ml.					1 tablespoon = 15 ml.					
1 ounce = 30 ml.					1 cup = 240 ml./.24 l.					
1 quart = 950 ml./.95 l.					1 gallon = 3.80 l.					
1 ounce = 28 gr.					1 pound = 454 gr./.454 kg.					
F.° 200	225	250	275	300	325	350	375	400	425	450
C.° 93	107	121	135	149	163	177	191	204	218	232

At 22¢ a pound for soybeans that give you three pounds of sprouts, a cup of soybeans costs you less than a penny. What else can give you so many nutrients for such a small cash investment?

Anyone who has been beefing about the high cost of natural and organic foods should take a closer look at some of the foods now being pushed all over the TV screen as the answer to a homemaker's dream or "how to make a gourmet meal without hardly trying." I did —and what I discovered will floor you. Those skillet dinner kits which contain everything but the meat and supposedly turn hamburger into a gourmet meal cost about $1.52 for five servings. And, even though they are ballyhooed as convenient quick-as-a-wink dinners, they take longer to prepare than the real thing and they cost more!

Here's what you get in Betty Crocker's Hamburger Helper: dehydrated vegetables (potatoes, onion, garlic), sour cream solids, salt, vegetable shortening, enriched flour (bleached), bouillon, hydrolyzed vegetable protein, sugar, natural and artificial flavorings, lactose, dextrins, beef extract solids, sodium caseinate, beef fat, caramel color, monosodium glutamate, potassium and sodium phosphates, citric acid, mono and diglycerides, disodium inosinate, guanylate, freshness preserved with sodium sulfite, BHA, and propylene glycol.

I have made Beef Potato Stroganoff at a cost of just $1.36 for five servings and the preparation time was only 20 minutes which is less time than you need using Hamburger Helper. This is the recipe I used:

Beef Potato Yogurt Stroganoff

¾ cup chopped onion (¼ pound)	5.5 cents
4 tablespoons oil	7 cents
1 pound hamburger meat	79 cents
1 cup beef stock or bouillon	negligible
3 pounds (4½ cups) sliced, raw potatoes (unpeeled)	30 cents
optional:	
salt, kelp, and a grating of nutmeg to taste	
½ cup yogurt	14 cents
	1.35.5 cents

Sauté onions in the oil very lightly keeping the lid on the skillet. Add meat and continue sautéing until the meat loses its red color. Now add the beef bouillon or stock and the

raw potatoes. A little salt, kelp, and a grating of nutmeg may be added at this point. Simmer gently for 30 minutes, or until potatoes are soft. Add yogurt when the mixture is ready to be served.
Serves five

(If you use homemade yogurt the cost will be 4.5 cents, making the total cost of the dish $1.25, or 25 cents a serving.)

You can considerably reduce the high cost of eating if you make your own fresh fruit cup and pass up the canned variety of fruit cocktail. I make a delicious fruit dessert using one orange, one banana, and two-thirds of a cup of unsweetened pineapple tidbits for a total cost of 36 cents for 16 ounces. Canned fruit cocktail sells for about 49 cents for 16 ounces and contains artificially colored red cherries and heavy syrup. You're paying for the sugar and water and artificial coloring which you don't want. Your homemade fruit cup goes much farther because all 16 ounces are fruit—no water, no sugar, and no dye.

If you're going to be baking your own cakes and cookies, you will have crumbs now and then. Save your crumbs and use them for crusts for cheesecake and cream pies.

I use watermelon rind in place of water chestnuts in Chinese dishes, in casseroles, and in stir-fry dishes. During the summer when watermelon is plentiful, I save the rinds, cutting off the outer green portion and any of the pink portion and then dice the remaining white section and freeze it in meal-size portions. All winter long you can enjoy this money-saving echo of summer's abundance.

Double Benefits

Saving money at the market can be a valuable ally in the good fight to bring better nutrition to your family. While they might fight the idea of improving their health with better food, they can't argue with a budget that won't stretch.

For instance, *Boy's Life* magazine surveyed its readers and found that the average boy scout drinks more than three bottles of pop a day; one out of twelve kids drinks an amazing eight or more bottles a day (*Center for Science Newsletter,* Fall 1972).

Let's say that your family is an average one and is therefore addicted to soft drinks. Let's say that no warnings, lectures, or preachments have been persuasive enough to turn them off. Just tell them in a tone that brooks no argument that at the price being asked for a six-pack you simply cannot afford it. And serve unsweetened pineapple juice at 73 cents for a big 46-ounce can. You will be providing some good nutrients while you are cancelling out all the sugar and artificial flavors and caffeine and other monstrosities in the soft drinks. You will be saving money on your food bill too.

But the real dividends—the ones that count the most —you will realize in other areas. You may find, as I did, that your children are coming home from their dental checkups with big no-cavity grins, that they don't get every cold that comes around, that the children's dispositions and yours are much sunnier, that the children are doing much better in school and somehow everyone seems to have more ability to cope—even with the high cost of living.

These are dividends you can't write a check for. Their value cannot be measured in dollars and cents.

Chapter 7

Creative Cooking for One

If you are going it alone, the temptation is to skip meals and live on snacks, or overdo the tea and toast thing. This can be the path to nutritional disaster and it frequently is—especially among older people.

I know it's no fun to cook for one. But you can make it fun. Pretend that that "one" is the Queen of England or the Duchess of Alhambra, or Golda Meir and cook for yourself as if you were a V.I.P., because you are. Set an attractive table. Use your best china and silver. What are you saving it for? Keep your favorite plant on the table.

There are quite a few advantages to cooking for *you*. You can always prepare exactly what you hanker for and fix it the way you like it. You can try out any new recipe that sounds exciting to you without having to be concerned about pleasing someone else.

There are some dishes that lend themselves to volume cooking—too much for one. Fine. Invite another person or two to share it with you. Or, freeze the unused portion in one meal sizes. Such dishes as rice pudding, black beans, and chopped liver freeze well. (Do not salt chopped liver before freezing, the salt attracts moisture and the liver gets mushy.)

If you're having liver, and you should have liver once

a week, make enough so you will have some left over for chopped liver for tomorrow night's dinner—or for freezing. Chop some toasted soy nuts into it for real crunch and more nutrition. When you have something scrumptious like this on the menu you have an urge to share it with an appreciative guest. Invite a friend. Your friend will be very grateful for your companionship and will return your invitation and before you know it, you're not cooking for one very often.

When you make brown rice, make a full portion and use some for rice pudding.

A Cure for that Nobody-Loves-Me Feeling

There's something about a good rice pudding that is a sure cure for that nobody-loves-me feeling that we all get at times—especially when the only shoes under the bed are yours. Even anticipating this gustatory pleasure lifts your morale. The following recipe makes six to eight servings. Freeze some in individual portions. (Set aside one serving for breakfast. Add a tablespoon of wheat germ and another of coarse bran, pour some milk over it and you have yourself a great battery charger.)

Having instant goodies like this in your freezer is just about the greatest spur to instantaneous sociability. When you meet someone exciting whose friendship you would like to develop, it's so easy to say, "Let's go over to my place. I've got some great rice pudding I'd like to share with you."

Rice Pudding, Plain and Fancy

2 eggs

2 cups milk

⅓ cup honey

1 teaspoon vanilla

1½ cups cooked short-grain brown rice

dash nutmeg

½ cup raisins (optional)

Beat eggs well with wire whisk. Add milk, honey, vanilla, rice, nutmeg, and raisins. Dust with more nutmeg. Bake in a one-quart casserole one to one-and-a-half hours at 350° F. Test for doneness by inserting a silver knife. If it comes out clean, the pudding is done. Chill it and serve plain or make it fancy topped with whipped cream or with fruit.

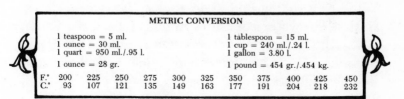

METRIC CONVERSION										
1 teaspoon = 5 ml.					1 tablespoon = 15 ml.					
1 ounce = 30 ml.					1 cup = 240 ml./.24 l.					
1 quart = 950 ml./.95 l.					1 gallon = 3.80 l.					
1 ounce = 28 gr.					1 pound = 454 gr./.454 kg.					
F.° 200	225	250	275	300	325	350	375	400	425	450
C.° 93	107	121	135	149	163	177	191	204	218	232

Whatever you do, do not use minute rice in this recipe, or ever. It doesn't have near the food value of brown rice. One woman to whom I gave this recipe wanted to know why her pudding didn't taste like mine or have the same consistency. The only change she made was to substitute minute rice for the brown. "Brown takes so long to cook," she said. Nonsense. It doesn't take any more of your time. You just start it earlier and go about your business.

How to Cook Brown Rice

Use a heavy pot with a tight-fitting lid. For one cup of brown rice, which will serve six people, use two cups of water and one teaspoon of salt. Cook until all the water has been absorbed (approximately 35 to 40 minutes). To test the rice, do not stir. Rub a grain between thumb and finger. If no hard core remains, the rice is done.

I like to use two-and-a-half cups of water and throw in a handful of wheat grains and a few mung beans. This combining of grain and legume increases protein values because the amino acids complement each other. Besides, it adds an extra wonderful dimension to the taste.

Another method of cooking your brown rice, suggested by Beatrice Trum Hunter, is to bring your liquid to a rolling boil, then trickle the rice in slowly so that the water continues to boil. Lower the flame, cover the pot and let it simmer for about 35 to 40 minutes. The rice comes out nice and fluffy and looks as light as white.

Plan to get double mileage out of lots of foods and you won't have to spend quite so much time in the kitchen but you will always have something ready to eat. This is important because it militates against the tea and toast habit.

For instance, cook a batch of black beans. Use some with rice tonight. Freeze the rest in meal-size portions. When Carla, a Rotary Exchange student from Brazil, stayed with us, we learned to enjoy black beans with brown rice, which Carla seasoned to a fare-thee-well and then added sliced bananas to cool the palate.

Black beans are the most flavorful and the meatiest of all beans, but if you don't have any, you can substitute any member of the bean family. They all provide complementary taste, texture, and nutrients. The beans are not cooked with the rice but are served with it. Carla would shovel up a scoop of the beans onto a mound of rice and enjoy the sight and the aroma before she dug in with gustatory enthusiasm. Try this recipe for Brazilian Black Beans and Rice. It will warm the cockles of your heart.

Brazilian Black Beans and Rice

2 cloves garlic

2 medium onions, chopped

2 tablespoons oil or butter

4 cups water, stock, or sprout water

1 cup black beans (carefully washed)

2 bay leaves

½ teaspoon paprika

1 teaspoon salt or kelp (or half-and-half)

2 stalks celery (including leaves), chopped

METRIC CONVERSION										
1 teaspoon = 5 ml.					1 tablespoon = 15 ml.					
1 ounce = 30 ml.					1 cup = 240 ml./.24 l.					
1 quart = 950 ml./.95 l.					1 gallon = 3.80 l.					
1 ounce = 28 gr.					1 pound = 454 gr./.454 kg.					
F.°	200	225	250	275	300	325	350	375	400	425	450
C.°	93	107	121	135	149	163	177	191	204	218	232

Put the garlic through a press or chop it
fine. In a heavy soup pot, sauté the garlic with
the onion in vegetable oil or butter. Add the
liquid, beans, bay leaves, and paprika. Bring
to a boil over high heat. Reduce the heat to
low, add the salt and celery and simmer partially covered for about three hours or until
beans are tender. Watch the liquid content.
Add more if necessary. Remove two tablespoons of beans and mash them to a smooth
paste using the back of a fork. Add the
mashed beans to the pot and cook a little
longer to thicken the whole mixture. Serve on
top of steamed brown rice. Deliciously satisfying.

In Cuba, thick, black bean soup is usually served with
side dishes of rice and cut-up raw onion. You thicken
the soup to your liking with the rice and sharpen it as
you like with the raw onions. Linda Wolfe, who wrote
The Cooking of the Caribbean Islands for Time-Life
Books, says that Cuba's black bean soup—thick and
dark and highly spiced, the beans as satisfying as any
meat—is the most memorable of dishes.

I found this recipe in a delightful book called *A Russian Jew Cooks in Peru* by Violeta Autumn (published
by 101 Productions, San Francisco, California, 1973).

If you have a good supply of soup stock in your
freezer, you can eliminate the first step in this recipe.
Simply cook the beans in the stock and proceed as
above.

Black Bean Soup

Soak one cup washed black beans in four cups of water for one hour. In the meantime make a broth of one pound of marrow bones and four cups of cold water. Bring to a boil, lower the heat, and simmer for an hour-and-a-half. Cool the broth, skim off the fat, then add the beans in their water, one sliced carrot, two tablespoons barley, one tablespoon dried mushrooms, and one teaspoon fresh hot pepper. (If you don't have hot pepper, substitute cayenne pepper.) Simmer until beans and barley are tender.

New Foods Add Days to Your Life

When you're living alone, good food is as sustaining as a good friend. Don't let your meals become monotonous. Try new foods you've never eaten before. The Japanese say that every time you eat a new food, you add 75 days to your life. Imagine! Have you ever tried millet, buckwheat, bulgur, or soy beans? There's a world of good eating in these unfamiliar foods and their many nutritional merits will add more life to your years. (See index for recipes for these foods.)

Get excited about what you're planning for dinner—not just for special occasions and weekends—but every night. You'll be surprised at how looking forward to an exotic meal will brighten your whole day. The very anticipation of sitting down to rice with chicken and cherries or a creamy mushroom *quiche* can have you stepping lively in the kitchen and will actually spur you on to new heights of creativity.

Mushroom Quiche

For Crust:

1½ cups whole wheat flour
pinch of salt
6 tablespoons butter
water

For Filling:

1 tablespoon onion, chopped
2 tablespoons oil or butter
8 mushrooms, sliced
3 eggs
½ pound cottage cheese
2 tablespoons fresh parsley, chopped
1 teaspoon salt
½ teaspoon kelp
pinch of pepper or paprika

Preheat oven to 400°F.

Make a crust by combining flour, salt, and butter. Add only enough cold water to make dough firm. Roll out and line a buttered eight-inch pie plate with it.

Sauté the onion lightly in a little oil or butter till soft. Add mushrooms and cook just until they begin to soften.

Beat the eggs and mix well with the cottage cheese. Add the mushrooms, parsley, and seasonings.

Pour into prepared pie crust and bake for 15 minutes at 400°F. Lower the heat to 350° F., and bake for 40 to 50 minutes or until the filling is firm.

This is high protein, inexpensive, and thoroughly delicious.

METRIC CONVERSION										

1 teaspoon = 5 ml.
1 ounce = 30 ml.
1 quart = 950 ml./.95 l.

1 ounce = 28 gr.

1 tablespoon = 15 ml.
1 cup = 240 ml./.24 l.
1 gallon = 3.80 l.

1 pound = 454 gr./.454 kg.

F.°	200	225	250	275	300	325	350	375	400	425	450
C.°	93	107	121	135	149	163	177	191	204	218	232

Chicken With Cherries and Brown Rice

3- or 4-pound chicken cut into 8 pieces

1 teaspoon salt

1 teaspoon kelp

1 teaspoon paprika

4 tablespoons oil or chicken fat

2 large onions, sliced

½ cup chicken stock

2 cups pitted bing cherries, fresh or frozen

2 tablespoons honey

2 tablespoons water or fruit juice

1½ cups long-grain brown rice

¼ cup chicken fat or oil

Combine the salt, kelp, and paprika and sprinkle over the chicken pieces. Heat the oil or chicken fat in a large skillet, and add the chicken pieces a few at a time. Cook for about

five minutes on each side to brown. Remove
the chicken, and brown the onions in the skillet just ever so lightly. Put the chicken pieces
back in the skillet, add the chicken stock and
bring to the boil, then reduce heat to low,
cover the pan and simmer for a half hour or
until fork tender.

While the chicken is simmering, put the
cherries, honey, and two tablespoons water or
juice in a saucepan over very low heat. Simmer uncovered for three minutes, stirring
frequently. Remove from heat.

Now partially cook the rice in a large saucepan. Bring four cups of water to the boil, add
the rice, and simmer for 20 minutes. Drain
the rice through a strainer (save the liquid for
soup or vegetable cooking).

Transfer the chicken pieces to a plate, re-
serving two tablespoons of the cooking liquid
and the browned onions.

Combine the reserved cooking liquid and
the quarter-cup chicken fat or oil in a large
oven-proof casserole and mix well. Put half
the rice in the casserole spreading it out
evenly. Add the chicken pieces, onions, and
half the cherries. Arrange the rest of the rice
on top of the mixture. Put in the remaining
cherries with their cooking liquid, cover the
casserole, and simmer for 20 minutes or until
rice is tender.

Presentation: Arrange half the rice on a
lovely serving platter. Arrange the chicken
pieces and the onions on top of the bed of
rice. Cover the chicken with the cherries and

half the remaining rice. Make an attractive
border with the rest of the rice.

This dish will delight your eye and your palate and if
you have invited dinner companions, their pure enjoyment will buoy your spirits for days. Freeze whatever
remains (if any) and enjoy it again when you're dining
alone.

The thing to remember is that there is pleasure to be
had in eating. Don't deny yourself that pleasure. Make
it happen—a nice atmosphere, relaxation, and whenever possible, friendly, laughing appreciative faces.

Above all, don't say, "I hardly cook anymore 'cause
there's only me." Say instead, "I plan my meals carefully—for good nutrition and for pleasure—because I'm
cooking for ME and I'm worth it!"

Chapter 8

Light and Lively Lunches

If you have been cooking with love and wheat germ at breakfast and at dinnertime, no doubt you have already witnessed some lovely changes in your family and yourself. But, you may be bothered, as I was, by this disturbing thought: What is the family eating away from home? What about lunches and those ever-present coffee breaks? When you finally get your family converted to the love and wheat germ principle, are you going to let them become junk food junkies once they leave the house? It's a challenge. After all, most of the commercial eating establishments available to your family at work and at school are not exactly run by a little old lady serving up Granny's homemade soup and brown bread.

In many business establishments the coffee cart comes rolling around every morning at 10, garlanded with Danish pastries, doughnuts, and other sweet temptations. These foods, laden with sugar, white flour, and a whole catalog of chemical additives, can seduce a person into obesity, diabetes, coronary crises, and other nasty problems we can live very nicely without.

I'm not going to suggest passing up the sociability or even the snacking at coffee break time. But there's absolutely no reason why you cannot make this snack a health builder instead of a health hazard. Slip a little bag of bran muffins into your, or your husband's, brief-case. That's what I did for my husband so he'd have something good to munch at coffee break time. Now he takes them himself and a few extra for his buddies who are hooked on them and have in fact requested my recipe.

These bran muffins are good in several ways. They are rich in fiber which, as you know, can be a great help to rapid transit of the food line thus preventing all kinds of digestive problems, diverticulosis, appendicitis, and cancer of the colon. My muffins also include all the ingredients of Dr. Rinse's formula for protection against atherosclerotic disease. (For the recipe see the Bless-Your-Heart Diet.) They are also very filling, thus discouraging overeating and preventing overweight. And, very important—they taste delicious.

The temptation to overdo the coffee thing is common to most business establishments. It seems as though the first piece of equipment a new company invests in is the coffeepot. But face it, coffee isn't the only thing to drink. And it surely isn't the best for you. So keep pack-ets of herb tea in your bottom drawer for a change of pace beverage. These teas have a most refreshing flavor and they don't play havoc with your blood sugar levels as coffee and regular tea do. Peppermint tea goes very nicely with bran muffins. I know.

Now what about lunch? Most restaurants and lunch bars are so crowded at the noon hour, that you might as well forget the whole concept of rest and relaxation while you're there. In fact, lunch-getting often becomes a hassle—a form of stress—which takes its own toll of your vitamin stores.

I have a simple solution to the problem of the lunch-time follies. Brown bag it. Pack a hot, nourishing, appetizing lunch for your spouse, yourself, and the children. How? Discover thermos bottle cooking. Start warming up a leftover soup or stew in the morning. (I always plan to have leftovers just for this.) Let it simmer while you're dressing or washing up or having breakfast. Then pour some in everybody's thermos where it will continue cooking and be hot and aromatic at lunchtime.

You will all enjoy a good tasting, highly nutritious lunch that will stick to your ribs. And considering the cost of restaurant meals, you'll save a barrel of money.

Goulash soup for instance can easily be poured into thermos bottles. Its fragrance will raise the A.I.Q. (Appetite Interest Quotient) even in poor eaters.

METRIC CONVERSION

1 teaspoon = 5 ml.
1 ounce = 30 ml.
1 quart = 950 ml./.95 l.
1 ounce = 28 gr.

1 tablespoon = 15 ml.
1 cup = 240 ml./.24 l.
1 gallon = 3.80 l.
1 pound = 454 gr./.454 kg.

F.°	200	225	250	275	300	325	350	375	400	425	450
C.°	93	107	121	135	149	163	177	191	204	218	232

Goulash Soup

2 tablespoons oil
1 cup finely chopped onion } *sauté till onion becomes translucent*
1 teaspoon minced garlic

2 teaspoons paprika

3 cups green pepper, cubed

1 teaspoon crushed caraway seeds

2 tablespoons whole wheat or soy flour

2 tablespoons nutritional yeast

1½ cups unpeeled potatoes,
    cut into small cubes

1 cup tomatoes, preferably home-canned

4 cups water, stock, or sprout soak water

2 cups cubed beef, (tiny cubes)

All you need do is combine all these ingredients, bring to a boil, and simmer 10 minutes. If you assemble the ingredients the night before, you might have time to do this in the morning. Distribute in thermos bottles. This amount will make four mini-lunches or two he-man meals.

Make sure you cut everything up fine and provide an iced tea spoon or a sturdy straw to facilitate getting the contents out of the thermos.

You can make lunches as varied as your imagination is fertile. Use any standard recipe for stews, soups, goulash, casseroles and follow the same procedure.

Thermos bottle cooking can be a blessing to you in your efforts to improve your whole family's nutrition—especially your schoolchildren. Because unless your children are among the fortunate few who attend a school where the Director of Food Service is really aware, chances are they are getting the usual fare in the school cafeteria: white bread (not whole grain), polished white rice (instead of brown), canned sweetened fruits usually topped with an embalmed and artificially colored maraschino cherry (rather than fresh fruit), hot dogs loaded with nitrates, nitrites and artificial colors (not simply cooked fresh meats), and fruit punches made from artificially flavored mixes (instead of plain fruit juice). Not only can these foods undermine your children's health, as you know, but they can also undo much of the good work that you have been doing in your campaign to establish good nutrition habits. Children, especially the little ones, tend to accept what is said and done at the school as gospel.

Of course, you must provide superior nutrition at home to compensate for any lack at school. But, in good conscience you must do more than that. With tact, diplomacy, and gentle persuasion, try to bring your knowledge of the importance of good nutrition to the school. There is, in fact, a movement in many schools throughout the country towards eliminating the junk foods, eliminating the sugar, white flour, and additives, and adding "love and wheat germ" to the school menu. This move in almost all instances was instigated by a concerned parent.

Until the food service at your school meets your good nutrition standards, the best thing to do is to pack the children's lunches and snacks so they can brown bag it healthfully.

A good lunch should include raw vegetables, a good hot soup or sandwich or both, some fresh fruit, and a nutritious goodie in the form of a cooky or some other confection that is as yummy as it is rich in nutrients. There are infinite variations on these themes so that every lunch can be a little different and always provide an exciting break.

For the sandwich in the lunch box, try whole grain bread spread with your own homemade mayonnaise topped with a good natural cheese with sprouts (they hold their crispness longer than lettuce). Cream cheese and walnuts on whole wheat bread are simply delicious. (Try making your own cream cheese, free of additives, by draining some yogurt in a cheese bag or in a strainer.) Peanut butter is still the "in thing" with youngsters. You can make your own peanut butter by whizzing peanuts in your blender and then adding a little oil. Or you can purchase good peanut butter that has nothing added to it at natural foods stores. It is not necessary to add sugar-loaded jelly to the peanut butter sandwich. Grated raw carrots go very well with peanut butter and they supply flavor contrast and moistness. Alfalfa sprouts are a nice partner for peanut butter; so are sliced bananas or applesauce. A handful of sunflower seeds gives a nice crunch along with some wonderful stay awake nutrients.

For raw vegetables, you could pack carrot sticks, celery sticks, cauliflowerettes, turnip slices, raw sweet potato slices, or a little container of sprouts. Try garbanzo sprouts, seasoned to your taste.

A cooky or yummy confection in the lunch box brings an element of surprise and delight, and it does not have to be an empty calorie trip to Cavity Corners. It can be supercharged with high power nutrients that taste great. Make these treats in double batches when you have time and cooperative youngsters on hand. Keep them in the freezer (the cookies, not the kids) and you will be free from the temptation to run to the store for sugar cookies for the lunch box.

Even if they don't eat lunch, they'll get a meal out of these cookies and a glass of milk.

Peanut Hootenannies

½ cup peanut butter, natural unhydrogenated

½ cup honey, unprocessed

½ cup chopped sunflower seeds

½ cup chopped English walnuts

½ cup wheat germ

coconut meal, for rolling

Mix together and shape into balls, then flatten with fork tines, first in one direction, then over them in the other direction, so you have grillwork on top of the cookies. Dip them in coconut meal, pack in a glass jar, and keep refrigerated.

Makes one dozen

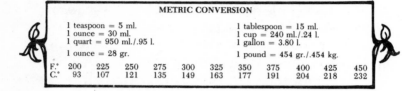

METRIC CONVERSION

1 teaspoon = 5 ml.   1 tablespoon = 15 ml.
1 ounce = 30 ml.   1 cup = 240 ml./.24 l.
1 quart = 950 ml./.95 l.   1 gallon = 3.80 l.

1 ounce = 28 gr.   1 pound = 454 gr./.454 kg.

F.°	200	225	250	275	300	325	350	375	400	425	450
C.°	93	107	121	135	149	163	177	191	204	218	232

High Protein Cookies

1 cup soy flour

½ cup brown rice flour

½ cup sunflower seed meal

½ cup wheat germ

½ cup rolled oats

½ cup raisins

½ cup apple juice

2 eggs

¼ cup vegetable oil

½ teaspoon salt

½ cup honey

¼ cup blackstrap molasses
½ cup peanut butter

Preheat oven to 350°F.
Combine dry ingredients and raisins. Stir in apple juice. Beat together: the eggs, vegetable oil, and salt, and add to mixture. Combine the honey, molasses, and peanut butter, and add to mixture. Spoon onto greased cooky sheet and bake 12 minutes in oven.
Makes two-and-a-half dozen

Sesame Raisin Squares

Combine in large mixing bowl:

2 eggs
⅓ cup tahini (sesame seed butter)
½ cup honey
Then add:
1 cup broken walnuts
1 cup oatmeal
¼ cup rice polishings
¼ cup wheat germ
½ cup finely ground
    unsweetened coconut
¼ cup sesame seeds
1 cup raisins

Spread in oiled, 9″ × 9″ glass baking dish. Bake about 20 minutes at 350°F. or until light brown. Cut in squares and remove to cooling rack. Makes 16 squares. Store in cooky jar. They get better with age.

METRIC CONVERSION										
1 teaspoon = 5 ml.					1 tablespoon = 15 ml.					
1 ounce = 30 ml.					1 cup = 240 ml./.24 l.					
1 quart = 950 ml./.95 l.					1 gallon = 3.80 l.					
1 ounce = 28 gr.					1 pound = 454 gr./.454 kg.					
F.° 200	225	250	275	300	325	350	375	400	425	450
C.° 93	107	121	135	149	163	177	191	204	218	232

Apricot Marbles

The kids will enjoy rolling these—right into their eager mouths.

1 cup sun-dried apricots

½ cup nut meats

1 cup ground coconut

4 tablespoons lemon juice

grated nuts (for rolling)

Put apricots, nut meats, and coconut through a food grinder. Add lemon juice, shape into balls, and roll in grated nuts. Refrigerate.

Makes one to one-and-a-half dozen

These muffins are moist and delicious and keep well (if you hide them).

Wheat Germ Muffins

1½ tablespoons dry yeast
½ cup warm water
3 cups raw wheat germ
4 cups rice flour
1 cup powdered milk
1 cup sesame seeds
1 cup whole wheat flour (or ½ cup
    whole wheat and ½ cup soy flour)
1 teaspoon salt
¾ cup oil
½ cup honey
4½ cups warm water
3 eggs

Preheat oven to 400°F.

Dissolve yeast in the warm water and let stand until dissolved. In a large bowl, mix wheat germ, rice flour, powdered milk, sesame seeds, whole wheat flour, and salt. Mix oil, honey, and warm water in another bowl. Slightly beat eggs and add to yeast. Add the oil, honey, and water mixture to yeast. Combine the liquid with the dry ingredients. Let stand about 10 minutes, then mix about one minute. Fill well-greased muffin tins with batter. Let stand 10 more minutes. Bake in oven for 20 minutes, lower heat to 350°F. and bake five more minutes.

Makes 30 muffins

You can vary these by adding raisins to some, nuts to some, sunflower seeds, chopped prunes, or apricots. You can also cut the wheat germ down to two cups and add one cup of bran.

Part 3

It's All In The Family

Chapter 9

When You Start Cooking for Two

You've just come home from your honeymoon with stars in your eyes and a firm resolve to make the honeymoon last forever. Love and wheat germ, at this stage of the game, can set you up for a smooth cruise on the sea of matrimony, a sea which can get pretty rough for some couples.

You've been flooded with good wishes, with casseroles, electric can openers, and silver trays. Now if your Aunt Sue shows up to welcome you home with a bottle of wheat germ, don't knock it. You will come to realize that Aunt Sue is one person who loved you enough to give you one of the things you need most. She knows that wheat germ has the nutrients to help you maintain a good heart and a pleasant disposition, and that spark which puts a special glow in marriage. Wheat germ is an excellent source of pantothenic acid, an anti-stress vitamin that will help you to cope with the excitement and the (sometimes) panic inherent in a new way of life.

Excitement—pleasant or unpleasant—is a form of stress. The excitement of preparing for your wedding, and the wedding itself, can deplete even a healthy person's supply of B vitamins and vitamin C, making him or her susceptible to any bug that happens to be hanging around.

Foods like wheat germ, brown rice, seeds, nuts, and grains can help to restore depleted supplies of vitamin B. They can also help to keep the magic in marriage because they provide the anti-fatigue vitamins of the B complex.

Every bride is so consumed with the responsibilities of fixing up her new home, learning to cook for two, and perhaps continuing her job at the same time, she is often exhausted when she gets to bed and wants only to sleep. Then it's "Not tonight, dear, I'm too tired." This kind of turnoff can quickly dim the lovelight in her husband's eyes.

Foods for the Sensual Side of Marriage

If she is going to keep the magic in her marriage, she must bear in mind that the sensuous woman does her homework in the kitchen, where she puts the emphasis on foods that are rich not only in the B vitamins, but in zinc, iodine, and other nutrients essential to love and life *and* love life.

The mineral zinc can help your man avoid the problem of impotence which plagues so many young men today. The medical profession is admittedly baffled by the increased rate of infertility and the increased lack of sexual spark among men in their prime who complain furtively of "bedroom fatigue."

Zinc is a necessary element for fertility and sexual vigor. Testosterone, the male hormone, cannot be produced without zinc. Like every other mineral, zinc is concentrated in the bran and germ portion of the cereal grains. This is removed in the refining process and fed to the animals. Female livestock have no complaints about their love life.

Zinc also plays a virtuoso role in orchestrating a woman's metabolism. Many enzymes cannot do their thing without zinc to spark their use by the body. But most girls do not get enough zinc. When the diets of high school girls and college women were analyzed to assess the zinc content, the majority of the diets contained less than the 15 mg. of zinc recently proposed as the RDA (Recommended Daily Allowance) for young women. In fact, many of the diets provided less than two-thirds of the RDA, according to the *Journal of the American Dietetic Association,* (March 1976).

When it comes to an important mineral like zinc, you're much better off by getting more than the RDA.

Wheat germ has the zinc that was removed from the flour that went into your grocer's white bread. Same goes for the bran. Add a tablespoon of each to your breakfast cereal. Add wheat germ and bran to hamburger whenever you use it. Use them also in your baked goods.

Another source of zinc is herring. Oysters too are rich in zinc, which may be one reason for their sexy reputation. But because of polluted waters the safety of eating oysters is questionable, so try to fill your zinc needs from other sources. Sweetbreads, the thymus gland of beef, calf, or lamb, are an excellent source of zinc. They have a delicate nutlike flavor and are simple to prepare:

Broiled Sweetbreads

Wash the sweetbreads and simmer them for about 20 minutes in salted water to cover. Let them cool in the liquid. Remove the skin and tough membranes, leaving tender, lobe-shaped pieces. Save the broth. Use it as stock or cook your vegetables in it.

Now pour a little oil or melted fat over the sweetbreads and brown on all sides in a heavy skillet or in the broiler. Sprinkle with a little salt, kelp, and paprika and serve on a bed of hot brown rice or garnished with parsley and lemon wedges.

Creamed Sweetbreads

After cooking the sweetbreads in salted water and cooling them slightly (as above) cut them into small pieces. Sprinkle with salt and a little whole wheat or soy flour and brown lightly in oil, butter, or chicken fat.

To make the sauce, blend three tablespoons of whole wheat flour with the drippings in the pan, stir in one to two cups of the liquid in which sweetbreads were cooked, add a half-cup of milk or cream and cook gently till smooth. Serve the sweetbreads on whole wheat toast, or brown rice. Pour the sauce on top. It's magic.

Perhaps your best source of zinc is seeds, particularly sunflower and pumpkin seeds. Seeds contain all the elements necessary to launch and sustain a new life. Therefore, they are rich in this substance which is so necessary to new life.

Seeds are also a remarkable source of vitamin F—the

essential unsaturated fatty acids, so very hard to get into our diet since most of the oils available today have had the vitamin F refined out of them. These fatty acids are very important to the machinery of sex—both male and female. They have been used effectively in the treatment of prostate disorders and menstrual disturbances.

You are just going into housekeeping, so now is the time to develop good patterns of eating—for both of you. The dividends which you will reap, in health, in happiness, in the achievement of your life's goals are incalculable.

Too few couples realize that the nutritional health of both parents at the time of conception greatly influences the health of the child. So the wife shouldn't wait until she conceives to try to build good health. She and her husband should be in radiantly good health long before pregnancy occurs.

On Setting Budget Priorities

Before you invest in a new rug or a lamp, pay attention to your pantry. Make sure there's money to set aside for fruit in season, fresh grains, raw nuts, sunflower, sesame and pumpkin seeds for stocking your refrigerator. This supply encourages healthful snacking habits and increases the zinc and magnesium content of your diet from the very beginning.

Incidentally, if you buy a refrigerator, get a big one. If your budget will stretch, invest in an extra freezer. You never have too much cold storage space. Freeze produce when it's in season and cheap. Make your own frozen dinners for quick heating up on rushed evenings. Store your whole grain flours, your seeds and nuts in the freezer. They are live foods and will keep much better if they are kept cold.

You're going to be so busy fixing up the place, painting, decorating, there will be a tendency to give your meals short shrift. Don't!

Make up your mind that the most important order of business is your nutrition plan. Before you pick up a paint brush or a tape measure, pick up a notepad and a cookbook and plan your menu for the next day and do what you can about it in advance.

Let's say you have decided on brown rice with meat sauce. Okay, get your chopped meat out of the freezer section so it will be ready for the skillet when you get home. Check your vegetable bins for the onion, celery, and green pepper you'll need. Plan to get the rice cooking as soon as you get in the house and then you won't be tempted, when you're both famished, to substitute something else because the brown rice takes too long to cook.

Now you have the ingredients and the plan for a good meal, but before you go back to paint-up, fix-up time, put some seeds up for sprouting. Soak your mung beans, alfalfa, and lentils. This takes only half-a-minute. And in less than three days they will provide you with the ingredients for a terrific salad and many life-giving nutrients for you, for your husband, and for the genes you will pass on to your children. (See Index for full directions for sprouting.)

If you are on a tight budget, as most young couples are, be sure to utilize the cheap but excellent nutrition of the bean family. Spend some time developing your skills with bean and grain combinations, and you will be well rewarded. You will be able to provide delicious high-protein meals without meat several times a week. They'll be a boon to your budget and your health.

Cash In on the Bean Bonanza

In the September 19, 1975 *Federal Register* the USDA proposed a "thrifty food plan" containing more meat, poultry, and fish, but less dry beans, potatoes, and grain products than were suggested in another plan called the "Economy Food Plan." The American Dietetic Association assailed the "thrifty" plan as inadequate in iron, zinc, folic acid, magnesium, and vitamin B_6. In other words, the diet high in bean and grains and potatoes with less meat contained many more essential nutrients.

It may surprise you to learn that beans are a good food for weight watchers. One hundred grams, or about 3.5 ounces (a half-cup) of cooked white or red beans is only 118 calories. The same 3.5 ounces of broiled choice porterhouse steak gives you a whopping 465 calories. The beans tend to fill you up. That little morsel of steak would hardly calm a hunger pang.

Beans can give both your wallet and your heart a break. The American Heart Association recommends that we cut our meat consumption by one-third. In their book, *The Benevolent Bean* (Doubleday and Company, Inc., New York, 1967), Dr. and Mrs. Ancel Keys describe studies which suggest a strong link between the low rate of coronary heart disease in Italy and the Italians' love of beans. Their observations tie in with the work of Dr. T. Kuo of the University of Pennsylvania, a leading investigator of the carbodydrate-heart link who observed that 90 percent of the subjects in his experiments reacted very favorably to a diet low in simple carbohydrates (sugar and refined flour products) but high in complex carbohydrates—such as beans.

Low in Fat, High in Protein

If it's fats you're avoiding, beans are made to order for you. Most beans contain less than two percent fat and this fat is low in saturates but high in essential linoleic and linolenic fatty acids.

Beans on the menu mean lots of good nutrients for your body—calcium, phosphorus, magnesium, and iron along with vitamins B_1 and B_2, niacin, and some vitamin C. They are also rich in protein. True, the protein of beans is not the same biological quality as meat protein, but when beans are combined with the cereal or grain family, with milk, cheese, or butter, they provide a complete protein with high biological value.

When you add lentils, soybeans, kidney beans, chickpeas, pea beans, split peas, pintos, mung beans, limas, or any of the thousand and one colorful members of the pulse family to a meat dish or to a soup, you put real pow into the nutritional wallop of the dish. It's a good idea, healthwise and budgetwise to use less meat and add beans to bridge the gap. Use the cheaper cuts of meat. Try to get the "utility" grade, the kind that comes from old cows that have been sent to pasture. These cows never get to the feedlots to be dosed with DES. Cook the meat slowly at low heat and it will be juicy and tender and tasty.

There's another terrific advantage in the bean family. You can always have a good supply of many varieties on hand without overcrowding your refrigerator and freezer. They have a long shelf life and need no refrigeration. Once the original package is opened, store the remainder in a tightly covered container—they look lovely in jars—and store them in a dry cool place where temperatures range from 50° F. to 70° F. It will give you a good feeling to know that come hail, or snow, or food shortages, your family will not go hungry.

Perhaps you have been turned off from using beans because usually the first step is "soak overnight." For those who plan ahead, this is no problem. If, however, you're looking for something for tonight's dinner, you can still use beans. Here is how:

Quickly wash a cup of dry beans and drop them into four cups of boiling water so slowly that the boiling does not stop. When you do this, the starch grains will burst, and break the outside covering of the bean. Then they can absorb the water more rapidly and cook more quickly. As soon as all the beans have been put into the water, lower the heat to a slow simmer to prevent toughening of the protein. Cook them at a simmer until they are tender. (Never add bicarbonate of soda even though it is recommended in some recipes. It harms a number of B vitamins.)

If salt, fat, or molasses are called for in your recipe, do not add them at the beginning of the cooking process. Fat tends to coat the outside covering and prevent moisture from passing into the legume. Acid present in molasses and tomatoes toughens the outside covering. Salt attracts water away from the legume rather than into it. Once the beans have become tender, add whatever seasonings are called for. Split peas and lentils are comparatively quick cooking and need no presoaking.

Beans Without Gas

Perhaps you are among those who get a lot of back talk from beans. If you prepare them according to a method devised by Dr. Joseph Rackis of the Northern Regional Research Laboratory in Peoria, Illinois, you can enjoy all the wonderfully creative bean dishes without fear of embarrassing flatulence.

The basic cause of the flatulence associated with beans, says Dr. Rackis, is the absence of enzymes in our systems which break down the trisaccharides (raffinase and stachyose) normally found in beans, into simple sugar. The undigested trisaccharides provide a banquet in the lower intestine for the natural bacterial flora which produce carbon dioxide and hydrogen—flatulence.

Dr. Rackis has figured out a way to enjoy beans without the offending trisaccharides, which, fortunately, are water soluble. The trick is to discard the soak water and the first cooking water and thus get rid of the little guys that are causing all the ruckus. Here's how you do it: Soak the beans in water for at least three hours. Throw away the soak water. Add boiling water to cover and cook for at least 30 minutes. Discard the cooking water. Add fresh water and resume cooking.

There is a slight loss in minerals, protein, and some water-soluble vitamins when you use this method. To compensate for this loss, add two tablespoons of nutritional yeast at the end of the cooking period.

Indian Dhal

(a hot and hearty dish)

Bring to a boil in a heavy pot with a tight-fitting lid:

1 cup Indian lentils, split peas, mung beans, or brown lentils

2 cups water

1 teaspoon salt

½ teaspoon turmeric

¼ teaspoon ground red pepper

Simmer until beans are tender and all the water is absorbed.
Fry together in a skillet:

1 onion, thinly sliced lengthwise

1 teaspoon cumin seeds

½ teaspoon ground coriander

3 tablespoons butter or crude safflower oil

When onions are golden, add them to the cooked beans, stir, cover the pot, and let steam for a few minutes. Serve with brown rice or bulgur. A delicious, sensual meal. Also cheap.

Serves four

METRIC CONVERSION										
1 teaspoon = 5 ml.					1 tablespoon = 15 ml.					
1 ounce = 30 ml.					1 cup = 240 ml./.24 l.					
1 quart = 950 ml./.95 l.					1 gallon = 3.80 l.					
1 ounce = 28 gr.					1 pound = 454 gr./.454 kg.					
F.° 200	225	250	275	300	325	350	375	400	425	450
C.° 93	107	121	135	149	163	177	191	204	218	232

Hummus, practically a national dish in the Middle East, combines the high lysine (an essential amino acid) of the garbanzo bean with the high methionine of the sesame seed. Together, they make a strong protein and a delightful dish.

When I brought a dish of hummus to a New Year's party, delighted merrymakers cleaned it up in 15 minutes. Dozens of tasty dips, spreads, and cheeses were still standing long after the hummus disappeared. I was literally besieged for the recipe. Here it is:

Hummus

Wash ½ cup (three ounces) garbanzo beans (chick-peas) in running water. Pick out any cracked or discolored beans. Soak washed beans in water to cover for two or three hours or overnight. If you're going to soak them overnight, in warm weather put the whole pot in the refrigerator to prevent fermentation.

Cook the beans in the soaking water with additional water to cover by one inch. Bring to a boil, then turn down heat and simmer for about two hours or until tender, in a partially covered pan. Add more boiling water as necessary to keep the beans covered. Do not salt until the beans get soft. Drain and season to taste. *Do not discard the cooking water.*

Makes one-and-a-half cups

You will also need:

½ cup lemon juice

1 large clove garlic

4 tablespoons tahini (sesame butter)

1 teaspoon salt

Put lemon juice, garlic, and salt in the blender and whiz till garlic is pulverized. Add the cooked chick-peas and half-a-cup cooking liquid, gradually until they are all blended. Add a little more cooking water if necessary.

When they are all blended, add the tahini and whiz again for an instant.

Spread the hummus in a flat bowl or plate and garnish with parsley, a few whole chick-peas, and some toasted sesame seeds. Enjoy, enjoy!

METRIC CONVERSION										

1 teaspoon = 5 ml. 1 tablespoon = 15 ml.
1 ounce = 30 ml. 1 cup = 240 ml./.24 l.
1 quart = 950 ml./.95 l. 1 gallon = 3.80 l.

1 ounce = 28 gr. 1 pound = 454 gr./.454 kg.

F.°	200	225	250	275	300	325	350	375	400	425	450
C.°	93	107	121	135	149	163	177	191	204	218	232

Famous Senate Restaurant Bean Soup

Bean soup always gets a majority vote in the Senate Dining Room, Mr. Louis Hurst, manager of the restaurant, told me. It is prepared every single day in a tremendous pot that is big enough to get into and pull the lid over your head.

Take two pounds of small Michigan navy beans. Wash and run through hot water. Put on the stove with four quarts of hot water. Add one-and-a-half pounds of smoked ham hock. Simmer slowly for three hours.

Braise one chopped onion in butter until light brown. Add to soup. Season with salt and pepper.

Serves eight

To avoid using nitrate-containing cured ham you may want to use instead a fresh tongue, a few bay leaves, a few crushed caraway seeds, and one minced clove of garlic.

If you prefer not to use any meat, add a half-cup of soy grits to increase the protein power. Softened soy grits should be added about 20 minutes before cooking is completed. You may need more water to accommodate them.

Unless you're cooking for a crowd, cut this recipe down to size. You're not feeding Congress. Remember that one cup of dry beans cooks up to three cups. And one pound of dry beans is about two-and-a-half cups. You can take it from there.

Treat your family to some of these marvelous bean dishes enjoyed throughout the world and make it a practice to put the emphasis on some member of the bean family at least once a week.

There are so many members of the legume family and so many tantalizing ways to prepare them, that anyone who says flatly he doesn't like them, just doesn't know beans about beans.

New Gadgets for New Cooking Habits

There are some appliances which can be a great help to you in your good cooking ventures. I would give top priority to a yogurt maker, a good blender, a little seed mill for grinding grains, nuts and seeds in small portions, and a *wok* for stir-fry dishes. Put these items on your wedding list or house-warming list to take the place of some of the silver and crystal which have to be polished and shined and insured, and which come out of hiding only on very, very special occasions, like 25th wedding anniversaries.

I am not unaware of the fact that a wife may have to change some of her new husband's eating habits, and perhaps some of her own. Now is the time to do it. How? Tenderly—with love and wheat germ.

Plan to try a new dish several times a week. On those days, always have ready something you know he loves. Serve the new dish first. Maybe it'll make a hit. Maybe it won't. Don't be devastated. Now bring out the dish he loves and the meal will end on a happy note. But even that irresistible dish that he loves should be made from highly nutritious substances and without no-no's. You don't have to depart from your favorite things. Simply convert them.

If a recipe calls for sugar, substitute honey and cut the amount in half. (I always use one-half cup of honey when a recipe calls for one cup of sugar, then, if I make the recipe often, I gradually cut the half-cup of honey down to one-quarter cup. You will find that your taste buds will rebel at the taste of excessive sweetness if you gradually cut down on the amount of sweeteners you consume.) You can also use date sugar as a substitute for sugar. This is made from ground dates and has all the nutrition of the date. Instead of chocolate, use carob. Carob is rich in minerals, has no fat and no oxalic acid, which can inhibit calcium absorption.

When a recipe calls for hydrogenated fats, substitute the least processed oil you can afford, (cold-pressed oils are best) or butter. Instead of white flour, use whole wheat flour. If you are not quite ready for whole wheat products, then use an unbleached flour and fortify it by adding wheat germ, bran, and soy flour.

Always add some soy flour to your wheat flour to enhance the protein value. The amino acid patterns of grains and legumes are complementary. The proportion can be 10 parts whole wheat to one part soy. But you will enhance the nutritional value even more if you make the formula five to one.

If a recipe calls for cornstarch as a thickening agent, use arrowroot or brown rice flour or soy flour instead. Let's say that he's crazy about Bavarian Cream. Who isn't? Okay. Make a carob-flavored Bavarian Cream and use honey instead of sugar. It's fantastic. He'll think he married a French chef.

This recipe is adapted from the *Mini-Guide to Living Foods* by Pat Connolly:

Carob Bavarian Cream

1 tablespoon gelatin, unflavored

½ cup water

4 egg yolks

½ cup carob powder

2 tablespoons honey

pinch salt

1½ teaspoons vanilla

4 egg whites

1 pint cream

METRIC CONVERSION										
1 teaspoon = 5 ml.				1 tablespoon = 15 ml.						
1 ounce = 30 ml.				1 cup = 240 ml./.24 l.						
1 quart = 950 ml./.95 l.				1 gallon = 3.80 l.						
1 ounce = 28 gr.				1 pound = 454 gr./.454 kg.						
F.°	200	225	250	275	300	325	350	375	400	425	450
C.°	93	107	121	135	149	163	177	191	204	218	232

Soften gelatin in water and warm over low heat till dissolved. Put egg yolks, carob, honey, salt, and vanilla in blender and whiz till well mixed. Beat the egg whites stiff. Whip the cream till satiny. Combine the three mixtures in a large bowl and whip together gently. Put in sherbet glasses and freeze. Serve some tonight. He'll melt.

Chapter 10
Ten Ways to Head Off the "Forties Blues" (Fat, Fatigued and Frustrated)

Remember how we used to say "life begins at 40?" We didn't believe it for a minute. It was an expression of sympathy for those who felt that at 40 they were getting fat, were always tired, and were frustrated because none of their early dreams had been realized.

Well, I have news for you. I'm going to show you how you can be slim, vital, and dynamic at 40 or 60 or at 80.

First, take a look at the calendar. Note the date. Put a red circle around it. There may be nothing special about this date—not yet. But you are going to change that. A year from now you will note this date as the anniversary of the *New You*.

Today you're going to take a giant step. You're going to do something "crazy." Not crazy—*mashigina* or insane—but crazy like an impossible dream seems crazy, because it will be something you have frequently dreamed of doing, but never really had the guts or motivation or the time to make a beginning. All of us have a whole catalog of activities we'd love to become involved in—if only. If only—what? No answer—just a faraway look, and we go on doing pretty much the same things today as we did yesterday and the day before. We watch TV, we go to a movie, we play bridge with the Smiths. There comes a time when all of us wonder "Is that all there is?"

No, that's not all there is. There's something out there that will make your spirits soar. Now's the time to try your wings on one or more of the 10 get-young ideas below:

1. For starters, just picture youself behind the footlights, the audience in the darkened theatre hanging onto your every nuance of speech and gesture as you transport them into another world. So it isn't Broadway. So, what? You've got a much better chance of making the footlights in a little theatre group in your own hometown. And for heaven's sake, don't be bashful about offering your services. They'll be delighted to discover you.

If you're not the type who can take the butterflies that go with performing, you might love it backstage where you participate in the excitement without the butterflies. Whatever aspect of theatre work you engage in, one thing is certain. In no other group will you ever find the wonderful spirit of camaraderie and fun that somehow always exists in the wings of a little theatre.

2. I'm going to make another suggestion that, on first blush, you may think is really zany. Get on the lecture circuit! Go ahead and laugh but don't knock it till you've tried it.

If there is a subject that really grabs you, become an expert on it. Research it, prepare a good talk on it and let the local organizations know you're available. Maybe it's handwriting analysis, stained glass, gourmet or natural food cooking, astronomy, astrology, a book review, or historical vignettes.

By the time you get this far into cooking with love and wheat germ you have a well-rounded knowledge of nutrition. Why not share it? PTA's are looking for good solid nutritional guidelines. Bring along a platter of snacks made without sugar, white flour, or hydrogenated fat. Audiences love to taste the evidence. Be sure to research your idea and use lots of humor. If you can help people to enjoy a big belly laugh, they'll love you for it and will accept your ideas much more willingly. Humorous speakers are in much demand. Look at Sam Levenson.

Almost any subject that is well thought out and well presented can be a hit on the lecture platform. If you have little children, don't let any of those cute things they say get away. Just by collecting the *bon mots* of four kids, I was able to put together a 40-minute monologue which I used for a long run on the local club circuit. Besides being a heck of a lot of fun to do, these engagements helped us to meet tuition bills and caused our firstborn to quip, "As soon as I opened my mouth, I started working my way through college."

No kidding. The lecture platform can put pow and prestige in your life and dollars in your pocket. John C. McCollister, who has been charming audiences for the past 10 years says that more and more retirees are discovering the potential of the lecture platform as a source of added income, (*NRTA Journal*, September-October 1975).

The activity which you begin today should be not a one-shot thing, but a continuing activity performed on a regular basis to which you can look forward with anticipation and pleasure.

3. If you are the sedentary type, if you wince and turn the page everytime you see an item about the importance of physical activity, or if you have been trying to trim down to bikini size, go to the phone right now. Call your "Y" or Community Center and register for gym and swim or yoga or slimnastics or belly dancing or folk dancing. No matter what the weather or distractions, let nothing deter you from going at least the first three times. Then it will be a habit programmed into your personal IBM and you will begin to realize some wonderful benefits. You will also make many new friends. Invite a few to dinner. Serve them a great vegetarian meal, or an all-natural meal based on love and wheat germ recipes. Spread your knowledge of nutrition. You'll enjoy it and do more good than you know.

Just the other day, I read a long newspaper story about treating "depression," called the most common of all diseases. But it's hard to recognize and hard to treat as such, said the story. The one universal symptom of every depression is the loss of pleasure and joy in those things and activities that, under normal circumstances, make life worth living. Things that used to give pleasure, don't anymore. A man who used to play tennis suddenly stops playing; a woman who used to enjoy bridge stops making dates to play.

I say, maybe they're depressed, but maybe they've just outgrown tennis and bridge.

If you feel well and eat a good diet and if your old activities still pall, by all means switch. Where does it say that the things that brought pleasure yesterday must do the same for us today? If a child can tire of a toy in a few days or weeks, why can't we grow weary of the same old activities after a period of years?

When we first moved to Pennsylvania and had no friends or connections, I was delighted to get together with the "girls" in the neighborhood for a weekly game of Mah-Jongg. It was a way to meet people, socialize, and swap recipes and baby stories. As soon as I became involved in little theatre and various "study" groups, the Mah-Jongg palled. I dropped it—not because I was depressed. Quite the contrary. I graduated from it. Don't hang on to any activity after it ceases to give you a lift.

A friend of mine, one of the most vital and dynamic people I know, makes it a point to pick up a new hobby every two years. He's been into photography, karate, *Tai Chi,* and oriental rugs, and he has continuing interest in nutrition. No, he's not flighty. He likes to expand his horizons. He never allows himself to get into a rut.

4. If you haven't yet quit smoking, for heaven's sake don't waste another minute. Don't say, "But I enjoy it." Nonsense. And don't say, "I can quit anytime, I'm waiting for my doctor to tell me." When your doctor tells you, baby, it's too late. If you have tried to quit and failed, call a Smoke Enders Clinic. Do this right away. Put some money on the line and sign up.

Then take the money you would have spent on the cancer sticks and put it in one of those slot banks that don't readily spill out their contents. Plan a trip to Hawaii financed by the money in that bank. Boy, will you enjoy booking your passage in the "No Smoking" section!

5. Make a patchwork quilt. We all have odds and ends of fabrics cut off the bottoms of skirts and dresses and slacks. That quilt could be a memorial to every outfit you have ever owned. Get your friends interested. Start an old-fashioned quilting bee.

Try a Friendship Pattern. Ask your very special friends to write their names on separate squares of fabric. Embroider over the writing and then add an applique representing your friends' special interest—a camera for a shutterbug; skis for those who slalom on the snowy slopes; a stethoscope for your doctor; a beautiful plant for your friend who parlayed her interest in growing things into a nice little business she calls "Plant Parenthood." This can be a fun venture and you'll end up with an heirloom piece that will enhance your bedroom decor and keep you warm in many ways. You could use this same friendship theme to make a tablecloth which could be an endless conversation piece.

How about original needlepoint? You can have canvases made to order to mark the birth of a new baby, a graduation, a wedding anniversary. Mr. Al Mintz who runs *Mazel Tov* in New York, a shop which deals in needlepoint canvases, told me that a friend of

Steve Lawrence and Edie Gorme presented the Lawrences with a needlepoint copy of the invitation to their son's *bar mitzvah*. Pearl Bailey did a canvas for President Ford illustrating his interests and those of his family. Some people do needlepoint chair seats to match their drapes. The possibilities are endless, the work is relaxing and seeing the finished product is a real thrill.

And get rid of the idea that needlework is exclusively a feminine activity. Many he-man types do terrific needlepoint and crewel embroidery. (Football linebacker Rosie Greer wrote a book on it!) I know medical students who find this kind of recreation not only extremely relaxing but helpful to them in improving their finger dexterity for surgery.

6. Try a new recipe today, one you have never attempted before. Make it a practice, at least one day a week, to try a brand-new recipe. (There are plenty in this book.) Invite some friends over to share it.

Think of cooking and homemaking, not as drudgery but as a creative art. Surely a person who makes a study of nutrition, continually seeking new ways to make good food attractive and delicious, earns high points for creativity.

In the book, *The Ulyssean Adult: Creativity in the Middle and Later Years* (McGraw Hill Ryerson, New York, 1976), psychologist Abraham Maslow tells of a woman, uneducated, poor, a full-time housewife and mother, who did none of the conventionally creative things. But, "with little money, her home was somehow always beautiful. She was a perfect hostess. Her meals were banquets. Her taste in linens, silver, glass, crockery, and furniture was impeccable. She was in all these areas original, novel, ingenious, unexpected, and inventive. I just had to call her creative."

Dr. Maslow's contact with this woman and others like her convinced him that, "A first-rate soup is more creative than a second-rate painting and that generally, cooking or parenthood or making a home could be creative, whereas poetry need not be."

To be even more creative, make a collection of your favorite recipes. Wherever you go collect recipes of dishes that are particularly appealing—from your Aunt Tilly, your mother-in-law, and even from restaurants. (Many restaurants are eager to share their recipes and flattered that you cared enough to ask.)

When your kids are married and on their own, they're going to ask you how to make that mushroom and barley soup, and what's your special trick for making chopped liver? It will be very nice to be able to hand them your collection (maybe as a wedding gift). And who knows, maybe you'll eventually get it published. That's how my first book, *Confessions of a Sneaky Organic Cook* was born.

7. Explore the mystery and fascination of foreign lands—without passport, luggage, or shots—and without cleaning out your bank account. How? Invite an exchange student to

share your home. This has been one of our most rewarding experiences.

Carla, our Brazilian daughter, a Rotary International youth exchange student, filled our home with that sparkling, lilting quality unique to the Latins. She brought us youthful excitement, involvement, a Brazilian beat which she drummed out on the too-long-silent piano, and black bean soup.

Rotary exchange students are high school age, 16 or older. They spend a year in this country with four different sets of parents. Thus, Carla stayed with us for three months. The student pays his own passage. Rotary provides a monthly stipend for the student and also sponsors parties, special trips, and events for all of the exchange students in the area. You provide tender loving care, good food, and parental supervision, same as you would for your own child.

You do not have to be a member of Rotary to be eligible as parents to an exchange student. You don't have to have children of similar age either. If your children have gone off to college, leaving empty beds behind, why not fill them up? Call your local Rotary club for details.

I have always had an aversion to unoccupied rooms and empty beds. I remember one time when we moved into our new home and the doctor came to call. I had two little ones and was big with the third. The doctor exclaimed at the size of our new home and asked "How many bedrooms do you have?"

"Five," I answered.

"Well," the doctor said sternly, "don't feel obligated to fill them all up."

I never did heed his advice. We filled them all up—with children and with strangers who became friends. Even when the children were little, we usually had a roomer occupying our third floor bedroom and bath which was meant to be maid's quarters. (*Alevai*—I should be so lucky!)

You can also enlarge your horizons, and get the spirit of youth into your home by making your empty beds available to college students in the area. This can be a good source of income. Every college is short of dormitory space and usually maintains a residence placement service to help students get located. You could offer room only, room and board, or room with kitchen privileges. Whatever suits you.

We have had students from India, Israel, and several far-away states. One of our students was a ham radio operator. He set up his paraphernalia and brought us voices from all over the world. One time we were guests at a long-distance wedding conducted over the airwaves.

8. Borrow or buy some books about herbs and plant yourself a lovely fragrant herb garden. Plant sweet basil, summer savory, dill, parsley, thyme, marjoram, oregano, coriander, chervil, sage, mints, and tarragon. Landscape your herb garden using stones to make a checkerboard design or go creative with your own design. Herbs require little care and aren't the least bit temperamental about the soil, and they reward you with

so many sweet aromas and savory meals. Or, choose just one herb, like peppermint or sage and become a *mayvin* on it. Read everything you can get your hands on. Cultivate the herb, harvest it, dry it, then put it up in colorful airtight tins or jars and give them to your friends to bring a very special fragrance on special occasions.

Here is a list of herbs suggested by *The American Herb Grower* back in 1947. (It sure pays to hang on to old publications.) Plant these seeds at the last possible moment in which the soil can be worked in the fall, and they will have a running start in the spring. The small seeds should be set in very shallow drills and tamped down firmly to prevent washing away.

Seeds to Sow in Late October

Annuals and Biennials

Ambrosia—*Chenopodium Botrys*
Borage—*Borago officinalis*
Caraway—*Carum carvi*
Chervil—*Anthrieus cerefolium*
Coriander—*Coriandrum sativum*
Dill—*Anethum grai colens*
Foxglove—*Digitalis purpurea*
Mignonette—*Reseda odorata*
Parsley—*Petroselinum latifolium*
Perilla—*Perilla frutescens*
Clary Sage—*Salvia sclarea*
Sweet Wormwood—*Artemisia annua*
Woad—*Isatis tinctoria*

Perennials

Angelica—*Angelica archangelica*
Lemon Balm—*Melissa officinalis*
Salad Burnet—*Sanguisorba minor*
Catnip—*Nepeta Cataria*
Sweet Cicily—*Myrrhis odorata*
Horehound—*Marrubium vulgare*
Hyssop—*Hyssopus officinalis*
Lamb's Ears—*Stachys lanata*
Lavender—*Lavandula vera*
Lovage—*Levisticum officinale*
Rue—*Ruta graveolens*
Sage—*Salvia officinalis*
French Sorrel—*Rumex Seutatus*

9. Go back to school. You're *not* too old. You have a remarkable mind which improves as the years bring wisdom. So, deliver a swift

kick to the conventional notion that once the bloom of youth has faded, school is out. A woman I know enrolled at 63 as a full-time student at our local Community College. She became an honor student and the darling of the campus. She says she never felt so good about herself.

Do some soul searching. Bring out that dream you put away because of the pressures of bringing up a family. If you kept a diary in your early years, read it to refresh your memory about the longings you had then, but couldn't fulfill. Now maybe you can. You always wanted to be a doctor or a nurse? Well, suppose it is too late to become a stethoscope-carrying doctor or a surgical nurse, you can still be a medical assistant, a dental hygienist, a laboratory assistant, a practical nurse. Enroll in one of the paramedical courses now being offered at many community colleges. One of my friends became a practical nurse at the age of 45. She's busy and involved, and the money comes in handy, too. I know of a woman whose children are now in school who went back to college to study midwifery. It will take her several years to complete the course. So what? One must make a beginning, and half the fun is getting there.

10. If the idea of going back to books doesn't particularly grab you, why not take up dancing or a musical instrument? At the Y.W.C.A. in our community, courses are offered in Hawaiian dancing, belly dancing, and ballroom dancing. They're inexpensive and so

much fun. You just can't be blue when you're moving to the music.

Do you like to sing? Join a barbershop quartet, or its distaff counterpart, the Sweet Adelines. For one or two nights a week you'll be an indispensable part of a team who will become your close friends. You'll travel to nearby towns together for fun evenings of regional competition and—who knows?—you might be the one who makes the difference that brings your quartet to the national finals!

I've given you a few suggestions to get you started. You can probably come up with some great ideas yourself.

If you've been cooking with love and wheat germ, you probably feel well and have boundless energy. But good nutrition is not an end in itself. It does not separate you from life. Rather, it enriches life—every aspect of it. It is a springboard from which you can and should sail into new vistas of joy and fulfillment. And if not now, when?

Chapter 11

The Bless-Your-Heart Diet

It's great to be told that you're not a candidate for a heart attack. That's the feeling my husband Harry and I enjoyed when our doctor marveled that even though we're old enough to remember the Flapper Age, our arteries are younger than springtime—supple, elastic, and free of cholesterol deposits.

I attribute our "young" arteries to our love and wheat germ diet and Dr. Rinse's breakfast mash. You will always find a batch in our refrigerator.

In my book, *How to Feel Younger Longer*, (Rodale Press, Emmaus, Pa., 1974) I told the story of Dr. Jacobus Rinse, the chemist who brews his heart medicine in his breakfast bowl. Since then there has been a tremendous wave of interest in Dr. Rinse's formula. Why not? It works!

One gentleman told me that he was only 10 days out of the hospital where he had been in intensive care for several weeks as a result of a serious heart attack. As soon as he came home, he started on Dr. Rinse's formula and, he said, nothing they did for him in the hospital helped like that. "I'm a new man," he said, making like Tarzan.

Dr. Rinse suffered a heart attack when he was 51 years old. Subsequently he was plagued by angina pains and the prognosis was that if he took good care of himself, he might live another 10 years. Last winter at the age of 76, Dr. Rinse took up a new hobby—skiing.

He attributes his current buoyant good health and vitality to a nutritional program based on a "mash" consisting of granular soybean lecithin, debittered brewer's yeast, raw wheat germ, bone meal, and polyunsaturated oil. In addition, he takes vitamin C, vitamin E, an all-purpose vitamin, and his diet includes other healthful foods such as bran, yogurt, and fruit.

Dr. Rinse wrote a report of his experiences (including his diet) and gave copies of it to friends. Later, many of them wrote to tell him about their success with it.

Mr. W. who survived a cerebral thrombosis and a heart infarct at the age of 53, started on the Rinse program right afterwards and was working again full time within six months. That was 15 years ago and he has had no relapse.

A Connecticut man wrote, "Fantastic results. Everyone was astonished about my vitality at 68. Before I felt like an old man—high blood pressure, very short of breath, dizzy, arms and legs always falling asleep. All complaints disappeared!"

Someone from Santa Barbara, California, wrote, "Cholesterol down to 264 after 315 when I started with your breakfast."

A gentleman from the Netherlands wrote . . . "At the age of 76, walking and climbing staircases became more and more difficult, I could not dress without help, I was also affected mentally by strong medicine. I started on your breakfast. Progress was noticed after one month. After three months I am completely changed. Now I live a normal life."

A grateful former cardiac victim of Red Oak, Iowa, wrote, ". . . within just a few days (after taking the breakfast mash) I noticed I could run upstairs again without puffing, I could walk a fast mile. The trouble that I previously had—my hands going to sleep while driving—has ceased. I had arthritis off and on in both knees for several years, also in my heels. All of this has now stopped."

Besides hundreds of reports like these from laymen, Dr. Rinse heard from physicians whose patients responded to the program. One of them, an internist, prescribes the breakfast to his older patients. "The results are spectacular," he writes. "Many of them resume their activities after having been invalids for a long time."

Another internist wrote that he owes his own life to the food supplements.

When I retell these experiences, many people are incredulous. "Why doesn't my doctor tell me these things?" A good question. While some physicians agree that cardiovascular problems can be the result of dietary deficiencies, the medical profession officially is still declining to sanction this theory. They say no definitive studies have been done. Most, however, willingly prescribe anticholesterol drugs. A recent report from the National Heart and Lung Institute states that after a 15-year investigation with more than 8,000 patients and at a cost of $40 million, it has concluded that no anticholesterol drugs are effective on patients who have suffered one or more cardiac attacks. The death rate is the same as with a placebo.

Dr. Rinse concedes that the lack of nutrients isn't the only heart-risk factor. Smoking, for instance, destroys vitamins and therefore may encourage atherosclerotic conditions. Obesity reduces physical activity and blood circulation. A sedentary life sometimes restricts food consumption and may result in shortages of some nutrients. Stress consumes large amounts of vitamins, particularly the vitamin B complex.

Heredity is a factor in heart disease—but one which can be overcome. Some people become affected earlier than normal because their bodies handle one or more nutrients inefficiently.

It is doubtful that avoiding dietary cholesterol makes sense. (Only 50 percent of heart disease patients have serum cholesterol levels above 220.) A better method, says Dr. Rinse, is based on the assumption that the diet should contain such elements as lecithin, linoleate oils, and sufficient vitamins and minerals, all of which work in the body to take care of any excess cholesterol.

This is confirmed by the Ireland-Boston Heart Study (1960–1970) conducted by J. Brown and 18 others from both the Department of Nutrition, Harvard School of Public Health, Boston, and the Department of Social Medicine, Trinity College School of Medicine, Dublin. Some 575 pairs of brothers between the ages of 30 and 65, born and raised for at least 20 years in Ireland were studied. One of the brothers of each pair had emigrated to the Boston area and lived there at least 10 years. The team of 19 researchers, including cardiologists and nutritionists ran controlled studies among 312 urban and 152 rural Irishmen not related to the paired brothers. In addition, they studied another 375 first-generation Americans whose parents had been born in Ireland.

The brothers who had remained in Ireland, in spite of eating a diet rich in butter, milk, cream, bacon, potatoes, mutton, and brown bread, *had lower incidence of heart disease* than those of their brothers in the Boston area. Autopsies from non-cardiovascular related deaths reveal that the hearts of brothers in Ireland on the average resembled those of American men 15 to 30 years younger.

The report revealed that the Irish diet contained greater quantities of vitamin E and magnesium. Apparently the food in Ireland is less processed and therefore richer in these nutrients. No difference in smoking habits nor in stressful situations was noted.

Dr. Rinse comes to these conclusions:

1. Atherosclerosis is a deficiency disease.

2. Human metabolism needs lecithin and polyunsaturated oils to prevent and dissolve deposits of cholesterol in the arteries.

3. Lecithin and oil should be consumed together with antioxidants (vitamins C and E).

4. Modern food, since it is often deficient in vitamins and minerals, should be supplemented with every known vitamin and mineral.

In the absence of specific medical advice to the contrary, says Dr. Rinse, there is no need to restrict consumption of cholesterol-containing natural foods—if the food supplements recommended in the breakfast mash are also taken.

Here is how the mixture is made:

To one tablespoon each of soybean lecithin granules, debittered brewer's yeast, and raw wheat germ, add one teaspoon of bone meal powder. You can make up a large quantity of this mixture, as Dr. Rinse does, and store it. Then for each serving mix in a bowl:

2 tablespoons of the above mixture

1 tablespoon dark brown sugar (we don't need the sweetness so we omit the sugar. If you do need sweetness, try honey)

1 tablespoon safflower, sunflower, or soybean oil. Add milk to dissolve the yeast and the sweetening agent. Add yogurt to improve consistency.

Add cold cereal (try granola) for calories as needed or put this mixture on top of hot cereal such as oatmeal or porridge. Raisins and other fruits may be added as desired. We prepare thermos-bottle oat, wheat, and millet cereal and top it with the Rinse formula plus one tablespoon coarse bran.

For severe cases of atherosclerosis, Dr. Rinse suggests that the quantity of lecithin should be doubled.

Dr. Rinse's formula does not have to be restricted to breakfast. We have been doing quite a lot of experimenting with Dr. Rinse's formula and have found that it can be added to meat loaf and other hamburger mixtures, omelets, breads, and cakes, and confections. Here are some recipes to get you started.

Blueberry Pancakes

1 cup buttermilk or yogurt

2 eggs

1 tablespoon honey

⅓ cup whole wheat flour

⅓ cup raw wheat germ

2 tablespoons bran

2 tablespoons lecithin granules

2 tablespoons nutritional yeast

2 teaspoons bone meal powder

pinch of salt

½ teaspoon kelp

½ teaspoon cinnamon

1 cup blueberries

2 tablespoons cold-pressed
   oil for the griddle

METRIC CONVERSION

1 teaspoon = 5 ml.					1 tablespoon = 15 ml.					
1 ounce = 30 ml.					1 cup = 240 ml./.24 l.					
1 quart = 950 ml./.95 l.					1 gallon = 3.80 l.					
1 ounce = 28 gr.					1 pound = 454 gr./.454 kg.					

F.°	200	225	250	275	300	325	350	375	400	425	450
C.°	93	107	121	135	149	163	177	191	204	218	232

Combine all ingredients adding the blueberries last. Cook on oiled griddle, brown on both sides. Serve with sour cream, yogurt, or blueberry syrup which you can make yourself, using a little honey as a sweetener. (Honey-sweetened syrups are available at natural food stores.) Or simply steam the blueberries in unsweetened blueberry or pineapple juice.

While you're making pancakes, try some with strawberries. Better than shortcake. Just follow the same pancake recipe as for blueberries, but without the blueberries. When pancakes are browned, spread sour cream or yogurt on each one and stack several on each plate. Top all with fresh strawberries.

Confections

(a la Dr. Rinse's Formula)

2 tablespoons honey

2 tablespoons very hot water

3 heaping tablespoons peanut butter

3 tablespoons wheat germ

3 tablespoons lecithin granules

3 tablespoons brewer's yeast

3 tablespoons coarse bran

3 teaspoons bone meal powder

2 tablespoons oil
    (safflower, soy, or sesame)

3 tablespoons carob powder

3 tablespoons sesame seeds

½ teaspoon grated orange or lemon rind

Add hot water to honey, add peanut butter, then the rest of the ingredients. Form into a dough. If it doesn't hold together, add a little more hot water. Break off small pieces and roll into little balls the size of small walnuts. **Makes 24 pieces**

Eight of these little confections a day would give you all the ingredients of Dr. Rinse's formula in the correct proportions.

Delicious Rinse-Burgers

1 pound ground meat

1 egg

1 clove garlic, minced

½ onion, grated

½ large raw white potato,
    or a whole small one, grated

2 tablespoons wheat germ

2 tablespoons brewer's yeast

2 tablespoons lecithin granules

2 teaspoons bone meal powder

1 teaspoon kelp

dash of basil and thyme

½ teaspoon paprika

½ teaspoon salt

Combine all ingredients. Form into patties and coat both sides with sesame seeds. Pan fry lightly in a little chicken fat or oil. Serve with potatoes baked or steamed in their jackets, steamed broccoli, or string beans, and a nice salad tossed with oil and lemon juice. Serve hot stewed or pureed tomatoes with the hamburgers and they'll never miss the ketchup.

Every now and then, it's nice just to spread something good on a slice of whole grain bread. There's nothing better than Dr. Rinse's Mash. Here are two spreads, developed by Anita Hirsch and other genies at the Rodale Press Experimental Kitchens, using Dr. Rinse's mash as a base.

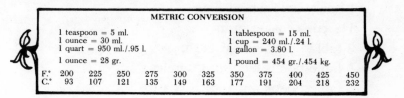

METRIC CONVERSION

1 teaspoon = 5 ml.						1 tablespoon = 15 ml.				
1 ounce = 30 ml.						1 cup = 240 ml./.24 l.				
1 quart = 950 ml./.95 l.						1 gallon = 3.80 l.				
1 ounce = 28 gr.						1 pound = 454 gr./.454 kg.				

F.°	200	225	250	275	300	325	350	375	400	425	450
C.°	93	107	121	135	149	163	177	191	204	218	232

Spread #1

2 tablespoons Rinse formula

1 tablespoon safflower oil

1 tablespoon honey

1 tablespoon peanut butter

2 teaspoons boiling water

Mix the above ingredients and spread on a slice of bread.

Spread #2

2 tablespoons Rinse formula

1 tablespoon blackstrap molasses

1 tablespoon safflower oil

2 tablespoons peanut butter

2 tablespoons rolled oats

Mix above ingredients and spread on bread.

Bran-and-Rinse Muffins

1 cup whole wheat flour
1½ cups coarse bran
3 tablespoons wheat germ
3 tablespoons lecithin granules
3 tablespoons nutritional yeast
3 teaspoons bone meal powder
1 teaspoon baking soda
½ teaspoon grated orange rind
½ teaspoon cinnamon
¼ teaspoon cloves
a few gratings of nutmeg
1 egg
½ cup raisins soaked in ¾ cup hot water
⅓ cup blackstrap molasses
½ cup sunflower seeds or chopped walnuts
3 tablespoons oil

Preheat oven to 350°F.

Combine all the dry ingredients. Beat the egg with the liquid from the raisins and add the blackstrap molasses to this mixture. Combine the two mixtures. Add the raisins and the sunflower seeds or walnuts. Bake in greased muffin tins for 20 minutes.

Yield: one dozen muffins

METRIC CONVERSION										
1 teaspoon = 5 ml.					1 tablespoon = 15 ml.					
1 ounce = 30 ml.					1 cup = 240 ml./.24 l.					
1 quart = 950 ml./.95 l.					1 gallon = 3.80 l.					
1 ounce = 28 gr.					1 pound = 454 gr./.454 kg.					
F.°	200	225	250	275	300	325	350	375	400	425	450
C.°	93	107	121	135	149	163	177	191	204	218	232

Chapter 12

When It's Just the Two of You After Retirement

Many of us look forward to retirement—all that lovely time on our hands to do as we darn please; no alarm clocks catching us in the middle of a dream; no more daily grind; lots of time to dawdle over breakfast and the morning paper; a chance to travel and see lots of enchanting faraway places.

It sounds lovely—and it can be if you shift gears to adapt to this new leisure. But if you don't plan them carefully these so-called carefree years can be the worst years of your life. Many people give up their sense of purpose, their sense of worth, and their appetites when they give up their jobs.

Decide right now that you're going to make your retirement years the best you've ever had. To accomplish your aim you must keep your body and mind in good running order. There are certain nutrients which can definitely help in this and I'll discuss them later.

If you are a married woman, chances are that it is your husband who has retired. You no longer have the house to yourself from nine-to-five. It's a big adjustment for you, having a man around the house all day. Many women complain that their retired husbands dog their footsteps and don't give them a moment's peace. Don't let it come to that. Encourage your man to take up an absorbing hobby long before he retires. Buy him "how-to" books as presents for birthdays and special occasions and make the package complete by including a few simple starter supplies.

Many older people have discovered creative abilities they never knew they had. I know of a very successful artist who is 90-years-old and planning four one-man shows within the next four months. But until he was 78 he never held a paintbrush in his hand. He held a baton. He was supervisor of music for the public schools in his community. He had always appreciated art but never knew that he had any talent until after his retirement when, on a whim, he bought a few cheap paints and tried copying Van Gogh's *Sunflowers.* He is now busier and happier than he has ever been.

Some people take up music, writing, ceramics, they spread their wings and glory in their newfound creativity. This is enriching and rewarding in terms of self-esteem.

True, there are basic changes that must be made in everyday living. A man around the house gets hungry three times a day and in between is apt to nosey around the kitchen for snacks. That can be a lot of work for his wife or a lot of fun for both depending on the approach.

If the wife has made a practice of keeping her man out of the kitchen and doing all the cooking herself, now is the time to change course. She should welcome him into the kitchen and give him a turn with the pots and pans. (Most men love to cook, given a good recipe and an opportunity.)

This is the perfect time to hatch a bread baker in the house. Anyone who has never baked a loaf of bread has missed out on one of life's most elemental joys. There is nothing like it. Not even winning an Oscar or getting an income tax rebate could put you on cloud nine like watching your guests devour a beautiful loaf of bread which you yourself have created out of flour, yeast, and sundry ingredients designed by nature to put a healthy glow on body and spirit.

As if the heady fragrance that fills the room weren't enough of an inducement, there is the knead, which many bread bakers look to as a form of therapy. What a great way to work out our aggressions! And if you don't have any aggressions, it's still darn good exercise.

And, of course, baking bread saves a lot of money. You get two beautiful, nutritious, chemical-free loaves of home-baked bread for what it cost to buy one mediocre whole wheat loaf ("with additives") at supermarket prices.

It's best to start slow, with recipes for basic breads, such as the one on p.125. Or try one from the many cookbooks which offer recipes for traditional breads. When the time is ripe for branching out, here are some innovations that will increase the nutritional value and improve the taste and beauty of the loaves.

Potato Bread

A winner at the Staff of Life bread-baking contest, Christifer Portner of Ambler, Pennsylvania, won top honors for his big, round, beautiful Potato Bread.

1 envelope yeast, 1 cake or 1 tablespoon yeast
 granules

¼ cup warm water

1 tablespoon honey

1 large potato, 11 ounces

1 cup water

1 tablespoon salt

⅓ cup butter, cut into cubes

⅓ cup honey

⅓ cup powdered milk

1 beaten egg, large

4 cups whole wheat flour

¾ teaspoon powdered cardamon

Preheat oven to 400° F.

Combine the first three ingredients. Peel and slice potato, cook in one cup saltwater until soft, and mash.

Combine butter, honey, powdered milk, egg, add mashed potatoes, and fluid from cooking.

Add yeast when potato mixture is warm, not hot. Combine three cups flour and cardamon and add to potato mixture. Work in an extra cup of whole wheat flour, knead until elastic. Let rise until double. Punch down and let rise a second time until double in the pan you plan to bake it in. Brush with milk glaze (brush once more while baking). Bake at 400° F. for 15 minutes. Bake 40 to 50 minutes longer at 325°F. (Note: Baking time will vary according to size and shape of loaf.)

Makes one large or two small loaves

METRIC CONVERSION										
1 teaspoon = 5 ml.					1 tablespoon = 15 ml.					
1 ounce = 30 ml.					1 cup = 240 ml./.24 l.					
1 quart = 950 ml./.95 l.					1 gallon = 3.80 l.					
1 ounce = 28 gr.					1 pound = 454 gr./.454 kg.					

F.°	200	225	250	275	300	325	350	375	400	425	450
C.°	93	107	121	135	149	163	177	191	204	218	232

Honey Wheat Loaf

This honey of a loaf was judged a winner in a bread-baking contest sponsored by Staff of Life of Springtown, Pennsylvania. It was baked superbly by 18-year-old Bonny Davis.

1 cake yeast or 1 tablespoon dry yeast

2½ cups warm water

4 tablespoons honey

3 tablespoons unrefined oil

6 cups whole wheat flour

2 teaspoons salt

1 teaspoon cinnamon

½ cup raisins

¼ cup sunflower seeds

2 tablespoons honey for glaze

Preheat oven to 350°F.

Dissolve the yeast in the water, add the honey, and oil. Blend the flour, salt, cinnamon, raisins, and sunflower seeds, and add to the liquid mixture. Knead, cover, and allow to rise until double in size. Push down, and form into two loaves. Place in oiled 9" × 5" × 3" loaf pans. Let rise again. Bake about 30 minutes. Brush with honey and return to oven briefly.

Onion Rye Bread

1½ packages cake yeast, or 1½ tablespoons
dry
1 cup warm water
2 cups milk
¼ cup honey
¼ cup salad oil
4 teaspoons salt
1 large onion, chopped
3 tablespoons caraway seeds
2½ cups rye flour
6 cups whole wheat flour

Preheat oven to 350°F.

Gently stir yeast into water. When dissolved and bubbly, stir onion, caraway, and rye flour into milk mixture. Add wheat flour, stirring until smooth and thick; knead dough well. Let rise, punch it down, and let rise again.

Grease three 4½" × 8½" loaf pans, and sprinkle with cornmeal. Punch down the dough again; divide and shape into three loaves, and place in pans.

Let rise in pans until doubled in volume, then bake in oven for about one hour.

METRIC CONVERSION										
1 teaspoon = 5 ml.					1 tablespoon = 15 ml.					
1 ounce = 30 ml.					1 cup = 240 ml./.24 l.					
1 quart = 950 ml./.95 l.					1 gallon = 3.80 l.					
1 ounce = 28 gr.					1 pound = 454 gr./.454 kg.					
F.°	200	225	250	275	300	325	350	375	400	425	450
C.°	93	107	121	135	149	163	177	191	204	218	232

Some men look upon retirement as the long-awaited opportunity to make all of their fish stories come true. Great, I say. But why not extend the tale beyond how the fish was caught to how the fish was cooked? Let the fisherman try his hand with the following recipes.

Fillet of Sole Francaise

6 fillets, 4–6 ounces each

Sauce

Combine:

2 tablespoons chicken base or equivalent (any good, dry concentrated soup)

½ teaspoon salt

1½ teaspoons garlic powder or about 3 cloves garlic, minced

Add to above mixture:

1½ cups dry white wine

1 cup lemon juice

Mix above ingredients well, preferably with a thin wire whisk or a fork.

Batter

4 eggs

1 cup white unbleached flour, or whole wheat flour

½ cup butter or ¼ cup
    butter and ¼ cup oil

Preheat oven to 350°F.

Heat the butter or butter and oil in a glass baking dish in the oven. Beat four eggs in a mixing bowl until fluffy. Dust fillets on both sides with flour. Then dip into the egg batter. Place the fish fillets flat in the heated butter. Heat for about three minutes on one side and then another two minutes on the other side. Drain off the butter and add approximately five tablespoons of the above sauce for each fillet. Heat fish and sauce until desired temperature is reached—it takes about two or three minutes. Top with finely chopped parsley and serve with the rest of the sauce. **Serves six**

Baked Yellow Pike

3 pounds yellow pike, dressed

½ teaspoon salt

¼ teaspoon pepper

2 tablespoons lemon juice

1 teaspoon onion, minced

¼ cup butter, melted, or salad oil

¼ cup parsley, finely chopped

Preheat oven to 350°F.

Wash and dry fish. Rub inside and out with

salt and pepper. Place in a well-greased baking pan, preferably one in which you can serve the fish. Combine lemon juice, onion, and butter or oil. Pour over fish. Bake 40 minutes, or until fish flakes easily when tested with a fork. Sprinkle chopped parsley over top. Serve hot with garnish of lemon wedges, beets, and horseradish, and boiled potatoes.

Serves six

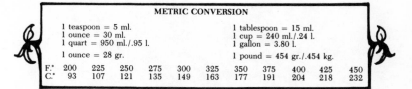

METRIC CONVERSION

1 teaspoon = 5 ml.	1 tablespoon = 15 ml.
1 ounce = 30 ml.	1 cup = 240 ml./.24 l.
1 quart = 950 ml./.95 l.	1 gallon = 3.80 l.
1 ounce = 28 gr.	1 pound = 454 gr./.454 kg.

F.°	200	225	250	275	300	325	350	375	400	425	450
C.°	93	107	121	135	149	163	177	191	204	218	232

Fish Newburg

¾ pound cooked fish, such as cod, halibut, or tuna; may be canned or fresh

¼ cup butter

2 tablespoons flour

1 teaspoon salt

¼ teaspoon paprika

dash of cayenne pepper

1 pint light cream

2 egg yolks, beaten

2 tablespoons sherry or any white wine

toast points

Flake fish or cut into cubes. Set aside until sauce is ready. Melt butter, blend in flour and seasonings. Stir until free of lumps. Add cream very gradually and cook until smooth and thick, stirring constantly. Stir a small amount of the hot sauce carefully into the beaten egg yolks, to bring up to a high temperature before adding to the sauce. Stir constantly over low heat until thick. Remove from heat and slowly stir in wine. Add fish and serve at once on toast points.
Serves six

Keeping Yourself Together

Just remember that both partners need "love and wheat germ" as much as ever at this stage of the game —perhaps even more. We all know that a house is no stronger than the materials that hold it up, and that it must be kept in constant repair as it ages. Well, the same goes for your body. And the stuff in your body that is comparable to mortar and cement in a building is called collagen, a very important gluelike substance that holds your cells together.

When your collagen is strong, you can look forward to fewer physical problems of old age. When it is defective, your body begins to break down—not all at once, perhaps, like the wonderful one-hoss shay, but little by little—with a touch of arthritis, muscle aches, or with serious destruction of bone or blood vessels.

Tissues that have the strength provided by collagen are better able to resist penetration by invading infections. But, if you are not getting the nutrients you need to manufacture collagen properly, your cell walls lose their firmness. The defective collagen goes to pieces, gets weak and weepy, and leaks uselessly into the bloodstream.

This happens quite frequently to those who are not eating carefully and leads to such debilitating conditions as low back pain, gout, and general inflammation of muscle tissues causing aches and pains. Other signs of collagen deficiency are receding and bleeding gums, wrinkling of the skin, and other stigmata of aging.

You will contribute immensely to your good collagen supply if you make sure to get optimal amounts of vitamin C and the bioflavanoids. Citrus fruits are great natural sources for both of these—especially if you eat the whole fruit. When you prepare grapefruit, score it to include lots of the white inner rind. This is a great source of the bioflavanoids. Instead of juicing your oranges, eat sections. The membrane on the fruit is a source of the bioflavanoids.

The older you are the more DDT, lead, food additives, and other toxic substances have accumulated in your system. These poisons slow down hormone and enzyme activity. Vitamin C is needed by the liver for the detoxification process. But it is used up with each job it performs and as you grow older, it is called upon to perform more and more jobs. Every time you worry, feel a chill, suffer a pain, smoke a cigarette (or breathe someone else's smoke), take a drug, inhale polluted air, or take a trip, your body undergoes a stress which uses up vitamin C.

As you age, you're going to need more vitamin C to protect your arteries against the kind of damage that could lead to cardiovascular problems. In fact, increasing your vitamin C is perhaps one of the best insurance policies you can take out upon retirement. Linus Pauling recommends three to five grams of vitamin C daily.

Other elements which are frequently lacking in the diets of older people but which are absolutely essential to health, are iron, zinc, manganese, and copper.

Animals that graze on soil deficient in manganese show the same skeletal and postural defects we often associate with the aged. Now we know that people eating manganese deficient diets tend to become stooped earlier in life.

Your best food sources for manganese are the dry legumes, such as peas and beans. So are blueberries, all nuts, and the bran portion of cereals.

Another element involved in metabolism of connective tissue is iron. The body needs about four grams of iron. That's about the size of a small nail. More than half of this is found in the blood. The rest goes about its business in various ways, and has a role in building collagen. Wheat germ is rich in iron—organic iron which the body utilizes fully and which does not interfere with your vitamin E. Other good sources of iron are liver, kidneys, turnip greens, beet greens, and blackstrap molasses. Try a teaspoon of blackstrap molasses in hot water as your morning beverage instead of coffee. It will give you a lift without a subsequent letdown.

When you achieve the age for retirement you need fewer calories, but more nutrients. You need foods that are rich in nucleic acids, the nutrients which help to preserve the blueprints of youth. Foods that are rich in nucleic acids are yeast, sweetbreads, and sardines. Take a yeast break instead of a coffee break. Put a tablespoon of brewer's yeast in a cup then fill it with hot water and add a dash of any good vegetable salt.

Someone once asked Bob Hope if there was sex after 65. "Oh yes," he answered, "very good, too, especially the one in the fall."

Many people put their sex life in mothballs when they get to the retirement stage. You don't have to. Thirty-five thousand men over 65 got married in 1975 and it wasn't just because they wanted home cooking. You're going to have more time for romance now that you're retired. Enjoy it. As Dr. G. E. Poesnecker of the Clymer Clinic in Quakertown, Pennsylvania, points out in *Creative Sex*, "There is within the creative centers of both men and women a resident power and energy which can be exchanged during the sexual union to build and strengthen the physical, mental, and emotional natures of each of the participants."

Just remember that your sex glands, to remain healthy, need all the nutrients your body needs, but they need specific nutrients as well. For example, the trace mineral zinc is indispensable to the health of the prostate gland. Thiamine, vitamin B_1, stimulates the sex glands indirectly through its action on the pituitary gland. Vitamin E is important for sexual health. These nutrients are found in wheat germ, wheat germ oil, pumpkin, and sunflower seeds. Good sources of zinc are sweetbreads and mushrooms. Zinc is present in all human tissues, especially the pancreas where it is associated with insulin. Serve a mushroom omelet frequently. Delicious.

Now that you are retired, you can devote more time to the preparation of meals. Experiment with new dishes you've never tried before. Make every meal special.

To invest dinner with a "special occasion" look and feeling, start by having drinks. Combine equal parts of chilled apple juice and carbonated water and serve in chilled champagne glasses. All the fun of the real thing without any alcoholic overtones—and no strain on the budget either. As an accompaniment serve crackers or thin toast made elegant this way: brush them with butter, sprinkle with poppy seeds, celery seeds, onion salt, or paprika and heat in a 300°F. oven for six minutes or until lightly browned. Serve them with mushroom caviar. These are extra touches that say "I want this evening to be special."

Mushroom Caviar

½ cup green onions, chopped, with tops
2 tablespoons butter
1 cup mushrooms, chopped
1 tablespoon lemon juice
⅛ teaspoon cayenne pepper
½ teaspoon salt
paprika
2 tablespoons dill, chopped
⅓ cup sour cream or yogurt
tomato slices

Sauté the onions in the butter for one minute. Add one cup chopped mushrooms, one tablespoon lemon juice and the seasonings. Sauté for four minutes stirring occasionally. Remove from heat. Stir in the two tablespoons chopped dill and the ⅓ cup sour cream or yogurt. Garnish with tomato slices. **Serves two romantically**

METRIC CONVERSION										

1 teaspoon = 5 ml.   1 tablespoon = 15 ml.
1 ounce = 30 ml.   1 cup = 240 ml./.24 l.
1 quart = 950 ml./.95 l.   1 gallon = 3.80 l.

1 ounce = 28 gr.   1 pound = 454 gr./.454 kg.

F.°	200	225	250	275	300	325	350	375	400	425	450
C.°	93	107	121	135	149	163	177	191	204	218	232

On birthdays and celebrations serve a lovely cake that does not do violence to your nutritional standards. This Mock German Chocolate Cake has lots of good nutrients, yet it is so delicious and festive, you'll be happy to serve it to company and to the grandchildren.

Mock German Chocolate Cake

(from *The Forget-About-Meat Cookbook*
Karen Brooks, Rodale Press, Emmaus, Pa., 1973)

1¼ cups boiling water

1 cup oats

½ cup butter

2 tablespoons molasses

1½ cups honey

1 teaspoon vanilla

2 eggs, slightly beaten

1½ cups whole wheat flour

3 teaspoons baking powder

½ teaspoon salt

¼ teaspoon cinnamon

¼ teaspoon nutmeg

Preheat oven to 350°F.

Pour water over oats in a large mixing bowl, and let stand for 20 minutes. Add butter, molasses, honey, vanilla, and eggs. Blend till smooth. Sift together flour, baking powder, and salt and add, with spices, to batter. Turn into large, shallow, greased cake pan, or two round cake pans for double layer cake. Bake for 50 to 55 minutes. Ice with Coconut Icing.

Coconut Icing

½ cup honey
¼ cup butter, softened
3 tablespoons cream
½ cup nuts, chopped
¾ cup coconut, shredded

In a small mixing bowl, cream honey and butter. Beat until smooth. Add the remaining ingredients and mix in thoroughly. Spread on cake and slip under broiler for a few minutes to toast coconut and let other ingredients seep into cake.

METRIC CONVERSION

1 teaspoon = 5 ml.
1 ounce = 30 ml.
1 quart = 950 ml./.95 l.
1 ounce = 28 gr.

1 tablespoon = 15 ml.
1 cup = 240 ml./.24 l.
1 gallon = 3.80 l.
1 pound = 454 gr./.454 kg.

F.°	200	225	250	275	300	325	350	375	400	425	450
C.°	93	107	121	135	149	163	177	191	204	218	232

Chapter 13

Do Some
Dining In the Raw...

"Is it true," someone asked my son, the doctor, "that an apple a day keeps the doctor away?"

"That depends on how good your aim is," he answered with a wink.

That an apple a day can keep the doctor away has never been proven definitively. But, if it does, much of the credit should go to the fact that the apple is consumed raw. Uncooked and unprocessed foods actually can heighten your powers of resistance, and if you have good powers of resistance, you rarely need a doctor.

According to a study by Swedish researcher, Dr. Henning Karstrom, raw foods can also protect you from disease. Even though you are careful to include every single one of the 50 known nutrients in your diet, says Dr. Karstrom in *Protectio Vitae* (February 1972), and you eat the correct proportions from the four basic food groups, you must also include many foods that are uncooked and unprocessed or your health will certainly suffer. You can stumble along on such a diet for years and not feel really sick. Neither will you feel entirely well. You will be in a state often referred to as mesotrophy—the twilight zone of ill health, or the incubation period—a sort of limbo of half health, half disease. Unfortunately this condition is common for about half of all Americans. Look around you. How many people do you see who appear to be enjoying total vibrant health?

I saw this kind of vibrancy in the children of a family living on a farm next door to the Rodale Farm in Maxatawny, Pennsylvania. They had an indefinable glow that was a pleasure to see. It did my heart good to watch those children as they rode their bikes and played and worked in the garden where they helped themselves to tomatoes, cucumbers, string beans, peas, and young onions right from the vine or the ground. They were certainly getting their fill of those substances which contribute to supernutrition.

"There is something in raw foods, writes Dr. Roger Williams, world famous biochemist and nutrition expert at the University of Texas, that contributes to supernutrition." Supernutrition contributes to glowing vital health. Cooking destroys many vitamins and a few heat-sensitive minerals such as magnesium. Enzymes too are destroyed by temperatures over 120° F., so you can see the importance of including many uncooked foods in your diet.

At the famous Bircher-Benner Clinic in Switzerland, where since 1897 they have been able to restore health to countless people, the goal is to serve at least half of all the food in an uncooked state, and to always start each meal with something raw. This is enzyme insurance and, in the long run, health insurance.

Take a little inventory. How many raw foods have you eaten today?

Here are some ways in which you can increase the raw food intake at your home and reap some very important health benefits, including increased resistance to infections.

Always have a tray of crisp raw vegetables ready for the children when they come home from school ravenous and ready to eat anything.

Vary the vegetables from day to day and add little surprises. Try raw sweet potatoes cut in thin rounds and spread with natural peanut butter. Make your own peanut butter from raw nuts; flavor it sometimes with raw honey. For a nice change, serve the vegetables around a little bowl of yogurt dip.

Yogurt Dip

Add to ½ cup yogurt and beat slightly:

2 to 4 tablespoons lemon juice or
    apple cider vinegar (omit if yogurt is tart)
1 green onion,
    finely chopped (or 1 grated onion)
½ teaspoon kelp
½ to 1 teaspoon paprika
1 clove garlic, minced

Combine all ingredients.

METRIC CONVERSION										
1 teaspoon = 5 ml.						1 tablespoon = 15 ml.				
1 ounce = 30 ml.						1 cup = 240 ml./.24 l.				
1 quart = 950 ml./.95 l.						1 gallon = 3.80 l.				
1 ounce = 28 gr.						1 pound = 454 gr./.454 kg.				
F.° 200	225	250	275	300	325	350	375	400	425	450
C.° 93	107	121	135	149	163	177	191	204	218	232

To make homemade peanut butter, you simply grind the peanuts in your blender or crush them with a rolling pin until very fine, then add enough oil to make the mixture spreadable. Keep it refrigerated.

Another interesting spread that will delight the chil-

dren is homemade raw cashew butter. This is particularly good stuffed into celery sticks. Blend one cup of
raw cashew bits with one tablespoon of sesame seeds.
Now add about one-third cup of soy or sesame oil and
mix thoroughly. Refrigerate.

Salads offer a wonderful opportunity to provide a
broad spectrum of raw nutrients. Learn how to make
a good Caesar Salad because that includes the benefit
of a raw egg. Use a good whole grain bread to make the
croutons, or else use sesame, sunflower, and pumpkin
seeds for a garnish to give it a good satisfying crunch.

Caesar Salad

1 clove garlic

¼ cup olive oil

½ cup croutons (optional)

1 head Romaine lettuce, and other greens

¼ cup grated Parmesan cheese, or
sharp cheese of your choice

½ cup good cold-pressed oil

¾ teaspoon kelp or salt

¼ teaspoon cayenne pepper

1 raw egg

¼ cup lemon juice

8 anchovies, cut up (this is optional)

Cut the garlic into four pieces and drop it
into the olive oil. Set this aside. If you are
going to use croutons, toast them until
golden. Now tear the lettuce and greens into

bite-size pieces and toss into a glass bowl. Refrigerate everything.

Just before serving sprinkle the greens with cheeses; now drizzle on the half-cup of oil mixed with kelp and pepper. Toss gently until every leaf shines. Break the whole raw egg onto the greens, and pour the lemon juice over all. Toss again until every sign of the egg disappears. Remove the garlic from the quarter-cup of oil that you set aside. Pour over the croutons. Toss the croutons and sprinkle them over the greens. If you want to use seeds and nuts instead of croutons, toss them in the garlic oil. Now add anchovies. Toss the salad and serve at once.

Serves four

METRIC CONVERSION										
1 teaspoon = 5 ml.					1 tablespoon = 15 ml.					
1 ounce = 30 ml.					1 cup = 240 ml./.24 l.					
1 quart = 950 ml./.95 l.					1 gallon = 3.80 l.					
1 ounce = 28 gr.					1 pound = 454 gr./.454 kg.					
F.°	200	225	250	275	300	325	350	375	400	425	450
C.°	93	107	121	135	149	163	177	191	204	218	232

Try to include several different greens in your salads. Remember the greener they are the more chlorophyll, vitamins, and minerals. Try to include some wild greens like dandelion, mustard greens, lamb's-quarters. Iceberg lettuce, while it does give a nice crisp quality to a salad, is not dark green, and therefore is not so desirable from a nutritional viewpoint. Bib lettuce, sometimes called Boston lettuce, the lettuce that looks like a green rose, is more nutritious than iceberg.

Care of Greens

When you buy watercress or parsley, open up the bunch as soon as you get it home, wash it quickly under running cold water, drain it and store it loosely, separate from your other salad greens in a covered jar in the refrigerator. Put the stem ends down and you'll get lots more crisp mileage from these nutrient-rich vegetables.

Watercress is a good complement for any salad. It can also be used as a garnish (be sure to eat your garnish) or instead of lettuce in sandwiches. Watercress is never treated with insecticides or raised with synthetic fertilizers. It just grows naturally in water. It is rich in vitamins and minerals and has a pleasant nippy flavor.

Spinach, especially when the leaves are young, is an excellent addition to your green salad. There is much confusion about oxalic acid. Dr. N. W. Walker says that "The oxalic acid in raw vegetables and their juices is organic, and as such is not only beneficial but essential for the physiological functions of the body."

Organic oxalic acid is one of the elements needed to maintain tone and to stimulate peristalsis, Dr. Walker points out in his book, *Raw Vegetable Juices* (Pyramid, New York, 1971). That is why raw spinach is an effective laxative food. Peristaltic action, a series of contracting and relaxing of the nerves and muscles, aids in the elimination process.

Another vegetable which you should include in your salad is parsley. Not only as a garnish but as a chopped green. Other greens which are lovely accompaniments for your salads are mint leaves, celery tops, beet tops, carrots tops, turnip tops, Swiss chard, Chinese cabbage, green and purple cabbage, and nasturtium leaves.

Whenever possible, says Ruth Kunz Bircher, "Every raw vegetable dish should combine roots—fruits—leaves." *Eating Your Way to Health* (Penguin, Baltimore, M.D., 1972).

Root vegetables include carrots, beets, turnips, radishes, kohlrabi, celeriac (celery root), and salsify. The fruit vegetables are tomatoes, cucumbers, zucchini, green and red peppers, and cauliflower. Don't peel cucumbers or zucchini, if they are organically grown.

Remember that salad greens should never be soaked in water. Wash them lightly and quickly in cold water, then drain in a salad basket or whirl them in an old pillowcase. They may then be stored in a refrigerator wrapped in a towel or in a plastic bag.

You can make your salad ahead of time, but do not add the dressing until just before serving. Agnes Toms makes this excellent suggestion in her book, *Eat, Drink and Be Healthy* (Devin-Adair, New York, 1963). "Five minutes before you are ready to toss with the dressing," she says, "put the salad bowl with the greens in your freezer. They will emerge wonderfully crisp."

To increase the nutrients, enzymes, and taste appeal of your salad, always add a fistful of fresh sprouts. Mung beans, alfalfa, wheat, rye, and lentils are excellent and easily sprouted. Remember, when a seed or grain sprouts, it multiplies values, and develops vitamin C which is not present in the original grain.

Use Fresh Fruits Liberally

One of the most important steps that you can take to promote better health at your home is to eliminate sweet desserts that are baked or cooked like pies, cakes, cookies, ice cream, and so forth. Instead serve fresh fruit in season. When melons are in season, use every variety you can find. Cantaloupe, honeydew, and watermelon are the usual fare. But have you ever tried a Casaba, a Crenshaw, a Christmas melon (this looks like a football), or a Persian melon? Each of these has a unique and delicious flavor. There is an old Japanese proverb that every time you taste a food that is new to you, you add 75 days to your life. So do be experimental and try the unfamiliar. Chances are that they contain different trace minerals. Use the seeds and pulp of the melons to make a delicious drink.

Try our variation on the famous Mexican drink called *horchata* which is made from melon seeds—cantaloupe, watermelon, even squash:

Horchata

1½ cups cantaloupe or other seeds
(save them up in the refrigerator)

¼ cup honey or date sugar

½ teaspoon cinnamon

3 cups water or unsweetened pineapple juice

Put seeds in blender with a little liquid until the power grabs the seeds. Then add more of the liquid by degrees. Strain the mixture through a very fine sieve or several layers of cheesecloth. Now taste it. Add honey and lemon juice until you have the right tang. A few mashed strawberries will give it a lovely pink color. You can make this *horchata* when melons are plentiful and freeze individual portions in sherbet glasses or paper cups and have a lovely nutritious surprise for some-one's birthday party.

METRIC CONVERSION										
1 teaspoon = 5 ml.					1 tablespoon = 15 ml.					
1 ounce = 30 ml.					1 cup = 240 ml./.24 l.					
1 quart = 950 ml./.95 l.					1 gallon = 3.80 l.					
1 ounce = 28 gr.					1 pound = 454 gr./.454 kg.					
F.° 200	225	250	275	300	325	350	375	400	425	450
C.° 93	107	121	135	149	163	177	191	204	218	232

Of course the fruits that you grow yourself and pick sunripened are full of natural sugars, vitamins, miner-als, enzymes, and flavors. If you don't grow your own, try to get fruit from organic gardens and orchards or organic merchants. If fruit is out of season in your area, you can usually arrange to have organic fruit shipped from Florida (for oranges, lemons, and grapefruit) or from Virginia (for apples).

For a delicious mineral-rich dessert or meat accom-paniment try this:

Raw Apple Sauce

¼ cup water, unsweetened pineapple juice, or apple juice

2 cups apples, quartered and cored (leave the skins on if they are organic)

½ cup raisins, unsulfured

pinch cinnamon

honey, if apples are tart

Put the water in the blender, add the apples and reduce to a pulp. Now add raisins and cinnamon and run for another minute. Add honey to taste, only if needed. This applesauce can be made when the apple crop is in, and frozen for later enjoyment throughout the winter when raw fruit is hard to obtain.

METRIC CONVERSION										
1 teaspoon = 5 ml.					1 tablespoon = 15 ml.					
1 ounce = 30 ml.					1 cup = 240 ml./.24 l.					
1 quart = 950 ml./.95 l.					1 gallon = 3.80 l.					
1 ounce = 28 gr.					1 pound = 454 gr./.454 kg.					
F.°	200	225	250	275	300	325	350	375	400	425	450
C.°	93	107	121	135	149	163	177	191	204	218	232

According to Dr. Karstrom, you will not only enjoy a better prognosis for health and longevity when you take the heat off your food, but, if you are careful to get your grains unprocessed with their full complement of germ and bran, you will actually enhance the quality of the genes you pass along to your children.

Some years ago Czechoslovakian physiologist Bernaseck gave his animals a diet containing every known nutrient in the right amounts and proportions. He observed completely normal growth and reproduction patterns in the first generation. In the second generation, certain irregularities could be noticed. In the third generation, malformation and stillbirth occurred. In the fourth generation, all offspring died. Autopsies of the dead offspring revealed degenerative abnormalities in the nervous system, in the reproductive system, and in the bone structure.

With another group of animals, Bernaseck added grain bran or grain germ to the same diet. Growth and reproduction tended to become normal. Bernaseck concluded that a diet which contained all the nutrients known at this time cannot guarantee normal reproduction nor normal growth. Bran and wheat germ and other factors in unprocessed natural products he says, represent an area of unknown nutritional factors. He calls these factors vital substances.

If you grind and soak your grains such as oats, rye, wheat, barley, even brown rice, overnight, you will have softened them without cooking. You can use these soaked grains as a foundation for a good cereal. Simply combine them with fruits, nuts, and yogurt for a delicious breakfast dish.

This is the basis for the famous mueslis served at the Bircher-Benner Clinic.

Apple Muesli

4 tablespoons water

2 tablespoons old-fashioned oatmeal

juice of half a lemon

½ cup yogurt

2 apples, (grated), unpeeled
    if they are unsprayed

2 tablespoons wheat germ

1 tablespoon raisins, unsulfured

2 tablespoons honey

2 tablespoons walnuts, chopped, or sunflower
    seeds

Soak oatmeal overnight in water. In the morning add the lemon juice and yogurt, mix well. Add grated apples and remaining ingredients. Mix it all up and enjoy immediately. **Makes one serving**

METRIC CONVERSION										
1 teaspoon = 5 ml.					1 tablespoon = 15 ml.					
1 ounce = 30 ml.					1 cup = 240 ml./.24 l.					
1 quart = 950 ml./.95 l.					1 gallon = 3.80 l.					
1 ounce = 28 gr.					1 pound = 454 gr./.454 kg.					
F.° 200	225	250	275	300	325	350	375	400	425	450
C.° 93	107	121	135	149	163	177	191	204	218	232

Fig Muesli

In the blender, put the following and whiz fine:

3 cups warm water

1 carrot, cut in chunks

1 cup almonds, unblanched

3 apples, unsprayed, cored,
    and cut in chunks

1 cup stemmed dried figs

This can be made quicker if you put the carrot and almonds and one cup of water in the blender first, reduce it to a fine pulp, then add the rest of the ingredients. Cover the blender tightly while whizzing, to keep the air out. Sprinkle with sunflower seed meal. **Serves three or four**

Raw Snacks

Your snacks too can contribute health, vitality, and lively enzymes if you substitute confections that are made with raw nuts, seeds, and other high-potency ingredients and throw away the usual empty calorie overprocessed, oversalted, oversugared snacks that are causing tooth decay, obesity, and other degenerative conditions.

These raw after-school snacks are the perfect answer to the perennial question, "What's to eat, Mom?" While they satisfy the sweet tooth, they also provide many marvelous nutrients.

Carob Halvah, Uncooked Taffy, and Vim Candy are delightful variations on the same theme. Make up an attractive tray of several varieties and serve them as TV snacks to delighted guests, and always put them in lunch boxes.

Carob Halvah

½ cup unsweetened coconut, finely ground

½ cup sunflower seed meal

½ cup raw wheat germ

¼ cup carob powder

¼ cup tahini (ground sesame seed)

¼ cup honey

Mix all together.

Separate into two portions. Place each on a piece of waxed paper and form into a one-inch thick roll. Wrap in the paper and keep in the refrigerator. Cut into one-inch pieces as needed. Variation: Omit carob from half the recipe. Make some plain halvah for contrast and variety.

METRIC CONVERSION										

1 teaspoon = 5 ml. 1 tablespoon = 15 ml.
1 ounce = 30 ml. 1 cup = 240 ml./.24 l.
1 quart = 950 ml./.95 l. 1 gallon = 3.80 l.

1 ounce = 28 gr. 1 pound = 454 gr./.454 kg.

F.°	200	225	250	275	300	325	350	375	400	425	450
C.°	93	107	121	135	149	163	177	191	204	218	232

Uncooked Taffy

½ cup natural peanut butter

½ cup honey

1 cup raw peanuts

soy powder

Blend the first three ingredients together. The peanuts may be chopped if desired. Then use only enough of the soy powder to make a stiff dough. Roll it in a long roll and place on a cooky sheet and chill overnight. In the morning, whack off inch-long pieces for the lunch pail, or for special treats.

Vim Candy

⅔ cup soy powder

¼ cup peanut butter

½ cup carob powder

¼ cup rice polish

2 tablespoons bone meal

½ teaspoon kelp

2 tablespoons brewer's yeast

2 tablespoons wheat germ

2 tablespoons vegetable oil

honey

chopped nuts

Mix first three ingredients together. Add enough honey to make consistency to knead. Spread in square dish. Press chopped nuts over top. Chill and cut in pieces like brownies.

More Raw Goodies

Here are some more raw food recipes that will help increase the ratio between raw and cooked at your home. Do try this raw potato soup. It's a favorite of Lori Stevens who runs a natural food catering service on West 57th Street in New York. It's truly delicious and gives you all the fine nutrients of the uncooked potato.

Lori's Raw Potato Vichysoisse

3 unpeeled potatoes,
     medium sized; light skinned

6 sprigs parsley (more to taste)

3 teaspoons dry vegetable
     broth or concentrate

1 sliced onion

½ teaspoon salt

cayenne pepper

½ cup cream (if you like a tart flavor—
use ¼ cup yogurt and ¼ cup cream)

chopped chives

paprika

METRIC CONVERSION										
1 teaspoon = 5 ml.					1 tablespoon = 15 ml.					
1 ounce = 30 ml.					1 cup = 240 ml./.24 l.					
1 quart = 950 ml./.95 l.					1 gallon = 3.80 l.					
1 ounce = 28 gr.					1 pound = 454 gr./.454 kg.					
F.°	200	225	250	275	300	325	350	375	400	425	450
C.°	93	107	121	135	149	163	177	191	204	218	232

Scrub the potatoes but do not remove skins. Slice them thin and pour boiling water over them just to cover. Put a lid on the pan and let it set for five minutes. Now add the parsley, vegetable concentrate, onion, salt, and cayenne. Pour all into a blender.

Blend until smooth. Taste and correct seasonings. Add cream. Blend again just for a second.

If you wish to serve this soup hot, heat it gently in a double boiler. Do not let it boil.

To serve it cold, refrigerate. Before serving, garnish with chopped chives and a dash of paprika. It should be a beautiful emerald green.

Develop Skill with Raw Soups

You will be making a significant contribution to your family's health if you develop your skill with raw soups. A blender makes them easy. A little ingenuity and creativity will increase the variety and your family's delight.

Here's a helpful hint: If you sauté about two table-spoons of onion in a little oil until just golden, then blend with the other ingredients, your raw soup will taste like you spent all day over the stove.

Here are some ideas to get you started in raw soups:

Put raw corn (scraped from the cob), fresh peas, cut-up celery, or carrot in the blender. Whiz till it is creamy. Season to taste and add water to desired consistency. Heat to serving temperature and no more.

To get body into your raw soups, add about one table-spoon of ground peanuts or a few tablespoons of sesame seeds and blend with the vegetables.

Changing lifetime habits is difficult, and it may be well nigh impossible in our state of civilization, to exist on a diet of all raw foods, unless you are a vegetarian. The methods by which meat and fowl are raised, transported, and stored under present conditions render them unsafe unless they are well cooked. The risk of salmonella is ever present.

Raw milk is certainly a source of important enzymes that are destroyed when the milk is pasteurized. But, unless you can find a source for safe raw milk, there is the danger of contaminants that can cause undulant fever. If you cannot find certified raw milk, then look for a dairy that has a permit to sell raw milk. There are several in my area and around your town too, I'll bet.

I am certain you can increase the amount and variety of foods that you consume in the uncooked state. You can make the salad bigger, more varied, and more important. Include in it some of the root vegetables in the raw—like beets, sweet potatoes, carrots, and Jerusalem artichokes. Try grating them and make mounds of different colors on your salad. Learn to sprout grains and seeds and then serve them in the raw with their full complement of valuable enzymes. If you cannot avoid processed foods completely, make sure you get a good portion of wheat germ or unhulled rice or some other whole natural food which gives you its full complement of germ and bran.

These are simple measures which you can take at once without upsetting the apple cart. Judging from all the evidence, the improvement in your well-being will keep the medical fraternity away far more effectively than the proverbial apple a day—even if you have lousy aim.

Part 4

Any Age, Any Time

Chapter 14
You Say You Love 'Em But You Can't "Wheat Germ" 'Em?

Getting a person to change poor eating habits isn't easy. Logic doesn't work. Nagging certainly doesn't work. Lecturing on the evils of white bread turns them off completely and then you have to go back to Square One. The guy who wrote, "You can lead a horse to water . . ." must have jotted it down right after he tried to get a friend to eat a better diet.

Don't despair and don't give up. But do stop hitting your target over the head with a healthy diet. Just "help" it to happen in a way that no one even notices the change.

It takes a little ingenuity, like the kind practiced by Catherine Gemmell, a nurse who runs Ocean View, a boarding home for the elderly in West Haven, Connecticut. She bakes all the bread using only whole grains and powerhouse natural ingredients. That's no problem. Her guests love it.

But Mrs. Gemmell did have trouble with the skins on the potatoes and the carrots and the zucchini and other vegetables. The guests objected to the skins being left on their food. There was no way to sell them on the idea that the skins held nutrition the guests needed. Catherine found another way. She made soup—and among the main ingredients: potato peelings, the outer skins of onions, a little lemon juice, tomatoes, and some marrow bones. So when the guests at Ocean View get mashed potatoes, they get the minerals from the skins in spite of themselves, in a nice hot soup that is served at the same meal.

I never peel potatoes. I bake them or steam them in their jackets. I save the water in which they were steamed and use it to cook another vegetable or I refrigerate it and use it when I make soup. This process salvages important minerals for your family and no one will object to it because nobody even knows. If the taste is affected at all it's for the better; it's richer, and more full bodied.

If you are just getting started with wheat germ and your family turns up its collective nose when wheat germ is detected in baked goods, try a device that I used when I was getting started. Put the wheat germ in the blender and pulverize it. Eagle eyes won't detect it and the family will never know how healthy they're getting.

The next time you make soup, add some nutritional yeast, maybe a teaspoon. Build it up till you're adding a few tablespoons to a pot of soup. Take it easy. Don't overdo. A little yeast enhances flavors. Too much overpowers the flavor of the soup.

If your family is accustomed to drinking soda, you can start forgetting to buy it. Stock lots of fruit juices (unsweetened apple, pineapple, grape, orange) as thirst quenchers. Make some great milk shakes. They may gripe. Expect it. But if they're thirsty they'll drink whatever you've got.

If the kids are already in high school and away from home a good part of the day, chances are they're going to be drinking soda at the corner hangout. That's what happened with our Bob when he went to an out-of-town prep school. He was the only one of our four who chalked up a bunch of cavities and a big dental bill that year. We put it to him this way. We'll budget $60 a year for your dental work. If your bill is less, you get to keep the difference. If it's more, it comes out of your allowance. You can bet your sweet sunflower seeds, he had no cavities the next year.

If there is someone in your household, perhaps an elderly person, who is constipated and refuses to take bran, work the bran into other foods—hamburgers, cooked cereals, muffins, cakes, and granolas or muesli. A doctor associated with St. Francis' Hospital in London reported in *The Lancet* (August 30, 1975) that when two dessertspoonfuls of bran were added to the foods given to all patients in a 30-bed ward, the patients did not "miss" the various laxatives they had been using.

If you have any candy in the house, throw it out—not gradually but all at once and right away. This is too much of a negative food to phase out gradually. Make some carob confections, some peanut butter balls, and some granola cookies. Put out dishes of "incredible edibles"—a mixture of seeds, nuts, and raisins. We haven't had a piece of candy in the house for maybe 15 years and nobody asks for it or misses it.

If you've been in the habit of baking pies, cut it down to special occasions and then use honey as your sweetening agent and only a very little of that. Instead of spending the time and energy making pies, serve the fruit fresh. Fresh blueberries with yogurt or whipped cream is delicious. To fancy it up, line a pie plate with crumbs made out of your own baked goods, add coconut flakes (unsweetened), a little wheat germ, and a little oil. Fill this shell with uncooked fruit—whatever is in season. Offer a dish of whipped cream (the real thing) and a dish of yogurt so that your weight watchers can join the fun.

Sprouts are a terrific food. Most kids love them. But, there could be a sprout-picker-outer in your family. The one who needs what they offer most will painstakingly pick the sprouts out of his salad. Keep his salad separate—without sprouts. Chop some sprouts—in the blender with herbs and lemon juice. Add to oil to make salad dressing and pour it over the salad. Chop up some sprouts and add them to soups—just before serving.

Start serving more and more foods "in the raw." Make the salad bigger and bigger. Nearly anything that can be eaten cooked, is better raw. Raw potatoes, or raw sweet potatoes, thinly sliced; raw broccoli, lots and lots of cabbage, both purple and white, spinach, carrot greens, radish tops (chopped), turnip tops (loads of calcium and vitamin A), and beet tops (loads of iron). Add them one at a time to your salad bowl and observe your family's reaction. If you get any flack, backtrack a little, then proceed at a less ambitious pace.

If your family objects to the rough texture of turnip greens, radish tops, carrot greens, and comfrey leaves in the salad, do this: Put all these greens in the water you used to steam vegetables. Then blenderize them with some sautéed onions, add a little cream, and some seasoning and you've got a delicious "spinach" soup. If they question you about what's in it, take the Fifth.

A little daring, a little ingenuity, and lots of love and wheat germ—and everyone in your family will soon be on the good food side. If you're flummoxed occasionally, and you will be, don't gnash your teeth. Eat some wheat germ and start all over again.

Chapter 15

You'll Find That Good
Food Makes the Party Better

It's great fun to go to dinner parties and you hate to
be a bore so you indulge in freaky food you wouldn't
feed to your cat in your own home. Like one time, our
hostess, knowing of my love affair with health, told me
confidentially that the yellow spread on the table was
not the real thing, so I didn't have to be afraid to eat
it; and the salad was dressed with a commercial dressing made from cottonseed oil which was approved by
the AMA. What are you going to do?

Once you become hooked on "love and wheat
germ," once you know how deficient, and even harmful, the usual party foods are, you are reluctant to eat
them when you are invited to dinner. You cannot, in
good conscience serve them to your friends either.

We have long nurtured a secret longing to enjoy dinner at someone else's home where everything that is
served is natural, where no maraschino cherries top the
fruit salad, no margarine drenches the vegetables, no
instant mashed potatoes parade as the real thing, where
nothing is made from a prefabricated mix, and the
bread has no propionate.

There are several successful gourmet dinner clubs in
every town, where the food is frequently too sweet, too
heavy, and too much. It takes a week to get over the

indigestion and the inflated calories of such a meal.

But it sure would be nice to enjoy real food that's all natural at a festive companionable dinner party. How?

The way to do it—on a regular basis—is to start a Natural Foods Dinner Club. Why not? It's the coming thing. You could even call it a Love and Wheat Germ Dinner Club. Invite as charter members those people who have expressed an interest, however slight, in natural foods. Or, put a notice on the bulletin board where you work. Your dinner club could operate in several ways. It could be "take turns at each others' home, with the hostess preparing the whole meal." It could be an "everybody brings a dish" affair: somebody makes the bread, somebody else makes the salad, somebody else makes the main dish, the dessert, and so forth. And once in a while, it could be a progressive party with one course at each home.

Sometimes it could be a meatless meal based on grains and nuts whose amino acid patterns complement each other. Many people would like to cut down on meat consumption but are unsure of how to plan well-balanced meals without it. And sometimes it could be meals based on ethnic specialties; like a Chinese night, a Greek night, a Jewish night, an Italian night, a Middle Eastern night, and so forth. Most of us enjoy the kinds of food that mama used to make. If we can take the old nostalgic delights and recreate them with only health-building ingredients, everybody is happy—and better for it.

Once you've agreed on a system of social rules, it's time to lay down some nutritional guidelines. Here are some suggestions:

Use organically grown fruits and vegetables—when they are available (no pesticide residues, and they taste better). When they are not, you can cut down on the spray residues on other fresh produce by dipping it into a vinegar bath (¼ cup vinegar to a large bowl of tepid water). Swish and rinse in clear water.

Use no margarine, either on the table or in anything that is served. Use butter or a good cold-pressed oil.

Add no sugar to anything that is served. Put out sugar in a bowl for those who insist on it. But honey should be provided. Suggested substitutes for sugar in baking: honey, date sugar, molasses, sorghum, or carob syrup.

Shortenings that are solid at room temperature are not acceptable. That means none of that white stuff that comes in cans. It's a hydrogenated abomination.

No bleached white flour. Unbleached may be used occasionally, but it should be accompanied with a dollop of wheat germ. Whole grain flour is preferred.

White rice is not acceptable. Use the brown.

Nothing that is tainted with BHA, BHT, or any chemical preservative is allowed.

Fruits canned with sugar syrup—not acceptable. Use fresh fruit or those fruits that are canned in their own juice without sugar.

Commercial breads that are loaded with emulsifiers and preservatives are not acceptable. Natural food stores provide whole grain breads that have no preservatives. Homemade bread is best of all.

Dry roasted nuts, salted nuts, commercial potato chips, corn curls, and things of that ilk—not acceptable. (Dry roasted nuts have a starch coating and other objectionables.) Serve unroasted, unsalted seeds and nuts.

Now those are enough restrictions to keep the menu healthful and yet not discourage the beginners. It's a good idea to keep a circulating library of natural food cookbooks to help the beginners over the hump, and to stimulate ideas for creative dishes and menu planning. *The Rodale Cookbook* is an excellent one; Beatrice

Trum Hunter's books on natural cooking are tops; the *Good Goodies* by the Dworkins, the *Forget About Meat Cookbook* by Karen Brooks, *Diet for a Small Planet* by Frances Moore Lappe and, of course, *Confessions of a Sneaky Organic Cook* and Table Talk columns from *Prevention*® magazine (modest, I'm not!).

This kind of natural foods dinner club could mushroom and pop in popularity and become the "in" thing, with everybody doing it. It has countless fringe benefits. Those people who think that natural food tastes like sawdust are in for some tasty revelations. Many people will sample things at a dinner party they would scorn at home—and then find they actually like them. There will of course be lots of questions, and discussion and more interest in the whole subject will be generated so that it could even evolve into an animated study and action group.

I have collected some recipes that are delicious and easy to make. Have a dip and dessert party, or a dinner party but do get a group together for next Saturday night and have a wonderful time—naturally—with love and wheat germ.

Dip and Dessert Party

Make everything ahead of time, and be a guest at your own party. This is a good way to entertain groups too large to sit comfortably around the dining room table, like holiday time when you feel like getting together with lots of old friends, or for study groups that meet at each other's homes. When the people in our Bible study group meet at our house, I plan a dip and dessert and I don't miss any of the fun and conversation.

Salmon Party Ball

Give it star billing on your buffet table because it is so lovely to look at. Serve with lots of crisp raw vegetables and thin whole wheat crackers.

2 cups salmon (1-pound can), drained
8 ounces cream cheese
1 tablespoon lemon juice
2 teaspoons onion, grated
1 tablespoon white horseradish
¼ teaspoon salt or kelp
¼ teaspoon paprika
½ cup pecans, chopped
3 tablespoons parsley, chopped

Thoroughly mix all ingredients except pecans and parsley. Roll into ball in wax paper and chill several hours. Then roll in combined pecans and parsley.

Re-chill until ready to serve, or freeze. Serve with a platter of raw vegetables, cut into convenient sizes for scooping into the salmon ball. Delicious and usually the most popular attraction at buffet parties.

Colorful Harlequin Dip

2 tablespoons milk

1 12-ounce carton cream-style cottage cheese

1 teaspoon lemon juice

½ teaspoon salt

1 teaspoon horseradish

1 medium carrot, cut in 1-inch pieces

3 radishes

3 sprigs parsley

Put milk, cottage cheese, lemon juice, salt, and horseradish in blender container; cover and blend until smooth. Add remaining ingredients; run blender again just until vegetables are chopped.

Yields one-and-one-half cups

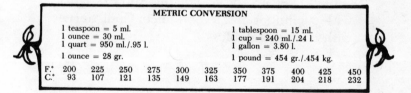

METRIC CONVERSION

1 teaspoon = 5 ml.	1 tablespoon = 15 ml.
1 ounce = 30 ml.	1 cup = 240 ml./.24 l.
1 quart = 950 ml./.95 l.	1 gallon = 3.80 l.
1 ounce = 28 gr.	1 pound = 454 gr./.454 kg.

F.°	200	225	250	275	300	325	350	375	400	425	450
C.°	93	107	121	135	149	163	177	191	204	218	232

Guacamole Dip

1 tablespoon lemon juice

½ cup mayonnaise, preferably homemade

½ small onion

½ teaspoon salt

½ teaspoon kelp

¼ teaspoon chili powder
½ teaspoon paprika
2 ripe avocados, peeled and pitted

Put all ingredients in the blender in order
listed. Whiz till smooth. Chill.

Pecan Yogurt Dip

5 pecans
1 clove garlic
1 tablespoon oil
1 cup yogurt
½ cucumber, diced
1 teaspoon lemon juice

Blend pecans, garlic, and oil. Add to yogurt
with cucumber and lemon juice. Chill. Serve
with crisp vegetables.

Fruit and Cheese Dip
(cool and refreshing)

1 cup cottage cheese
1 tablespoon lemon juice
2 tablespoons yogurt
½ cup crushed pineapple
¼ teaspoon ginger
¼ teaspoon cinnamon

Put all ingredients in blender until smooth. Mound in an attractive bowl and surround with fruits on toothpicks for dipping. Try peaches, apples, oranges, strawberries, melon —whatever is in season.

Tomato-Yogurt Dip

A lovely coral color—zippy flavor

½ cup tomato sauce or three ripe
   tomatoes from the vine

½ cup yogurt

½ teaspoon kelp

¼ teaspoon salt

1 onion, sliced

¼ cup horseradish (prepared)

Blend all ingredients together until smooth. Garnish with parsley, chives, or watercress. This is a good sauce for fish as well as a great dip for vegetables.

METRIC CONVERSION										
1 teaspoon = 5 ml.					1 tablespoon = 15 ml.					
1 ounce = 30 ml.					1 cup = 240 ml./.24 l.					
1 quart = 950 ml./.95 l.					1 gallon = 3.80 l.					
1 ounce = 28 gr.					1 pound = 454 gr./.454 kg.					

F.°	200	225	250	275	300	325	350	375	400	425	450
C.°	93	107	121	135	149	163	177	191	204	218	232

Green Onion Dip

½ cup green onions, finely chopped
¼ cup parsley, chopped
½ teaspoon powdered ginger
1 tablespoon tamari soy sauce
2 tablespoons walnuts, chopped
1 cup yogurt or sour cream
2 tablespoons mayonnaise

Combine all ingredients. This is especially good with raw zucchini slices, raw cauliflower, and raw broccoli.

Cranberry Dip

(It's a lovely pale pink and perfect for fruits.)

½ cup cranberry sauce, cooked
½ cup mayonnaise
½ cup sour cream or yogurt

Blend until smooth. Mound it in a bowl, chill, and serve surrounded by pineapple chunks, apple slices, pieces of melon, and whole strawberries. Very festive.

Your dessert table can be just as sensational as your dips and just as nutritious.

Berry Ambrosia

A most gracious way to say "Welcome" to your guests or just to make your family feel they're "special" is to serve fresh berry ambrosia. Try this recipe but don't limit yourself to the fruits I suggest. Use whatever is in season to create a colorful, pretty-as-a-picture medley.

1 pint sour cream

1 pint yogurt

crushed pineapple, unsweetened (20-ounce can or 2 cups fresh)

1 cup strawberries, sliced

1 cup blueberries

2 or 3 peaches, sliced

½ cup walnuts

½ cup coconut, unsweetened

1 banana, sliced

2 oranges

Drain pineapple. Peel and section oranges. Combine the yogurt and sour cream in a large glass bowl. Add the coconut and walnuts. Fold in the rest of the fruit. Garnish with a few whole strawberries and a few walnut halves.

METRIC CONVERSION										
1 teaspoon = 5 ml.					1 tablespoon = 15 ml.					
1 ounce = 30 ml.					1 cup = 240 ml./.24 l.					
1 quart = 950 ml./.95 l.					1 gallon = 3.80 l.					
1 ounce = 28 gr.					1 pound = 454 gr./.454 kg.					

F.°	200	225	250	275	300	325	350	375	400	425	450
C.°	93	107	121	135	149	163	177	191	204	218	232

Pineapple Banana Bake

A touch of Hawaii in a delicious pie with a banana crust.

3 tablespoons butter

1 tablespoon honey

1 can (20 ounces) crushed pineapple (unsweetened) with juice

1 teaspoon lemon rind, grated

¼ teaspoon mace

½ teaspoon cinnamon

2 teaspoons arrowroot starch

1 tablespoon cold water

3 bananas

coconut

½ cup cooky crumbs or granola

Preheat oven to 350°F.

Melt butter in a medium-sized saucepan. Stir in the honey, the pineapple with juice, the lemon rind, mace, and cinnamon.

Mix the arrowroot and water. Stir this into the pineapple mixture. Heat to boiling. Boil for half-a-minute, stirring constantly. Cut bananas in half and then lengthwise, and place in a buttered nine-inch square baking dish. Sprinkle with coconut. Pour the pineapple mixture over the bananas and coconut and top with cooky crumbs or granola. Bake for 15 minutes. Lovely.

Oatmeal Walnut Cake

This recipe is great for family or for company. Make it when you have some spare time and store it in the freezer. It defrosts quickly and tastes especially delicious when it is cold.

1 cup oatmeal (not the instant)

1½ cups boiling water

½ cup butter

¾ cup honey

2 eggs

1¼ cups whole wheat flour

2 tablespoons coarse bran

2 tablespoons lecithin granules

2 tablespoons wheat germ

2 teaspoons bone meal powder

1 teaspoon baking powder

1 teaspoon baking soda

1 teaspoon cinnamon

½ cup chopped walnuts

METRIC CONVERSION

1 teaspoon = 5 ml.					1 tablespoon = 15 ml.					
1 ounce = 30 ml.					1 cup = 240 ml./.24 l.					
1 quart = 950 ml./.95 l.					1 gallon = 3.80 l.					
1 ounce = 28 gr.					1 pound = 454 gr./.454 kg.					

F.°	200	225	250	275	300	325	350	375	400	425	450
C.°	93	107	121	135	149	163	177	191	204	218	232

Preheat oven to 350°F.

Pour boiling water over the oatmeal and let it cool. Cream the butter and the honey, add eggs, then the slightly cooled oatmeal. In another bowl combine the flour with the rest of the ingredients and blend this thoroughly with the other mixture. Bake in a greased and floured, nine-inch square baking pan for 40 minutes.

This cake is delicious just as it is, but if you want to fancy it up, try this topping.

METRIC CONVERSION

1 teaspoon = 5 ml.
1 ounce = 30 ml.
1 quart = 950 ml./.95 l.

1 ounce = 28 gr.

1 tablespoon = 15 ml.
1 cup = 240 ml./.24 l.
1 gallon = 3.80 l.

1 pound = 454 gr./.454 kg.

F.°	200	225	250	275	300	325	350	375	400	425	450
C.°	93	107	121	135	149	163	177	191	204	218	232

Topping for Oatmeal Walnut Cake

6 tablespoons butter

¼ cup light cream

¼ cup honey

1 cup coconut

½ cup nuts, chopped

1 teaspoon vanilla

Mix these ingredients together then spread on cooled cake. Brown under broiler briefly.

Cheese Pie

This one makes a hit at every party

For the crust use about 18 zwieback biscuits crumbed in the blender. One-eighth pound of butter and one teaspoon of cinnamon. Combine the ingredients for the crust in a large pie plate. Spread it around and press it down to form a shell.

Put the following ingredients in the blender for a few minutes:

½ pound cream cheese

½ pound cottage cheese, drained

½ cup honey

2 eggs

½ teaspoon vanilla

½ teaspoon lemon

½ teaspoon almond flavoring

Preheat oven to 375°F.

Pour the mixture into the prepared shell. Bake for five minutes. Take pie out of the oven and let it cool.

For a lovely topping whip slightly less than one pint of sour cream or yogurt or a combination of both with two tablespoons of honey and a little vanilla. Pour on top of the cheese pie and bake for five minutes. When you take it out of the oven, sprinkle chopped nuts all over the top. You could also use crushed pineapple, cherries, or strawberries on top.

It is best to make this pie ahead of time and keep it refrigerated until you're ready to serve it. It also freezes well. This pie makes any meal festive. And it is substantial enough to satisfy those who only grabbed a quick snack before coming to your dip and dessert party.

Carrot Coconut Cake

(A cake with body—try it with cream cheese, also good for a brunch party.)

3 eggs

¾ cup oil

1 teaspoon vanilla

2 cups carrots, shredded

1 cup coconut, shredded

1 cup walnuts, chopped

½ cup honey

1 cup raisins

1½ cups whole wheat flour

½ cup oat flour

1 teaspoon baking powder

1 teaspoon baking soda

1 teaspoon cinnamon

½ teaspoon salt

METRIC CONVERSION

1 teaspoon = 5 ml. 1 ounce = 30 ml. 1 quart = 950 ml./.95 l.	1 tablespoon = 15 ml. 1 cup = 240 ml./.24 l. 1 gallon = 3.80 l.
1 ounce = 28 gr.	1 pound = 454 gr./.454 kg.

F.°	200	225	250	275	300	325	350	375	400	425	450
C.°	93	107	121	135	149	163	177	191	204	218	232

Preheat oven to 350°F.

In electric mixer beat eggs until light. Stir in oil, vanilla, carrots, coconut, walnuts, honey, and raisins. Mix flours, baking powder, baking soda, cinnamon, and salt. Add to first mixture. Do not overmix. Spread in greased 9″ × 5″ × 3″ loaf pan and bake for 70 minutes, or until done. Let stand 10 minutes until cooled and turn out right side up. Cool thoroughly.

Apple Crisp

Wash, core and slice enough apples or pears (or a combination of the two), to fill a nine-inch square baking pan. (Peel the fruit if it is not organically grown.) In a large skillet, sauté the fruit in a small amount of oil over high heat for five minutes, stirring constantly. Salt lightly. Turn heat to medium-low and cook 20 minutes, again stirring often. Add two tablespoons of dry white wine. Cover and cook another five to 10 minutes until apples are soft. Sprinkle the mixture lightly with arrowroot flour and mix it in. Pour the apples into the lightly oiled nine-inch square pan. If desired, you may also add the juice of half a lemon, cinnamon, or a few raisins to the cooked apples. This filling is also delicious in pies or knishes.

Sprinkle with topping.

Topping for Crisp

½ cup whole wheat flour
½ cup rolled oats
1 teaspoon cinnamon

¼ cup oil

4 teaspoons water or apple juice

Preheat oven to 450°F.
Mix dry ingredients and cut in oil. Sprinkle
in water or apple juice. The mixture should be
moist, but not wet or sticky. Crumble the mixture over the apples and bake, uncovered, in
oven until topping is browned, about 10 to 15
minutes.

METRIC CONVERSION

1 teaspoon = 5 ml.	1 tablespoon = 15 ml.
1 ounce = 30 ml.	1 cup = 240 ml./.24 l.
1 quart = 950 ml./.95 l.	1 gallon = 3.80 l.
1 ounce = 28 gr.	1 pound = 454 gr./.454 kg.

F.°	200	225	250	275	300	325	350	375	400	425	450
C.°	93	107	121	135	149	163	177	191	204	218	232

Go Ethnic!

If you want to add some special interest to your party,
why not introduce your guests to some ethnic dishes?
Every country has its own delicious specialities. You'll
find them easy to make and they will be the topic of
conversation among your guests for weeks after the
party's over.

Here are a few of my favorites. They always make a
hit, whether you build a whole ethnic meal around
them or serve them as the main course at any dinner
or buffet.

Spaghetti Roma

8 ounces thin whole wheat spaghetti
water
¼ cup olive oil
¼ cup butter
1 small clove garlic, minced
½ teaspoon oregano
½ teaspoon salt
3 hard-cooked eggs, chopped very fine
½ cup parsley, chopped
grated Parmesan cheese

Cook spaghetti in water as directed on the package. Drain and keep warm. Heat oil and butter in a small saucepan. Add garlic, oregano, and salt; cook five minutes. Sprinkle oil mixture, egg, and parsley over spaghetti; toss to mix well. Turn into a serving bowl. Serve sprinkled with cheese.
Makes six servings

Vegetable Stew De Casa

1 eggplant, unpeeled, cut into ⅛-inch thick
    round slices
½ cup whole wheat flour
¼ teaspoon salt
¼ teaspoon pepper

¼ teaspoon paprika

olive oil

butter

2 onions, diced

2 potatoes, diced

1 pound peas, shelled

2 carrots, diced

2 zucchini, diced

¼ pound green beans, cut in pieces

1 pepper (sweet or frying pepper), diced

3 ripe tomatoes, diced

3 cloves garlic, crushed or minced

1½ teaspoons salt

½ teaspoon pepper

3 tablespoons olive oil

METRIC CONVERSION										
1 teaspoon = 5 ml.					1 tablespoon = 15 ml.					
1 ounce = 30 ml.					1 cup = 240 ml./.24 l.					
1 quart = 950 ml./.95 l.					1 gallon = 3.80 l.					
1 ounce = 28 gr.					1 pound = 454 gr./.454 kg.					
F.°	200	225	250	275	300	325	350	375	400	425	450
C.°	93	107	121	135	149	163	177	191	204	218	232

Preheat oven to 350°F.

Butter a one-and-one-half quart casserole or shallow baking pan. Dredge eggplant in a mixture of flour, salt, pepper, and paprika.

Heat one tablespoon oil and one tablespoon butter in a skillet. Brown eggplant slices on both sides. Use more oil and butter as needed.

Layer half of the slices along the bottom

of the baking dish. Reserve the other half.

Blend all other vegetables, seasonings and oil. Place vegetables on eggplant. Cover with the layer of reserved eggplant. Bake for 45 minutes, uncovered for 15 minutes.
Yield: six to eight servings

Baked Chicken Piquant, Provencale

1 ready-to-cook broiler-fryer, cut in quarters

1 lemon, cut in half

⅛ teaspoon each dried thyme leaves, crushed, and dried basil, crushed

pepper and salt to taste

Preheat oven to 400°F.

Place chicken quarters in shallow baking pan. Squeeze juice from ½ lemon over chicken. Sprinkle with half the thyme and sweet basil; season with salt and pepper. Bake, uncovered, for 40 to 50 minutes.

Turn chicken; squeeze juice from remaining lemon half over quarters, then sprinkle with remaining herbs and salt and pepper to taste. Bake 25 to 35 minutes more, or until chicken is done.
Serves four

Spiced German Pot Roast of Beef

2 tablespoons fat or cooking oil

4 to 5 pounds beef, boned rump or sirloin tip

1 tablespoon cinnamon

2 teaspoons ginger

2 tablespoons honey

1 tablespoon vinegar

2 cups tomato juice

1 cup onion, chopped

1 large bay leaf

1½ teaspoons salt

⅛ teaspoon pepper

½ cup cold water

¼ cup whole wheat or soy flour

METRIC CONVERSION										

1 teaspoon = 5 ml.   1 tablespoon = 15 ml.
1 ounce = 30 ml.   1 cup = 240 ml./.24 l.
1 quart = 950 ml./.95 l. 1 gallon = 3.80 l.

1 ounce = 28 gr.   1 pound = 454 gr./.454 kg.

F.°	200	225	250	275	300	325	350	375	400	425	450
C.°	93	107	121	135	149	163	177	191	204	218	232

Heat fat in a Dutch oven or sauce pot over high heat. Add meat and brown well on all sides. Combine cinnamon, ginger, honey, vinegar, tomato juice, onion, bay leaf, salt and pepper. Pour over meat. Bring to boiling; reduce heat to low and simmer, covered, about three hours or until meat is tender. Place meat on a platter and keep warm. Take out bay leaf.

Measure the liquid in the pan; add water, if necessary, to make two cups. Return to pan.

Mix cold water with the flour and make a smooth paste. Slowly stir into liquid. Bring sauce to a boil and cook until thickened, stirring constantly. Serve separately.
Makes 10 to 12 servings

Japanese-Style Beef

1 pound round steak, very thinly
    sliced across the grain

2 tablespoons oil

¼ cup beef or vegetable bouillon

3 tablespoons soy sauce

1½ cups asparagus,
    cut into 2-inch lengths

1 bunch scallions,
    cut into 2-inch lengths

½ Spanish onion, thinly sliced

½ pound mushrooms, thinly sliced

½ pound spinach, washed and drained

In a skillet, brown the beef quickly in hot oil. Add the bouillon mixed with the soy sauce. Cover and simmer gently two minutes.

Add the asparagus, scallions, onion, and mushrooms. Place the spinach on top, cover and cook until spinach is done, about 10 minutes. Serve with rice.

Yield: about five servings

East Indian Stuffed Fish

3 pounds cleaned boned whitefish or bass
1 teaspoon salt
⅛ teaspoon black pepper
2 tablespoons fresh onion, minced
¼ teaspoon garlic powder
1 teaspoon curry powder
¾ to 1 teaspoon salt
⅛ teaspoon black pepper
2 cups soft whole grain bread crumbs
¼ cup celery, finely chopped
1 tablespoon parsley, chopped
2 tablespoons butter, melted

Preheat oven to 350°F.

Sprinkle inside of fish with half the salt and pepper mixed together.

Combine the rest of ingredients, tossing lightly. Spoon into cavity of fish. Close opening with skewers or toothpicks, and lace with strong thread.

Sprinkle skin of fish with reserved salt and pepper.

Bake in buttered baking pan for 35 to 40 minutes or until fish flakes.

Serves six

Malayan Chicken

1 2½-pound chicken, cut into serving pieces

¼ cup salad oil

1 small clove garlic, finely chopped

1 teaspoon ginger

1 teaspoon salt

1 8-ounce can of pitted ripe olives,
    drained and halved

1 5¼-ounce can of water chestnuts,
    drained and sliced

¾ cup dry white wine

½ cup chicken broth

2 tablespoons arrowroot starch

Brown the chicken pieces in the hot oil with the garlic. Add the remaining ingredients except the starch, cover and cook gently until the chicken is done, about 30 minutes. Remove the chicken to a warm serving platter and keep hot.

Mix the starch with enough water to form a smooth paste. Add to the cooking liquid and cook, stirring, until thickened and translucent. Serve with the chicken.

Serves four to six

METRIC CONVERSION

1 teaspoon = 5 ml.		1 tablespoon = 15 ml.
1 ounce = 30 ml.		1 cup = 240 ml./.24 l.
1 quart = 950 ml./.95 l.		1 gallon = 3.80 l.
1 ounce = 28 gr.		1 pound = 454 gr./.454 kg.

F.°	200	225	250	275	300	325	350	375	400	425	450
C.°	93	107	121	135	149	163	177	191	204	218	232

Russian Vatrushki
(Cheese-Filled Tarts)

Pastry:

1½ envelopes dry active yeast

¼ cup warm water

¾ cup warm milk

1 cup (two sticks) butter, melted and
clarified by pouring off yellow liquid
to use and discarding the white sediment

2½ cups whole wheat flour

¼ teaspoon salt

Filling:

1 pound farmer cheese

2 eggs, lightly beaten

2 tablespoons sour cream

1 tablespoon flour

Preheat the oven to 400°F.

Dissolve the yeast in the warm water. Add
milk, butter, flour, and salt. Work into a dough
with the hands until smooth and a consistency
that can be rolled.

Mix the farmer cheese with one egg and
sour cream until smooth. Beat in the flour.

Roll out the dough on a lightly floured
board or cloth to about one-quarter-inch
thickness. It may be easier to divide into two
or more batches. Cut out rounds three to four
inches in diameter. Place one tablespoon of

the filling in the middle of each round. Draw up the border or edge of the dough and pinch in scallops, leaving the cheese filling partly exposed. These are open tarts.

Place tarts on lightly greased baking sheet, brushing pastry and filling with remaining egg. Bake about 25 minutes or until lightly browned and cooked. Cool on a rack.
Yield: About four dozen vatrushki

METRIC CONVERSION

1 teaspoon = 5 ml.	1 tablespoon = 15 ml.
1 ounce = 30 ml.	1 cup = 240 ml./.24 l.
1 quart = 950 ml./.95 l.	1 gallon = 3.80 l.
1 ounce = 28 gr.	1 pound = 454 gr./.454 kg.

F.°	200	225	250	275	300	325	350	375	400	425	450
C.°	93	107	121	135	149	163	177	191	204	218	232

Piroshki Ivan

(Savory Pastries)

1½ pounds boneless breast or
    neck of veal, cut into small cubes

¾ cup water

2 onions, chopped

salt and pepper

1 pair sweetbreads

1 calf's brain

½ pound mushrooms

3 cups cooked brown rice

¼ cup snipped, fresh dill weed

2 recipes yeast pastry as for the vatrushki

1 egg for glaze

Place veal, water, onions, salt and pepper in a heavy saucepan. Bring to a boil, cover, and simmer gently until tender, 35 to 45 minutes. Add more water if necessary, but at the end of cooking the mixture should be as dry as possible. Evaporate extra liquid by boiling.

Cover sweetbreads with cold water, bring to a boil, simmer 10 minutes, drain, remove connective tissue.

Drop the brain into a pan of boiling water. Leave 10 minutes, drain, and skin.

When veal is cooked, put it through a food chopper with sweetbreads, brain, and mushrooms. Mix with rice and dill; test for seasoning.

Preheat the oven to 425°F.

Prepare the pastry. Roll out one-quarter of the dough to one-quarter-inch thickness on a lightly floured board. Cut into three-inch rounds. Place about two teaspoons of the filling in the middle of each round. Fold over dough, making a crescent shape, and seal.

Brush with egg, prick, and bake on a greased sheet about 10 minutes. Reduce the heat to 400°F. and bake 15 minutes longer or until cooked. Repeat with remaining dough and filling.

Yield: About 75 piroshki

METRIC CONVERSION										
1 teaspoon = 5 ml.					1 tablespoon = 15 ml.					
1 ounce = 30 ml.					1 cup = 240 ml./.24 l.					
1 quart = 950 ml./.95 l.					1 gallon = 3.80 l.					
1 ounce = 28 gr.					1 pound = 454 gr./.454 kg.					

F.°	200	225	250	275	300	325	350	375	400	425	450
C.°	93	107	121	135	149	163	177	191	204	218	232

Middle Eastern Eggplant Dish

½ cup whole wheat flour

2 tablespoons soy flour

½ teaspoon salt or vegetable salt

2 tablespoons sesame seeds

2 medium eggplants

½ cup lemon juice

2 cloves garlic, minced

2 onions, finely chopped

1 cup grated cheese (optional)

1 cup tomato sauce

Preheat oven to 375°F.

Combine all the dry ingredients to make a seasoned flour. Wash and slice the eggplants thickly. Do not peel. Dip each slice in the lemon juice and then the seasoned flour. Sauté in hot vegetable oil, not too fast, until the slices are crisp on both sides, then drain them on paper towels. While the eggplant is crisping up, sauté two crushed garlic cloves and two chopped onions. Butter a deep baking dish and arrange the eggplant slices alternately with layers of onion and garlic and half-a-cup of grated cheese (optional). Pour in one cup of tomato sauce, cover with more cheese, and bake in oven for about half-an-hour or until the top is bubbly.

My Favorite Regulars

No matter how many parties I give, no matter how many new recipes I try, some dishes turn out to be regulars on my table. I feel comfortable about them. They fit in with almost anything else I'm serving and I know how they'll come out. Best of all, my guests never fail to tell me how good these dishes tasted to them.

Try serving one or two to your family and friends— you'll see what I mean.

Rice Salad

1 cup brown rice

6 tablespoons olive oil

3 tablespoons apple cider vinegar

salt and pepper

½ teaspoon dried tarragon

¼ cup green pepper or pimiento, chopped

¼ cup parsley, chopped

¼ cup onion, finely chopped

½ cup green peas, cooked

¼ cup chopped chives (optional)

METRIC CONVERSION

1 teaspoon = 5 ml.	1 tablespoon = 15 ml.
1 ounce = 30 ml.	1 cup = 240 ml./.24 l.
1 quart = 950 ml./.95 l.	1 gallon = 3.80 l.
1 ounce = 28 gr.	1 pound = 454 gr./.454 kg.

F.°	200	225	250	275	300	325	350	375	400	425	450
C.°	93	107	121	135	149	163	177	191	204	218	232

Cook the rice. While still hot, add oil, vinegar, salt and pepper to taste, and tarragon. Cool. Add remaining vegetables and mix well. Chill. At serving time, pile rice salad on platter in the shape of a pyramid. Surround with wedges of tomato and hard-cooked eggs. A good main dish for summer luncheon, or in small portions for hors d'oeuvre.

Casserole Marie-Blanche

(With a salad and fruit it makes a great meal. It also goes very well with fish dinners.)

1½ pounds cooked, drained noodles

½ cup wheat germ

1 cup cream-style cottage cheese

1 cup sour cream

½ teaspoon salt

⅛ teaspoon pepper

⅓ cup chopped chives

1 tablespoon butter

Preheat oven to 350°F.

Combine all ingredients except the butter. Pour into a buttered two-quart casserole and dot top with one tablespoon butter. Bake about 30 minutes, until noodles begin to brown. Serve immediately.

Serves six

METRIC CONVERSION

1 teaspoon = 5 ml.	1 tablespoon = 15 ml.
1 ounce = 30 ml.	1 cup = 240 ml./.24 l.
1 quart = 950 ml./.95 l.	1 gallon = 3.80 l.
1 ounce = 28 gr.	1 pound = 454 gr./.454 kg.

F.°	200	225	250	275	300	325	350	375	400	425	450
C.°	93	107	121	135	149	163	177	191	204	218	232

Danish Tuna-Cucumber Salad

Toss together lightly:

2 cups cucumber, thinly sliced

½ teaspoon salt

⅛ teaspoon pepper

2 tablespoons onion, finely chopped

2 regular size (6½ ounce) or
    1 giant size (12½ ounce) can tuna fish

Mix:

1 cup sour cream

2 tablespoons lemon juice

Pour over tuna mixture and combine lightly but thoroughly. Place in lettuce-lined salad bowl. Garnish with tomato wedges.

Cucumber Almond Salad

Combine:

2 cucumbers, pared and thinly sliced

½ teaspoon salt in a bowl

Let stand about 15 minutes. Drain.

Combine in a small bowl:

  1 cup sour cream or yogurt

  ⅓ cup slivered almonds

  1 teaspoon onion, chopped

  1½ teaspoon lime juice

  Pour sour cream mixture over cucumbers; toss to mix well.
Serves six

Red Cabbage Slaw

  1 cup red cabbage, finely shredded
  3 cups green cabbage, finely shredded
  ½ cup mayonnaise
  ½ to ¾ teaspoon dill seeds
  ¾ teaspoon salt
  dash pepper
  few grains paprika
  ¼ cup sour cream

  Put the red and green cabbage in a bowl. Combine mayonnaise and remaining ingredients in another bowl. Pour mayonnaise mixture over cabbage; toss to mix, then chill.
Serves six to eight

Tomato Aspic Salad

4 cups tomato juice
1 bay leaf
1 teaspoon salt
dash cayenne
2 stalks celery, sliced
2 tablespoons onion, grated
2 envelopes unflavored gelatin
½ cup cold water
2 tablespoons lemon juice
crisp salad greens

Combine tomato juice and the next five ingredients in a saucepan. Bring to a boil; simmer 10 minutes. Sprinkle gelatin over cold water and let stand to soften. Add softened gelatin to tomato mixture; stir until dissolved. Add lemon juice. Remove bay leaf. Pour into a one-quart ring mold. Chill until set. Unmold on a serving plate and garnish with salad greens. If desired, fill center with potato salad or cottage cheese.

Serves six

METRIC CONVERSION										
1 teaspoon = 5 ml.					1 tablespoon = 15 ml.					
1 ounce = 30 ml.					1 cup = 240 ml./.24 l.					
1 quart = 950 ml./.95 l.					1 gallon = 3.80 l.					
1 ounce = 28 gr.					1 pound = 454 gr./.454 kg.					

F.°	200	225	250	275	300	325	350	375	400	425	450
C.°	93	107	121	135	149	163	177	191	204	218	232

Macedoine of Vegetables

A very colorful dish. Use any leftover vegetables. It's great for a vegetarian dinner. But since you never know who's a vegetarian these days, it's a good idea to provide a dish like this whenever you entertain large groups.

2 cups cold, cooked cubed potatoes

2 cups cold cooked peas

2 cups cold, cooked green beans,
    cut into one-inch pieces

2 cups cold, cooked small lima beans

2 cups cold, cooked cubed carrots

1½ tablespoons wine vinegar

½ teaspoon kelp powder

¼ teaspoon dry mustard

1 teaspoon salt

½ teaspoon freshly ground pepper

½ cup pignolia nuts or
    sunflower seed kernels

1 tablespoon fresh lemon juice

1 cup mayonnaise

3 hard-cooked eggs, sliced thin

2 medium tomatoes, cut in wedges

Place cooked vegetables in large mixing bowl. Combine wine vinegar, kelp, dry mustard, and salt and pepper in a small bowl and pour over cooked vegetables.

Toss gently and allow to cool at room temperature. Add one-half cup pignolia nuts or sunflower kernels to mixed vegetables. Sprinkle one tablespoon of lemon juice over top, and stir in enough mayonnaise to moisten the vegetables well. Taste and correct seasoning. Garnish with sliced eggs and tomato wedges.

Serves eight

METRIC CONVERSION

1 teaspoon = 5 ml.		1 tablespoon = 15 ml.
1 ounce = 30 ml.		1 cup = 240 ml./.24 l.
1 quart = 950 ml./.95 l.		1 gallon = 3.80 l.
1 ounce = 28 gr.		1 pound = 454 gr./.454 kg.

F.°	200	225	250	275	300	325	350	375	400	425	450
C.°	93	107	121	135	149	163	177	191	204	218	232

Ginger Baked Mushrooms

Preheat oven to 400°F.

Soften a tablespoon of butter, but do not melt it, and add a pinch of ginger. Blend well and then rub this mixture all over, inside and outside, of fresh raw mushroom caps. Place the caps, cup side up, in a glass pie plate, keeping them nestled closely together. Bake in oven for eight to 10 minutes—no more. Spear with picks and pass them hot. They are a real favorite. Make plenty.

Cheese Vegetable Rarebit

(This one is for a crowd—serves 25)

½ cup onions, chopped

½ cup green peppers, chopped

¼ cup celery, chopped

¼ cup salad oil

4 cups milk

¼ cup arrowroot starch

salt

2 pounds, 2 ounces cheese, grated

8 eggs, beaten

1 teaspoon dry mustard

1 tablespoon tamari soy sauce

1 teaspoon paprika

1 teaspoon garlic salt

¾ cup ketchup

Sauté onion, green pepper, and celery in oil until golden. Mix arrowroot starch with milk and add to vegetables, stirring constantly. Heat to simmer while stirring. Add salt and cheese. Heat until cheese is melted. Stir some of the hot cheese into beaten eggs, then add eggs to remaining cheese mixture. Add the ketchup.

Cook and stir constantly about six minutes, or until temperature of mixture has returned to simmer. Serve over toast.

Serves 25

Dinner Party for Celebrating

This is the menu for my favorite dinner party. It's the kind of meal that a modern-day Fiddler on the Roof might serve to celebrate a successful "match" or any happy occasion. This menu rates many a *mazel tov* and you don't have to be Jewish to relish it. Best of all—everything can be fixed ahead of time. Even if you have no hired help (I don't) you can be a relaxed guest at your own dinner party and savor every moment of your guests' enjoyment and every compliment.

MENU

(Dinner for Eight)

Hummus Dip (*see Index*) with Raw Vegetables

Brisket of Beef

Kasha with Mushroom Gravy

Carrots and Pineapple

Cabbage and Cranberry Coleslaw

Stir-fry String Beans Almondine (optional)

Fresh Fruit Ambrosia *(see Index)*

Whole Wheat Crescent Rolls

Herb Teas

Assorted Confections *(see Index)*

Nuts and Seeds to go with tea and conversation

METRIC CONVERSION										

1 teaspoon = 5 ml.
1 ounce = 30 ml.
1 quart = 950 ml./.95 l.
1 ounce = 28 gr.

1 tablespoon = 15 ml.
1 cup = 240 ml./.24 l.
1 gallon = 3.80 l.
1 pound = 454 gr./.454 kg.

F.°	200	225	250	275	300	325	350	375	400	425	450
C.°	93	107	121	135	149	163	177	191	204	218	232

Roast Brisket

Great for a dinner party because everybody likes it. (Can be made ahead and reheated.)

3 onions, sliced

2 ribs celery, including tops, diced

1 carrot, sliced

3 bay leaves

few drops water

5–6 pounds brisket of beef

1 clove garlic

½ teaspoon salt

paprika

1 can tomato sauce, about 4 ounces

1 4-ounce can mushrooms, undrained

{ or 1 can tomato-mushroom sauce

Preheat oven to 350°F.

Place the onions, celery, carrots, and bay leaves in bottom of roasting pan. Add water. Rub the brisket with the cut clove of garlic and salt. Mince whatever garlic remains and toss into the roasting pan. Sprinkle the meat generously with paprika. Roast for two-and-a-half hours, but turn the meat over after the first hour. When slightly cool, refrigerate. The day of your party, slice the meat thinly (electric knife works well here). Arrange the slices in a large heat-proof casserole that can go to the table, add the pot juices and vegetables, mixed with tomato sauce, and mushrooms, and heat to serving temperature. The hearty aroma will raise the cockles on everyone's appetite.

Whatever you have left can be made into sandwiches with mustard or horseradish. It can also make another meal.

Kasha

(Goes great with brisket)

1½ cups coarse buckwheat groats

1 egg

3 to 4 cups boiling water

1 teaspoon salt

1 teaspoon kelp

1 onion, diced

mushrooms (optional—but very good)

2 tablespoons chicken fat or oil

Add the egg to the groats and mix well with a fork. Heat a heavy frying pan over moderate flame and add the groats mixture. Stir to prevent burning, till groats are dry and toasty. Add boiling water gradually, while stirring. Add seasoning. Cover the pan and reduce heat for 15 minutes or until the grains fluff up and are tender. If necessary, add more boiling water, a little at a time. While the groats are cooking, brown the onion and some mushrooms in the fat, then add them to the groats. If you make this dish a day ahead, put it in a heat-and-serve dish. Next day, put it in the oven for 15 minutes while you're heating the brisket. Add some brisket gravy to keep it from drying out.

When you serve the kasha, add some of the brisket gravy to each serving. So good!

METRIC CONVERSION										
1 teaspoon = 5 ml.					1 tablespoon = 15 ml.					
1 ounce = 30 ml.					1 cup = 240 ml./.24 l.					
1 quart = 950 ml./.95 l.					1 gallon = 3.80 l.					
1 ounce = 28 gr.					1 pound = 454 gr./.454 kg.					
F.° 200	225	250	275	300	325	350	375	400	425	450
C.° 93	107	121	135	149	163	177	191	204	218	232

Carrots and Pineapple

(a great marriage)

1 can pineapple tidbits, unsweetened
3 or 4 large carrots

Scrub the carrots (do not peel), cut into slices and steam them, using the juice from the pineapple tidbits as the liquid in the steamer. If there isn't enough liquid, add a little water.

When carrots are crisp tender, add the pineapple chunks and heat. Serve in a pretty bowl, garnished with sprigs of parsley or watercress. No matter how much of this dish I make, there's never any left over.

Cabbage Cranberry Slaw

3 cups shredded cabbage

1 cup cranberry orange relish
    (2 cups cranberries, 1 orange or ½ cup orange juice and ½ cup honey—blenderized)

1 teaspoon salt

1 teaspoon kelp

2 tablespoons apple cider or wine vinegar

Combine all ingredients. Chill. It is best to make this salad a day ahead to allow flavors to meld. You can serve this dish as your salad to save yourself last-minute preparations.

METRIC CONVERSION										
1 teaspoon = 5 ml.					1 tablespoon = 15 ml.					
1 ounce = 30 ml.					1 cup = 240 ml./.24 l.					
1 quart = 950 ml./.95 l.					1 gallon = 3.80 l.					
1 ounce = 28 gr.					1 pound = 454 gr./.454 kg.					
F.° 200	225	250	275	300	325	350	375	400	425	450
C.° 93	107	121	135	149	163	177	191	204	218	232

Stir-Fried Green Beans Almondine

3 tablespoons oil
12 almonds (chopped or slivered)
1½ pounds green beans (leave them whole)
2 green onions, chopped (optional)
3 tablespoons chicken broth
    or vegetable water
1 tablespoon tamari soy sauce

Heat the oil in a skillet or *wok*. Add the almonds; when they are golden remove them to another dish with a slotted spoon. Add the beans and green onions to the same skillet you removed the almonds from and stir fry till they are well coated with oil. Mix the broth or vegetable water and soy sauce and pour over the vegetables. Cover the skillet or *wok* and cook over low heat about five minutes or until the beans are crisp tender but still bright green. Garnish with the toasted almonds. A lovely dish—if it is not overcooked.

Whole Wheat Crescent Rolls

4 teaspoons dry yeast
1 cup lukewarm water
1 teaspoon honey
1 cup oil
3 tablespoons honey

2 teaspoons salt

1 cup boiling water

2 eggs, beaten

6 cups whole wheat flour (more, if necessary, for rolling out crescents)

1 egg, beaten

½ teaspoon water

4 tablespoons sesame seeds (toasted for about 20 minutes in a 200°F. oven)

METRIC CONVERSION										
1 teaspoon = 5 ml.					1 tablespoon = 15 ml.					
1 ounce = 30 ml.					1 cup = 240 ml./.24 l.					
1 quart = 950 ml./.95 l.					1 gallon = 3.80 l.					
1 ounce = 28 gr.					1 pound = 454 gr./.454 kg.					
F.° 200	225	250	275	300	325	350	375	400	425	450
C.° 93	107	121	135	149	163	177	191	204	218	232

Dissolve yeast in lukewarm water. Add one teaspoon honey.

In large bowl, mix oil, three tablespoons honey, salt, and boiling water. When lukewarm, add two beaten eggs, then dissolved yeast. Gradually stir in whole wheat flour, mixing well, but do not knead. Put in refrigerator to chill until firm.

Divide dough into three parts and roll each one out on a floured board into a large circle, as thin as possible. Brush with beaten egg to which ½ teaspoon water has been added. Sprinkle sesame seeds over the surface. Cut each circle into wedges about two inches wide at the outside edge. Roll each wedge toward the center, lift off board, dip top in egg mixture, and then in sesame seeds. Place on oiled cooky sheet, leaving enough room for each crescent to rise. Let rise in draft-free

place for 1½ hours. Meanwhile, preheat oven to 425°F. Bake for 25 minutes until golden brown. Serve warm.
Yield: four dozen delicious rolls

I usually make two dozen rolls and two dozen *rogelach* using the same basic dough. To make *rogelach*, you sprinkle the rolled-out dough with raisins, chopped nuts, a little date sugar and cinnamon. Then proceed the same as for crescent rolls. The *rogelach* look great on my confection platter and they taste—how do they taste? Like granma's in the kitchen.

What's to Drink?

I have found that you can toast the health of your friends and the spirit of the season without a bloody mary, screwdriver, or a whiskey sour in your hand. You can even bring in the New Year with liquid refreshment that will bring on pink cheeks not pink elephants; drinks that make you peppy, not punchy.

You can get a happy "high" on drinks that have nothing to do with alcohol.

If you have a vegetable juicer, you're in business. You can make some great drinks at the flip of a switch. Have ready some scrubbed beets, carrots, and apples, carbonated water, some unsweetened pineapple juice, orange juice, grape juice, lemons and limes, and go creative. Have a tasting party.

This list from Brownie's Natural Foods Restaurant in New York City, will give you some ideas for drinks to spark a party or to sparkle your own spirits any day of the year.

Half-and-Half—fresh carrot and celery juice
Cooler—fresh cucumber, red radish, celery
Orange Blossom—fresh carrot, apple, and orange
Eye Opener—fresh celery, spinach, lemon, and to-
    mato
Old-Fashioned Garden Cocktail—fresh carrot, cel-
    ery, spinach, parsley
Grasshopper—fresh spinach, escarole, celery, and
    parsley
Dubonnet Cocktail—fresh apple and grape
Honi-Lulu—fresh pineapple, orange, and carrot
Tiger's Milk Flip—Tiger's Milk, fresh orange, and
    pineapple with dash of papaya
Protein Jubilee—soy milk, brewer's yeast, skim
    milk, blackstrap molasses, and honey

I've tried these drinks which are included in
Brownie's book, *Cooking Creatively with Natural
Foods* (Hawthorne Books, New York, 1972), and en-
joyed them. I think your guests will, too.

Trinidad Shake

You don't need a juicer to make the Trini-
dad Shake. Everything goes into the blender.
This one is a real eye-opener and full of good
nutrients. You really shouldn't wait for a party
to enjoy one.

1 cup canned unsweetened
    pineapple juice
2 eggs
½ cup canned unsweetened
    crushed pineapple

⅔ cup milk

2 tablespoons tahini

1 teaspoon Barbados molasses

1 teaspoon date sugar

2 tablespoons soybean powder

2 tablespoons powdered nonfat dry milk

½ teaspoon vanilla extract

Whiz all ingredients in blender for one minute.

Serves six (one-and-one-half quarts)

METRIC CONVERSION

1 teaspoon = 5 ml.	1 tablespoon = 15 ml.
1 ounce = 30 ml.	1 cup = 240 ml./.24 l.
1 quart = 950 ml./.95 l.	1 gallon = 3.80 l.
1 ounce = 28 gr.	1 pound = 454 gr./.454 kg.

F.°	200	225	250	275	300	325	350	375	400	425	450
C.°	93	107	121	135	149	163	177	191	204	218	232

Minty Apple Cup

1 cup apple juice

1 diced McIntosh apple with skin

⅔ cup buttermilk or yogurt

2 tablespoons powdered nonfat dry milk

2 teaspoons toasted wheat germ

1 tablespoon papaya syrup concentrate

1 teaspoon mint flakes or ½ cup mint tea

Whiz all ingredients in blender until smooth.

If you have a lovely punch bowl, use it for a double batch of this tangy, mint-flavored apple refresher. Surround the punch bowl with little bowls of nuts, seeds, and raisins and your guests will breathe pretty compliments into your ears between nibbles (on the food). **Serves four (one quart)**

Carob Freeze

For a delightfully different drink that will have your friends trying to divine the ingredients, try the Carob Freeze or Brown Velvet, both from Brownie's "natural cocktail bar."

½ cup water

½ cup crushed ice cubes

½ cup powdered nonfat dry milk

¼ cup carob powder

1 tablespoon honey

1 tablespoon brewer's yeast

Whip all ingredients in blender for one minute.
Serves two

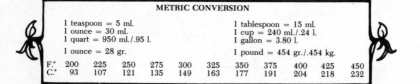

METRIC CONVERSION										
1 teaspoon = 5 ml.					1 tablespoon = 15 ml.					
1 ounce = 30 ml.					1 cup = 240 ml./.24 l.					
1 quart = 950 ml./.95 l.					1 gallon = 3.80 l.					
1 ounce = 28 gr.					1 pound = 454 gr./.454 kg.					
F.°	200	225	250	275	300	325	350	375	400	425	450
C.°	93	107	121	135	149	163	177	191	204	218	232

Brown Velvet

2 cups milk
¼ cup carob powder
2 tablespoons powdered milk
2 teaspoons rice polishings
2 teaspoons lecithin
2 tablespoons tahini
2 tablespoons honey
½ teaspoon vanilla extract

Whip all ingredients in blender for one minute.
Serves three

If you don't have a juicer or a blender, don't despair. You can still give a great natural party. We all love this Apple Ginger Fizz.

Apple or Grape Ginger Fizz

Pour a good-quality, unsweetened apple juice or white grape juice into champagne glasses—half full. Add a teaspoon of lemon juice to each glass and dust with powdered ginger. Fill each glass with carbonated mineral water. *Skoal!*

Toast the new year with a creamy eggnog that is smooth as velvet and full of ambrosial flavors. Here are a few recipes to choose from:

Velvety Orange Eggnog

6 egg yolks

3 tablespoons honey

1 cup heavy cream

2 cups milk

1 cup orange juice

2 cups heavy cream

6 egg whites

2 tablespoons honey

grated rind of one orange (organically grown if possible)

nutmeg

Beat egg yolks with three tablespoons of honey. Add one cup of cream and all the milk and continue beating. Add the orange juice slowly to prevent curdling. Whip remaining two cups of cream. Fold into orange mixture. Beat the egg whites until soft peaks form, then add remaining two tablespoons of honey. Beat again until honey is mixed into egg whites. Fold into the eggnog. Garnish with the grated orange rind and the nutmeg. **Serves 16**

Carobnog

3 teaspoons carob powder

1 tablespoon honey

1 beaten egg

2 cups milk

¼ teaspoon vanilla

½ cup heavy cream, whipped

Combine carob, honey, and beaten egg and beat or blend. Add milk and vanilla and blend again. Top each serving with a dollop of whipped cream.

Makes eight punch glass servings

METRIC CONVERSION										
1 teaspoon = 5 ml.					1 tablespoon = 15 ml.					
1 ounce = 30 ml.					1 cup = 240 ml./.24 l.					
1 quart = 950 ml./.95 l.					1 gallon = 3.80 l.					
1 ounce = 28 gr.					1 pound = 454 gr./.454 kg.					
F.°	200	225	250	275	300	325	350	375	400	425	450
C.°	93	107	121	135	149	163	177	191	204	218	232

Cherry Drink

1 pint cherry concentrate

12 cups water

½ cup honey (heat with some of the water to dissolve)

⅛ teaspoon salt

In an electric blender combine ingredients in order listed.

For variation:

Mix two parts of above with one part of any of the following:
pineapple juice
frozen orange juice (diluted)
orange-pineapple juice
Yield: 14 cups or 28 servings

Carrot-Pineapple Cocktail

2 cups unsweetened pineapple juice

2 medium carrots, washed and scraped, cut into one-inch pieces

1 slice lemon, ¼-inch thick

1 cup ice, crushed

In an electric blender combine the unsweetened pineapple juice, carrot pieces, and slice of lemon. Cover and blend until carrot is liquefied. Remove cover from blender and add the crushed ice. Cover and continue to blend until ice is liquefied. Sweeten with honey if desired. Serve in cocktail glasses; garnish with a slice of orange.
Yield: Approximately three cups

Apple Julep
(Who needs champagne?)

4 cups apple juice, unsweetened

2 cups pineapple juice, unsweetened

1 cup orange juice

¼ cup lemon juice, freshly squeezed

Combine ingredients and chill before serving. Pour mixture into punch bowl; garnish with lemon slices and fresh sprigs of mint. **Yield: Approximately one-and-three-fourth quarts**

METRIC CONVERSION										
1 teaspoon = 5 ml.					1 tablespoon = 15 ml.					
1 ounce = 30 ml.					1 cup = 240 ml./.24 l.					
1 quart = 950 ml./.95 l.					1 gallon = 3.80 l.					
1 ounce = 28 gr.					1 pound = 454 gr./.454 kg.					
F.° 200	225	250	275	300	325	350	375	400	425	450
C.° 93	107	121	135	149	163	177	191	204	218	232

Pineapple Cocktail

1 bunch watercress

2 cups pineapple juice, unsweetened

3 tablespoons honey

1 tablespoon fresh lemon juice

1 piece fresh lemon peel
   (½ inch by 3 inches)

1 cup ice, crushed

Wash and drain watercress, remove long stems. Reserve six sprigs for garnishing. In an electric blender combine watercress, pineapple juice, honey, lemon juice, lemon peel, and crushed ice. Blend until smooth and frothy. Serve immediately in cocktail glasses. Garnish with a sprig of watercress. **Yield: six cocktails**

Melon Cooler

1 small cantaloupe
1 can (20 ounces) crushed
    pineapple, unsweetened
12 ice cubes, crushed for easier blending
mint sprigs for garnish
pineapple juice, unsweetened

Peel and seed cantaloupe; cut fruit into chunks. In an electric blender combine crushed pineapple, ice and about one-third of the cantaloupe cubes. Blend at high speed, adding the remaining cantaloupe cubes gradually. Blend until smooth.

Thin with unsweetened pineapple juice to the consistency desired. Pour into glasses and serve garnished with mint sprigs.

This melon cooler also makes a very refreshing cold soup.

Yield: six servings

METRIC CONVERSION										
1 teaspoon = 5 ml.						1 tablespoon = 15 ml.				
1 ounce = 30 ml.						1 cup = 240 ml./.24 l.				
1 quart = 950 ml./.95 l.						1 gallon = 3.80 l.				
1 ounce = 28 gr.						1 pound = 454 gr./.454 kg.				

F.°	200	225	250	275	300	325	350	375	400	425	450
C.°	93	107	121	135	149	163	177	191	204	218	232

Chapter 16

Your Own Training Plan for the Family Athlete

When a youngster, a teenager, or an adult takes on a heavier than usual athletic program—like weight lifting, wrestling, jogging, tennis, a place on a basketball, baseball, or football team, gymnastics, intensive ballet training, or even cheerleading—the requirement for certain nutrients skyrockets. That's the time when love and wheat germ can do more good than liniment by the quart or whirlpool baths by the hour.

Take "sports anemia" for example. Of course you don't think of big strapping athletes as being anemic, just the opposite in fact. However, the rigors of a heavy physical training program frequently induce an iron deficiency leading directly to that condition. It is particularly common among male athletes, according to an address delivered by Dr. Kvanta of Sweden to an international symposium on the nutrition of athletes held in Leningrad *(Physician and Sports Medicine,* January 1975). He pointed out that perspiration contains .3 to .4 mg. of iron per liter. Therefore a vigorous athlete who loses nine to 12 liters of perspiration daily loses 2.7 to 4.8 mg. of iron above his normal losses. His iron loss would be equal to, or greater than, that lost by a woman monthly through menstruation.

When a daily capsule of beef hemoglobin supplying

a highly absorbable form of iron was administered to runners in experiments, their hemoglobin levels increased by 20 to 40 percent and their serum iron levels by 25 to 30 percent.

It is important that you be aware of this threat to your in-house athletes' iron stores and keep pitching with liver, apricots, dark green vegetables, wheat germ, and blackstrap molasses, all of which are good sources of iron. It may be necessary to add an iron supplement, which I prefer to get from organic sources. Inorganic iron is a vitamin E antagonist. If you are taking both, take one in the morning and the other at night.

What about Special Drinks for Athletes?

I am often asked about the value of drinks like Gatorade as a booster of athletic performance. Certain natural and manufactured solutions do revive hot and thirsty athletes faster than water, if the chemicals and the water are in the same proportions in which they occur in perspiration, say the editors of *Food for Fitness* (World Publications, Mountain View, California, 1975).

When three leading commercial preparations were analyzed, all of them—Gatorade, Sportade, and Half-Time Punch—were found to have similar salt content —about the same as that found in a glass of whole milk. Potassium was highest in Sportade—five to ten times more than in Gatorade or Half-Time Punch—but still only half the potassium level of whole milk or orange juice.

Of the synthetic "sweat drinks" analyzed, Dr. George Sheehan, author of the *Encyclopedia of Athletic Medicine,* rates Sportade first, Half-Time Punch second, and Gatorade a distant third. But he thinks another solution, E. R. G. (Electrolyte Replacement with Glucose) runs well ahead of the three. A good homemade substitute, says Dr. Sheehan, would be a glass of orange juice with a weak salt solution. Most physiologists agree that the artificial concoctions are a waste of money.

Good sources of potassium to include in your athletes' diet, are sprouts, seeds like sunflower, sesame, and pumpkin seeds, and all kinds of nuts and fruits, particularly bananas and oranges.

Perfect your skills with milk shakes which you can load up with wheat germ or wheat germ oil, protein powder, nutritional yeast, and blackstrap molasses. You can put bananas and eggs in milk shakes, too. Make a big batch to keep in the refrigerator. After a session of weight lifting, for instance, when your youngster is depleted, a healthy draft of such a shake will slake his thirst and replace lots of the nutrients he has lost, and keep him from devouring lots of empty calorie snacks —the kind that add weight without nutrients.

Here is a group of what I call Great Drinks—to refresh the athlete, improve athletic performance, and replace minerals lost in physical exertion.

Cranberry Punch

In the blender put the following:

½ cup red raspberries
2 cups sweet cider
½ cup raw cranberries
1 banana

½ cup sunflower seeds

honey to taste

This one really packs a punch with the enzymes of the raw cranberries and the food energy, vitamin A, and potassium in the banana.

METRIC CONVERSION										
1 teaspoon = 5 ml.					1 tablespoon = 15 ml.					
1 ounce = 30 ml.					1 cup = 240 ml./.24 l.					
1 quart = 950 ml./.95 l.					1 gallon = 3.80 l.					
1 ounce = 28 gr.					1 pound = 454 gr./.454 kg.					

F.°	200	225	250	275	300	325	350	375	400	425	450
C.°	93	107	121	135	149	163	177	191	204	218	232

Fruit Blender Drink

In the blender put the following:

1 cup raw pineapple, fresh or frozen

3 cups water

½ cup honey

4 peaches, washed and pitted

Blend, adding ice cubes until you have a thin, chilled drink.

When peaches are in season, this is a great way to get lots of vitamin A while you're quenching your thirst.

Banana Drink

In the blender put the following:

2 tablespoons soya powder
1 pint water
1 large banana
1 tablespoon honey
½ teaspoon vanilla

Soya powder gives this beverage protein power and unsaturated fatty acids that are so good for heart and muscle health.

Dried Fruit Shake

In the blender put the following:

2 tablespoons soya milk powder
1 pint water
4 dates, figs, prunes or ¼ cup raisins
2 tablespoons blackstrap molasses

Besides the protein and unsaturated fatty acids of the soy, the molasses in this drink provides the iron, calcium, potassium, and 13 vitamins so vital to energy and well-being. Dried fruit provides even more zip and flavor.

Virginia Fruit Punch

1 cup apple juice
1 cup water
1 cup grape juice
honey to taste
1 tablespoon lemon juice

Mix all ingredients together and chill well. The fructose in grapes supplies quick energy, and loads of minerals, especially potassium. In addition to taste, honey contributes extra energy and its own share of trace minerals.

METRIC CONVERSION										
1 teaspoon = 5 ml.			1 tablespoon = 15 ml.							
1 ounce = 30 ml.			1 cup = 240 ml./.24 l.							
1 quart = 950 ml./.95 l.			1 gallon = 3.80 l.							
1 ounce = 28 gr.			1 pound = 454 gr./.454 kg.							

F.°	200	225	250	275	300	325	350	375	400	425	450
C.°	93	107	121	135	149	163	177	191	204	218	232

Orange Shake

In a blender put the following:

2 cups milk
½ small can frozen orange
   juice (undiluted)

Carob Shake

1 ½ cups milk
1½ teaspoons carob powder
1 tablespoon oil
    (safflower, soy, or corn)
1 teaspoon honey
1 teaspoon vanilla

Dissolve carob in oil, add a little milk, and heat briefly to cook the carob. Blend carob mixture, milk, honey, and vanilla until smooth, and serve cold.

Banana Kugel

(Athletes like to eat, too. This cake is mineral rich and goes great with a milk shake.)

½ cup butter
1 cup honey
2 eggs, beaten
½ cup yogurt or sour cream
1 cup bananas, mashed
½ cup walnuts, pecans,
    or sunflower seeds, chopped
1½ cups whole wheat flour
¼ teaspoon salt
1 teaspoon vanilla

Preheat oven to 350°F.
Cream together the butter and honey. Add

eggs and yogurt or sour cream and beat well. Add mashed bananas and chopped nuts, then the flour, salt, and vanilla and mix again. Pour into greased and floured nine-inch square, cake pan. Bake 35 to 45 minutes.

Consequences of Potassium Depletion

It is especially important to be aware of the need for minerals that are lost in perspiration during summer work outs. An athlete, even when he is seriously potassium depleted, may feel fine. But if he goes too far, he may cross the dangerous muscle destroying threshold. About 50 percent of those admitted to the hospital for "heat stroke" after intense exercise are potassium depleted, Dr. James P. Knochel of the University of Texas Southwestern Medical School told a symposium of the American Heart Association in Dallas, November 21, 1974. "The danger is that depletion beyond a certain level can cause irreversible death of muscle."

In hot weather, hard exercise can lead to a loss of all the potassium consumed in an average day through sweating alone. Add to this the loss through urine of about half the daily dietary intake, and it is easy to see how the overall loss quickly uses up any stores. Athletes are likely to become potassium depleted by the second week of training during the summer, the Texas scientist said.

Note this: feeling hot and sweating are not the only indications that an athlete might be losing potassium. Swimmers frequently suffer severe muscle cramps which can be traced to the loss of potassium, even though they do their thing in cool, refreshing water.

It is commonly assumed that sodium is the nutrient which needs replacement during the hot weather but Schamadan and Snively tested workers in the hot fields of Arizona and Israel and found that the main electrolytes lost were potassium and magnesium—not sodium *(Food for Fitness,* World Publications, Mountain View, California, 1975).

You don't have to be an athlete to suffer from losses of essential minerals during the summer. During a 14-day period of uncomfortable heat in Michigan, Dr. Stanley H. Schoeman and Dr. George W. Williams of the Medical University of South Carolina and the Department of Biostatistics, School of Public Health, University of Missouri, studied the biochemical profiles of 631 outpatients and compared them with profiles of 698 outpatients taken during a preceding cool period (*Ecology of Food and Nutrition,* Gordon and Breach, Great Britain, 1974). They found a statistically significant shift in as many as 17 biochemical variables. Two essential electrolytes—potassium and calcium—were significantly lower during the hot period. Their findings suggest that changes in dietary levels of potassium and calcium may be associated with heat waves. No wonder you wilt when the thermometer soars. "Poorly balanced meals (tea and toast, beer and pretzels) are probably more widely consumed during hot humid weather than during normal seasonal conditions," said the report.

Put the emphasis on foods that are rich in potassium, calcium, and magnesium—not just for the athlete but for the whole family. You will enhance everybody's health and performance—athletes and non-athletes alike—if you put the emphasis on big, beautiful salads.

And you will make things easy for yourself at the same time.

Use all kinds of green leaves, the deeper the green, the better. Use spinach, dandelion greens, escarole, kale, watercress, parsley, comfrey leaves if you have some in your garden, chicory, lettuce, romaine. Wash them quickly and dry them. Salad oils will cling to dry leaves sealing in the chlorophyll and preventing the leaves from wilting. This keeps your salad fresh, crisp, and appetizing.

To make a delightful salad dressing, try combining several oils—safflower, sesame, or sunflower are excellent. Since the use of vegetable oils increases the need for vitamin E (to prevent peroxidation of the oils in the body), it's a good idea to squeeze the contents of a 400 I.U. vitamin E capsule into a quart of oil. I also add a tablespoon of fresh wheat germ oil, a great energy food, rich in unsaturated fatty acids.

For a pleasant change of taste, spike your salad bowl with a tablespoon of minced fresh basil, watercress, chopped green pepper (include the seeds), mint leaves, or a handful of violets. Here are some great salad bowl combinations which are beautiful to behold, crunchy, and delicious to eat, and provide you and your athletes with lots of pep-up nutrients.

Six Succulent Salad Bowl Combinations

Apples, cabbage, chopped celery, fresh or dried mint, avocado, sunflower seeds, and alfalfa sprouts.

Grated cauliflower on romaine lettuce, thinly sliced carrots, Jerusalem artichokes, radishes, pumpkin seeds, and mung bean sprouts.

Chopped red cabbage, fresh or unsweetened pineapple, watercress, sliced zucchini, sesame seeds, and lentil sprouts.

Raw spinach leaves, sliced raw mushrooms, sliced Bermuda onions, grated carrots, and wheat sprouts.

Chopped apples and walnuts, a touch of cinnamon, and grape juice to moisten—served on a bed of chopped greens and alfalfa sprouts.

Grated carrots, walnuts, raisins, moistened with your special supercharged mayonnaise, garnished with marinated garbanzo sprouts.

Add any good protein to enrich the mixture—bits of tuna fish, salmon, chicken, hard-cooked eggs, sardines, cottage cheese, or good, natural hard cheese. Throw a handful of sunflower, sesame, or pumpkin seeds into any salad and you greatly increase potassium, magnesium, and calcium values. A handful of sprouts enhances vitamin, enzyme, and protein values. Use mung bean, alfalfa, lentil, and garbanzo sprouts liberally. Garbanzo sprouts are said to be a great source of energy. Marinate them for a day or two in your salad dressing for a real zesty treat.

Serve your salads with good wholesome bread, or, for a change, try these bread sticks. They are loaded with nutrients.

Bread Sticks

1½ cups whole wheat flour
½ cup soy flour
1¼ cups milk
½ cup vegetable oil

2 cups raw wheat germ

1 tablespoon honey or blackstrap molasses

1 teaspoon vegetable salt

Preheat oven to 350° F.

Mix and knead all ingredients. Roll the dough about one-quarter inch thick. Cut into sticks about five inches long. Place on an oiled cooky sheet. Sprinkle some of the sticks with caraway seeds, some with poppy seeds, and others with sesame seeds. Bake about 35 minutes, or until golden brown.

Here is another dish which will insure ample supplies of potassium for you and your physically active family:

Hi-Mineral Broth

1 cup celery, finely shredded (leaves and all)

1 cup carrots, finely shredded

1 tablespoon nutritional yeast

1 tablespoon parsley or chives, chopped

1 quart water (or vegetable cooking water or water from soaking seeds for sprouting)

1 cup tomato juice

1 teaspoon vegetable salt

1 teaspoon honey

Put all the shredded vegetables into a quart of water. Cover and cook slowly for 30 minutes. Then add thick tomato juice (or tomatoes), vegetable salt, and honey. Let cook for five more minutes. If you want a clear broth, strain and serve. I like to put the whole thing in the blender, one cup at a time and whiz it. This makes a thicker but very appetizing broth and will include all of the nutrients.

METRIC CONVERSION										
1 teaspoon = 5 ml.						1 tablespoon = 15 ml.				
1 ounce = 30 ml.						1 cup = 240 ml./.24 l.				
1 quart = 950 ml./.95 l.						1 gallon = 3.80 l.				
1 ounce = 28 gr.						1 pound = 454 gr./.454 kg.				
F.° 200	225	250	275	300	325	350	375	400	425	450
C.° 93	107	121	135	149	163	177	191	204	218	232

If your vigorous athletes, ballet dancers, and perpetual motion children are at home, you can, following these guidelines, provide a diet which will help them maintain muscle tone, pep, energy, and endurance.

For Athletes Living at School

But what about the family's athletes who are living away from home in college dormitories? Herb Wilf, a wholehearted advocate of the "love and wheat germ" principle, made an intensive study of nutritional needs and supplements and devised a program for his son who was on the swimming team and whose athletic activities included two two-hour workouts every day.

Charlie, who was six feet tall and weighed 165 pounds, started practicing with the swim team with light workouts in October and built up to heavier schedules in November and December. The official season began December-January. Between October and December, Charlie's weight dipped to 155 pounds. He fainted on two occasions. He became irritable, tired, and short-tempered. He then developed a pain in his right knee that kept him from effective swimming.

When Charlie came home for Christmas vacation, his father devised a food program to correct his problems. At school he ate at the student union where the diet was strongly starchy and overcooked. But he did have facilities in his apartment, including a stove, sink, blender, and refrigerator.

The program which his father devised took into consideration the fact that after studies, swimming, and social commitments, Charlie had little time to spend on food preparation and learning about food values.

Mr. Wilf sent me a copy of the letter and program which he sent to his son:

Dear Charlie:

Find enclosed vitamins, minerals, protein food, high-protein supplements.

1. **Vitamins**

E—200 I.U.–two per day (more if you like) not at the same time, (one at breakfast, one at lunch).

B complex–two per day.

All-purpose vitamins–therapeutic formula—one per day.

Pantothenic acid—do not use now—start at exam time or when training.

2. **Minerals**

Kelp—use as you would salt or pepper. Twenty known minerals—in balance and intact in their natural form (comes from seaweed).

Blackstrap molasses—high in organic iron, calcium, phosphorus, copper. Also vitamins: two to three tablespoons per day—minimum daily requirement for iron. Too much has laxative effect.

3. **Protein**

Desiccated liver—enclosed are two types: powder and tablets. I would prefer that you take powder as food rather than tablets. However it may not be convenient because of your meal structure. Therefore, take the tablets. This is the most nutritionally complete food. It is a tremendous source of natural body and blood building food available. Take every day.

Liver is also good for vitamin A, B complex, and C.

Brewer's yeast—this is a better tasting kind than you had before. Start with small quantities (a half-teaspoon) and build up gradually. (Great protein plus 17 vitamins, 14 minerals, and 16 amino acids.)

Soyagen (soybean milk)—three tablespoons in eight-ounces water in blender. I often make nine ounces in 24 ounces of water and store in milk bottle in refrigerator. Add flavor or use in cereal like milk.

Soya granules—additional good protein, minerals, and vitamins.

4. **High protein supplements**

Tiger's Milk—contains all amino acids plus (see label on can) all kinds of things. Try TM shake in water or fruit juice. (I use it in my carrot juice or in yogurt and molasses.)

Powerhouse 32–information is included with package. Read it.

Charlie, I was unable to secure sunflower seeds. The store was out of stock. This is a great protein food. I will mail you a supply when I can get some.

In addition to the above, excellent protein sources are: milk, yogurt (plain and flavor it with molasses or honey), cottage cheese, fresh fish (broiled or baked), canned fish (sardines or tuna), nuts (almonds, unsalted and raw), and wheat germ.

Very, very important that you have much
raw vegetables. Raw fruit in addition to all the
above. Also include in your diet vegetable oil as in
salad.

A good breakfast would be:

Piece of fruit or juice and the following cereal.
1 cup milk or 1 cup soy milk
1 tablespoon brewer's yeast
¼ cup wheat germ
2 tablespoons soya granules
1 raw egg yolk
　Run through blender, then add molasses.

The following are some desserts or snacks:

Plain yogurt and molasses.
Plain yogurt and molasses, or honey and Tiger's
Milk.
Tiger's Milk shake with honey or molasses.
Powerhouse 32 shake with honey or molasses.
Almonds and raisins—good amino balance and
great dessert.

Salads—a big one every day—add following to your
salads:

2 tablespoons wheat germ
1 tablespoon lecithin
1 tablespoon vegetable oil
kelp (use as salt and pepper)
garlic powder (use as salt and pepper)
lemon juice to taste

Charlie, do you remember the headstand, deep relaxation, and deep breathing of yoga? If so, practice daily.

The most important thing of all, more important than all the foregoing is the manner of your meal.

a. Surroundings and atmosphere—must be relaxed and pleasant.

b. Chew your food completely and thoroughly.

c. Drink no water while eating.

d. Enjoy your taste and sight of your food; and remember the source of this blessing.

Love,
Mom and Dad

Chapter 17
What I Tell My Friends When They Ask How to Handle Common Health Problems

It was a long time coming, but I've finally achieved peer recognition as a prophet who was way ahead of her time. Friends who once laughed at my penchant for love and wheat germ as a *michigas* (a crazy notion) are now bringing me their health problems, their mother-in-law's health problems, their cleaning woman's health problems and even, believe it or not, Fido's health problems.

Since I have a gut level urge to see the glow of health shining all around me, I am always happy to share whatever knowledge I have accumulated over the years. And I don't ask for Blue Cross cards.

One of the problems which seems to beset a great many people judging by their "private consultations" with me, is hemorrhoids. To them I suggest three things: get more bran into your diet; take lots of bioflavonoids with rutin (many people have told me that the rutin quickly stops the bleeding); and use vitamin E suppositories (available at natural food stores) for healing and lubrication. More than one person credited this three-way recommendation with helping to avoid surgery.

Another private question I get a lot: What can I do for constipation? I've heard about bran but I don't know how to use it.

Bran Controls Constipation

Perhaps you'd be interested in the experience of one woman who had been taking laxatives regularly every night for 50 years. Sometimes even a dose of salts in the morning. After reading an article I wrote for *Prevention®* magazine, "Some Delicious Ways to Enjoy Your Bran," in which I suggested using coarse bran, available in any natural food store, she tried it and it worked. She took her bran in a glass of half orange juice and half water while watching the late news. And so to bed. She said it worked like a charm.

For most people, one or two teaspoons of bran a day, in cereal, on toast, or in juice will do the job very well. Start with small amounts and add more if needed. Give your system a chance to get used to the added roughage slowly.

Sinus congestion is a common problem in our area of Pennsylvania, and in many other areas of the country, I'm sure. Bioflavonoids and lots of vitamin C usually help this condition in a gratifyingly short time. One woman who suffered for many years with a sinus postnasal drip which caused a chronic irritation in her throat, was constantly getting head and chest colds in spite of many visits to the doctor, and lots of drugs and cough medicines. She began chewing 100 mg. tablets containing natural vitamin C from acerola berries, and she took a supplement of natural citrus bioflavonoid complex with wild rose hips. The rapid rate of improvement and relief was absolutely fantastic, she said.

Many mothers want to discuss menstrual problems with me because their teenage daughters are having debilitating cramps. More calcium, vitamin B_6 and vitamin E, I say. And that goes for menopausal problems mom might be having too.

Bone meal is a good source of supplementary calcium, but it is not the only one. Some people have insufficient hydrochloric acid in their stomachs and can't assimilate the calcium from bone meal. If you suspect that you do have such a deficiency, try taking your bone meal tablets with a mixture of apple cider vinegar and honey in a glass of water, with the proportions adjusted to make a solution palatable to you. I like two teaspoons of the vinegar to one teaspoon of the honey. Make sure that your diet includes calcium-rich dark green vegetables, sesame seeds, and wheat germ. Vitamin B_6 is plentiful in pecans and in seeds but you just can't get enough in your food to have a therapeutic effect on menstrual and menopausal problems. I take 100 mg. of B_6 daily. Be sure to take some source of the whole B complex when you take B_6, since the B's work best when they are all present to help each other. I back my B_6 up with brewer's yeast. A heaping tablespoon in a cup of hot water seasoned with vegetable seasoning. This is my "coffee break" refreshment. As for vitamin E, I suggest a minimum of 100 I.U. daily for young people and at least 400 I.U. for women going through the menopause. If by chance you have high blood pressure, start your vitamin E at a lower dosage level, like 50 I.U. daily and increase gradually.

The Sore Back Story

"Oh my aching back," is a groan I hear all the time, especially on Monday mornings. I pass on the prescription which was given to us by a doctor who practices metabolic nutrition: Four bone meal tablets, one dolomite tablet, four vitamin C (500 mg. each), and four calcium pantothenic (100 mg. each) to be taken every hour until you feel better. Or, until you can get professional help.

It's a good idea to saturate your tissues with vitamin C before the weekend whirl begins. Then you might spare yourself the misery of a backache. Dr. James Greenwood, Jr., of Baylor University College of Medicine, Houston, Texas, recommends up to 2,000 mg. of vitamin C a day if heavy exercise is anticipated.

Sometimes a good stretch will reposition whatever it is that is giving you an aching back. People get relief by chinning themselves either from a chinning bar or from a door holding on to the top with both hands and letting the feet dangle. This maneuver frequently permits whatever has slipped out to slip back where it belongs.

One of my friends was a bikini dropout—not because she had suddenly become puritanical. It's just that she got so tired of explaining how she got those black and blue marks. The fact is she didn't know herself. Many easy bruisers don't realize they are actually suffering from a condition known as purpura, the disease of the purple spots. This colorful (and embarrassing) condition could be a manifestation of a vitamin E deficiency. There has been a lot more of it since the increasing use of estrogens both for birth control and as a menopausal crutch. Estrogens are a vitamin E antagonist.

Vitamin E was used experimentally by a researcher in Japan on seven patients with purpura between the ages of 16 and 54. All of them appeared to be well nourished and showed no signs of scurvy (capillary fragility, sometimes a precipitating factor in purpura which can be the result of a vitamin C deficiency). When Dr. Takaaki Fujii of the Utsunomya Hospital in Japan administered vitamin E to all of these patients in dosages of 400 to 600 mg. orally every day, he noted quick recoveries and disappearance of all spots in two to four weeks.

I gave this information to my "spotted" friend who quickly upped her vitamin E intake. In a few weeks the only spots on her were the ones printed on her leopard-skin bikini.

Lumps in the Breasts

The problem of lumps in the breasts is a frequent and terrifying one for more and more women. My friend, Maggie, told me that she was forming lumps in her breasts so frequently that, even though her doctor had diagnosed them as benign, he was thinking of surgery. On her own, Maggie increased her intake of vitamin E. When she saw her doctor the following month, there was no sign of a lump. "What have you been doing he asked in amazement?"

"Taking vitamin E," said Maggie.

"I don't believe it."

"Do you want me to go off the vitamin E?"

"Yes," said the doctor. Maggie went off the vitamin E and when she was examined the next month her lumps were back. "Okay," the doctor said, "now go back on vitamin E." She did, and the following month there was no sign of a lump.

"You've convinced me," said the doctor, "I'm going to recommend vitamin E to all my patients with that problem." A few months passed and when Maggie saw her doctor again, he said, "I'm not getting the same results with my other patients."

"How much vitamin E are you prescribing?"

"Two hundred units a day."

"I've been taking 2,400 units a day. I'll bet I wouldn't get results with 200 units either."

I haven't heard from Maggie since, but I do hope her doctor upped his recommendations for vitamin E. In many cases large doses do a lot of jobs that don't respond to ordinary amounts.

Getting Rid of Warts

Warts cause plenty of annoyance and embarrassment, even though they seldom add up to a serious ailment. Those who ask me about them say doctors are puzzled too. They remove one and another pops up.

When our Dan, as a youngster, had a flush of warts on his hand, we increased his vitamin A to 50,000 units a day and within two months he had no sign of a wart. Warts are of viral origin and they seem to disappear when the body's immunologic mechanism is strengthened.

Some people have said good riddance to warts by using vitamin E topically. A woman who had a big wart on her ribs where clothing rubbed it constantly, tried several disappointing remedies. Then she pierced a 100 I.U. capsule of vitamin E, rubbed some directly on the wart and squeezed the rest onto an adhesive bandage and applied it to the wart overnight. Next morning she repeated this process and left the bandage on all day. On the morning of the fourth day of this treatment the wart had disappeared leaving no mark or scar of any kind.

Vitamin E also worked for a man who had a series of plantar warts on both feet. He had had them burned off several times but they always came back. It took just three weeks of the vitamin E treatment to bring about a complete cure. He first soaked his feet in mild soapy water. Then he applied the vitamin E and put on clean, white cotton socks overnight.

Cold sores, fever blisters, and canker sores are the kind of common and annoying problems people call me up about on the night before a dinner party or a charity ball when they've just got to look great—"New gown, new hair style, and a red sore on my upper lip!" they cry. Antibiotic therapy can bring these sores on. You can swiftly clear them up and even prevent them if you eat yogurt—the acidophilus kind—or take some yogurt tablets. Usual commercial yogurts do not have the acidophilus culture. A brand of yogurt called Erivan is made with acidophilus and is available at some natural food stores. The dry yogurt culture also includes the acidophilus strain.

If the canker sore is in the mouth, it is a good idea to take a mouthful of yogurt as frequently as possible allowing the yogurt to cover the ulcer for a minute or two. The lactic acid in the yogurt accelerates healing.

Migraine Headaches

I guess everybody has at least one acquaintance who gets migraine headaches. I have several. Persons with migraine often feel dizzy—as though they were seasick on dry land—and some develop full-blown Meniere's disease with its attacks of vertigo, ringing noises in the ears, and loss of hearing. Dr. Myles Atkinson, formerly of New York University, now retired, told me that he saw signs of severe chronic vitamin B deficiency in both conditions and relieved both with intensive vitamin B treatment. At the Mayo Clinic they found that head noises associated with Meniere's were responsive to large doses of vitamin C and bioflavonoids plus large doses of the B complex. Anyone who suffers from migraines or Meniere's should avoid salt (because it makes the tissues retain fluid and swell), and preparations high in sodium like sodium bicarbonate, sodium solicilates, and sodium nitrite, a food preservative which is identified as the cause of "hot dog headache." You should also avoid tyramine which is a troublemaker that is found in some cheese and some wines, and monosodium glutamate, which has been identified as the cause of "Chinese restaurant syndrome" headache —which could be a mild migraine.

Cystitis, an infection of the bladder, is probably the condition that I am most often asked about. It is very common in females and it can be painful and uncomfortable. One has a burning sensation during and after urination, and a need to run to the bathroom frequently.

I got my first attack of cystitis when I was in summer stock one season when June was as cold as January. Between curtain calls, we huddled around the coffee pot backstage. Since the only bathroom was across the yard in a nearby hotel, our bladders didn't fare very well. My doctor prescribed the usual medical treatment—Gantrisin, a sulfa drug which clears up the infection quickly but leaves you so drowsy and heavy headed, that all you want to do is sleep. Sleep is contraindicated when you're due on stage. So naturally, as soon as the infection disappeared, I would go off the Gantrisin. And naturally I'd come down with another case in a month. Then I heard about cranberry juice and yogurt from a young intern who had just returned from a symposium on urinary problems. It worked as advertised.

For several years I had no recurrence of the cystitis. Then, after weeks of hectic activity, on the eve of my daughter's wedding, I felt those old crazy symptoms again. I dreaded having to take the Gantrisin because

I didn't want to sleep-walk down the aisle. No time for concentrated yogurt-cranberry juice therapy. So I started to gobble vitamin C—I took two grams every hour. I woke twice during the night and took two grams each time. Then in the morning I started on the vitamin C again until it was time to leave for the nuptials, at which time the mother of the bride was feeling no pain. P.S. It was a gorgeous wedding.

Many people are forced to have their wisdom teeth removed. Afterwards, they suffer excruciating pains in the gums. I know of a person who was in such pain that she was almost hysterical. Her mother fixed some epsom salts and hot water and had her gargle with it quite a few times. She says it worked like magic. Every time the pain started to come back, more epsom salts and hot water. After about a day the pain was completely gone. I tried it myself after a painful session at the dentist's office. And it really does work.

My Stay-Slim Techniques

I am frequently asked how I manage to stay slim. In my previous book, *Confessions of a Sneaky Organic Cook* (Rodale Press, Emmaus, Pa., 1972), I gave some basic rules for weight control and they still hold true:

1. Never eat what the kids don't finish—just because it's a shame to throw it out. If you just can't stand this kind of waste, get a dog, feed the birds, or start a compost pile.
2. Always eat a good high-protein breakfast.
3. Go to bed early if you're the type to get snack happy with late night television.
4. Never eat an empty calorie—that means noth-

ing made with sugar or refined flour—and you'll never need to count calories.

One of my friends who's continually waging a losing battle with her bulges, told me she could not understand why she gains weight because she never eats anything between meals. She is making the three meal mistake. Studies show that frequent small meals make weight control and weight loss easier. Also smaller meals tend to reduce levels of blood cholesterol and improve glucose tolerance, an important factor to those who would like to lose weight, to those who are diabetic, to those who suffer with hypoglycemia (low blood sugar). These benefits cannot be realized by taking the same amount of food in three large meals. Nibbling, then, is better than feasting.

Here are a few more weight control tricks to try:

When you go out to dine, don't nibble on crackers or bread sticks. If you're famished, eat something before you leave the house—some yogurt, a piece of cheese or a hard-cooked egg. This fortification will keep you from going overboard. Choose broiled fish frequently. Skip the potato unless it's freshly baked. Most restaurants serve baked potatoes that are wrapped in foil and have been reheated. They're soggy and not worth the extra calories in the butter or sour cream you must doctor them up with. Get doubles on the salad instead. For dessert, ask for fresh fruit—melon in season, a pear or apple and cheese, or fresh fruit cocktail—not the canned. If you feel like something a little wicked, cheesecake is a good choice. But don't eat the crust.

When you go to one of those lavish affairs—weddings, *bar mitzvahs,* receptions, open house buffets—enjoy the sights and sounds and sociability. Don't feel obligated to taste everything. I once counted 48 different hot dishes at a pre-dinner cocktail hour, besides the specialties that were being brought around on silver platters. I go for the mushrooms and the fish dishes. At the dinner that follows, I eat everybody's pineapple, the salad, and skip the meat, and any vegetables that look candied or overcooked. When the lights are dimmed, the trumpet blasts and the Viennese breakfast parades in, I thoroughly enjoy the show, and a piece of fresh fruit. And since I never sit out a dance, I manage to navigate the oceans of food without adding a ripple to my waist and believe me, long after the other guests have wilted, I'm still ready for a waltz or a fast polka.

"What can I do about swollen ankles?" Eat lots of parsley, I tell them. It's a gold mine of potassium which fights water retention and the edema it causes. Also cut way back on salt.

Garlic for Remembering

One of the big after-sixty complaints is, "I keep forgetting things." Well, join the crowd and try garlic. It's an ancient folk remedy for failing memory. It is said that Eleanor Roosevelt was also a member of the club, and to keep the facts straight and people's names tripping lightly from the tongue, she ate three honey-covered cloves of garlic every morning. I wouldn't go to that extreme. But be sure to rub garlic on the inside of your salad bowl, marinate it in your salad dressing and add a garlic perle to your vitamin rations, morning and night. You may even remember your dreams.

Try adding crushed garlic, chopped parsley, chopped chives, and caraway seeds to cottage cheese. Serve it as a dip with crisp raw vegetables (celery, turnip slices, cucumber) or as a side dish on greens.

When you buy garlic, select a firm bulb with brittle skin. Store it in a container that is not airtight and keep it in a dry spot preferably at room temperature.

You've heard of people who wear a copper bracelet for stiff arthritic joints. Well, I'm one of them. I'm sure some day medicine will find justification for this practice. Meanwhile, why take a chance by being without one? It helps a great many people. A friend of mine gave away her last copper bracelet because she was planning a trip to Israel, the land of Solomon's copper mines. Once there, she scoured every jewelry store on the tour for a copper bracelet. Her fingers were beginning to ache and swell. In desperation she asked the tour guide where she could buy a copper bracelet. "You mean a rheumatism bracelet?" he asked. "You buy it in a pharmacy." Sure enough, she found her copper bracelet at the next drugstore. Jewelry or therapy or both? Like I said, I wear one. When my friends ask, I tell them to wear one too.

In addition to the copper bracelet, you may be interested in a dietary regime that works wonders for some people. A doctor who practices nutrition told me that the following dietary pattern, first devised by Dr. Swinburne Clymer, for whom the famous Clymer Clinic is named, has proven very effective for some of his patients. One woman who could hardly walk because she was so cripped and overweight, after a period of three months, had lost 20 pounds, walked with alacrity and looked years younger. Here's the program:

1. Apple cider vinegar (two teaspoons) in water between meals twice a day.
2. Each day eat one of these foods: stewed tomatoes, baked apple, okras, or celery juice.
3. Eat no sugar.

4. Eat no citrus. (For some reason it seems to aggravate osteoarthritis.)

5. Limit your dairy products (yogurt is OK).

People who have diabetes (hyperglycemia—high blood sugar) or hypoglycemia (low blood sugar) are generally stymied when it comes to desserts. "I'm not allowed to have sugar, honey, or dried fruits," my seat partner on a bus trip wailed. "I don't want to resort to artificial sweeteners, but once in a while I get a yen for something besides a piece of fruit for dessert. Do you have any ideas?"

Do I? Try making applesauce using unsweetened pineapple juice as your liquid instead of water. The applesauce will be plenty sweet. Then use this applesauce mixed with a touch of cinnamon, nutmeg, and a little lemon rind on a bed of oatmeal flakes, coconut, chopped nuts, and a little oil or butter. Reserve some of this mixture to scatter on top of the applesauce and place in the oven for about 20 minutes.

Another very good dessert is frozen carob bananas. Make a paste of a few tablespoons of carob powder and a little bit of water. Divide some very ripe bananas into thirds. Roll them in the carob paste and then in unsweetened coconut. Arrange in a pie plate and freeze. When they are frozen they can be bagged individually and enjoyed anytime. You can also make a banana pie using a little water, gelatin, and bananas whizzed in the blender poured over a layer of sliced bananas in a pie plate. You could top it with whipped cream and nuts for a really fantastic dessert.

If you sprout wheat and then dry it in a very low oven overnight, then pulverize it in a seed mill, you have a malt which is very sweet and can be used in some recipes instead of sugar.

Appendix
A Step-By-Step Plan for Converting Your Kitchen to Love and Wheat Germ (For Less Than $25)

After my lectures, somebody always says to me, "I wish I could take you home with me. I'd like to convert my kitchen and cook your way, but I don't know how to begin." Well, I can't go home with everybody, but I can tell you what I'd say if I went home with you.

My first piece of advice is—don't do it all at once, unless you have the complete and enthusiastic cooperation of your family—everyone urging you to make a clean sweep. Otherwise, the idea is to substitute.

Okay, let's go over your kitchen for some easy, basic changes. Here is a step-by-step plan:

Do you use minute rice? Buy brown rice to replace it on your next shopping trip. Brown rice actually costs less than the minute kind, though it may cost a little more than regular white rice. Nutritionally speaking, brown is beautiful—and your best buy.

Bleached white flour? Switch to whole wheat flour—freshly ground at a co-op or natural food store if you can get it. This flour should be refrigerated or frozen. While you're thinking flour, also put soy flour on your shopping list.

Do I see maraschino cherries? Out. That's the easiest

item to get rid of. And don't try to feed them to the birds or the Audubon Society will get after you.

Let's look into your pantry. You've got quite an assortment of canned vegetables and fruits. Don't throw them out, but don't restock them. Frozen vegetables are better for you (and better tasting) than canned. Fresh are better than frozen. Canned fruits that are packed in sugar syrup should be drained of the syrup and washed in a colander. Then mix some fresh fruits with them for fruit cocktail. If you need more juice, add the juice of an orange.

Now, let's look at your breakfast cereal cupboard. You offer the kids five different varieties of cereal. Not too bad. Some homes make room for 10 and 15. At least one package of your cereals should be free of additives. If you have the heart, get a large garbage bag and fill it up. Or let the kids eat their way through this batch and next time you shop buy these: oatmeal flakes, wheat germ, bran, raisins, sesame seeds, sunflower seeds, honey, and cold-pressed oil. Now—make your own granola (see p. 76). If the family is going to get in an uproar over *no* box cereal, let them taper off by stocking only the additive-free brands and making the granola available to try.

You have now achieved Level Number One. You have spent less than $10 on the change. Would you like to try for Level Number Two?

The sugar bowl has got to go, eventually. Wherever possible in cooking use honey, date sugar, or blackstrap molasses.

Is that hydrogenated shortening in that big can on the shelf? Maybe it can be used for polishing furniture or greasing the lawn mower. Just don't eat it. You don't want hydrogenated (clogged) arteries. Get some cold-pressed oil for shortening.

Let's look under your sink. What, nothing sprouting? Well, let's get started. On your shopping list: mung beans, alfalfa seeds, wheat grains, lentils, garbanzos. You say you have garbanzos? No, no. Not the canned ones, honey. They won't sprout. Get the dried beans at co-ops, natural food stores, or ethnic shops.

You have now reached Level Number Two. Want to go on to Three?

Take one of those shelves you're no longer using for canned goods. Haunt the delicatessen for gallon-sized jars (if you are a large family). If not, the quart-size Mason jars will do. Now get an assortment of beans: cranberry, fava, lima, split peas, marrow, and navy and fill up those jars.

You know something? Yours is beginning to look like a natural foods kitchen.

But, wait, let's look in your refrigerator. Soda? Out. I don't care if it is sugarless. It's full of fake colors and chemicals. Don't worry about what you're going to drink. Ever hear of water? Or fruit juices? Oh no, not Tang. It has nothing whatever in common with an orange, except maybe the phoney color. Want orange juice? Buy some oranges. Get some unsweetened apple juice, pineapple juice, grape juice, and cranberry concentrate. It's more expensive, but a little goes a long, long way.

You have spent less than $25. Now your savings begin. Your meat bill will go down because you're going to be serving smaller quantities and several meatless meals every week. That's where the beans and brown rice come in.

Are those store-bought cookies? Uh-huh—synthetic coloring and flavoring and the first ingredient is sugar. Get the big garbage bag. What are you going to give the kids? Okay; put on your shopping list: raw nuts, sunflower seeds, raisins, dried prunes, and apricots. Get some bananas. Keep them on the table. They should be the first thing the children see when they come home from school. Get some apples, too.

That's probably as much as I could do on a single blitz through your kitchen. You have to take over from there. I make most of my decisions on the basis of this simple fact: Natural Is Best. Use that as your motto and you won't need any more help from me in keeping the most healthful kitchen in town.

Tips On How To Convert
Metric Measurements

If you know Fahrenheit temperature, you can find Celsius (Centigrade) by subtracting 32, then multiplying by 5 and dividing by 9. For example 200° F. = (200−32) × 5 − 9= 93° C.

If you know ounces, you can find grams by multiplying by 28.

If you know pounds, you can find kilograms by multiplying by 0.45.

If you know ounces, you can find milliliters by multiplying by 30.

If you know cups, you can find liters by multiplying by 0.24.

If you know pints, you can find liters by multiplying by 0.47.

If you know quarts, you can find liters by multiplying by 0.95.

If you know gallons, you can find liters by multiplying by 3.8.

INDEX

A

appliances, for cooking, 181
Apricot Marbles, 164
arthritics, diet for, 329, 330
arthritis, copper bracelets and, 329
Aspic Salad, Tomato, 280
atherosclerosis, Rinse formula and, 203
athletes, anemia in, 301, 302
  beverages for, 302–308
  bread sticks for, 311
  breakfast for, 316
  broth for, 312
  desserts for, 316
  foods for, 301–317
  iron deficiency in, 301, 302
  minerals and, 301–303, 308–310, 314 *(see also name of mineral)*
  protein supplements for, 315, 316
  salads for, 310, 311, 316
  at school, advice for, 313–317
  snacks for, 316
  vitamins for, 314

B

baby(ies). See also *children*
  acid milk for, 11, 12
  anemia in, 7
  blackstrap molasses for, 39, 40
  bottle feeding and, 12, 13
  brewer's yeast for, 39, 40
  cereals for, 15, 16
  fluorides and, 8
  formulas for, 11, 12
  iron for, 14, 15, 39
  lullabies for, 16, 17
  meat for, 41
  milk for, 11, 12
  nursing of, 2–4. See also *nursing*
  as problem eaters, 41–43
  rice for, 15, 16
  solid foods and, 40, 41
  vitamin E and, 6, 7, 11, 15
baby formulas, 11, 12
back, aching, relief from, 320, 321
Baked Chicken Piquant, Provencale, 267
Baked Yellow Pike, 216, 217
baking, of bread, as retirement activity, 210, 211
Banana Drink, 305
Banana Kugel, 307
banana pie, pineapple and, 258
bananas, beverage from, 305
  cake from, 307, 308
  pineapple pie and, 258
  as snack, 80
Bavarian Cream, Carob, 183
Bavarian custard, 134
Bean Soup, Black, 151
  Senate Restaurant, 180
beans, advantages of, 174–176
  black, recipes with, 149–151